DUBLIN

CAMILLE DeANGELIS

Contents

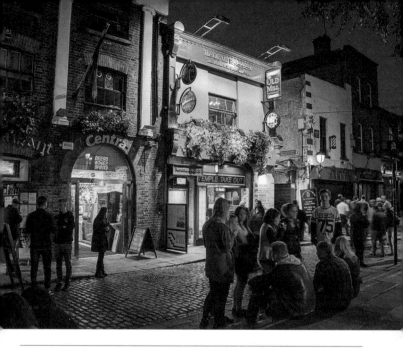

Clockwise from top left: Ha'penny Bridge; Temple Bar quarter; St. Kevin's Church in Glendalough; a view across the River Liffey.

DISCOVER
Dublin

apital of the Irish Republic, vibrant Dublin is as fast-paced and cosmopolitan as any European metropolis, yet it offers its own singular pleasures. Tour the Old Jameson Distillery and go for a pub crawl, to soak in the atmosphere and listen to rollicking traditional music—but be sure to seek out culture *outside* the pubs, too. Art, architecture, archaeology, and book lovers can occupy themselves for days at places like Trinity College (where the Book of Kells, Ireland's most famous illuminated manuscript, is on display), the grand neo-Gothic Christ Church Cathedral, and the National Museum of Archaeology and History, with its spectacular collection of Irish treasures. And it's worth passing an hour or two on St. Stephen's Green just watching the city go by.

Whether you're looking for a fresh pint of Guinness or glimpses of a storied past, Dublin has got you covered.

Clockwise from top left: Trim Castle; St. Patrick's Cathedral; St. Cassán's monastery at Donaghmore; Temple Bar; Christ Church Cathedral.

Planning Your Trip

When to Go

Ireland can be beautiful at any time of year. **July** and **August** are **peak months,** when the sheer volume of tourists in popular destinations can be downright irritating.

Do those tour buses really get on your nerves? Visit during the **spring** or **autumn**—the **"shoulder seasons"**—or in winter, better yet.

Want to get **off the beaten track? Late spring** or **early autumn** is best, but transportation can be limited to more remote locales between November and April. Note that late autumn can be the rainiest time of year.

There is much to be said for a **winter** visit. New Year's is a good choice; listening to a live traditional music session with a pint in hand sure beats watching the ball drop. Irish winters are milder than those of New England—the low/high temperatures run 0-11°C (32-52°F)—and the rare snowfall wreaks both magic and chaos (the former in the landscape; the latter in the national bus system). Aer Lingus and other airline carriers post their lowest fares in January and February, and many hotels, B&Bs, and hostels offer better off-season rates, though many others close altogether.

You may also wish to time your visit to coincide with a particular event, such as the **Dublin Theatre Festival** in early October.

Know Before You Go

Passports and Visas

Upon arrival, an immigration official will stamp your passport for a **three-month tourist visa.** Come prepared with proof of departure within the 90-day window.

What to Pack

Bring lots of comfortable clothing to wear in **layers,** as well as a **water-proof jacket.** Pack a couple of **sweaters** even in summertime—but don't let the threat of rain keep you from applying **sunblock.** On lucky days when the temperature's in the high 20s C (80s F), you'll find the beaches (or "strands") crowded with pasty-skinned locals of all ages reveling in the sun.

Dress is quite **informal,** even in the fancier pubs and restaurants. Though **raingear** is sensible, you will find that the Irish don't wear galoshes unless farming is their business. Getting soaked, followed by drinking tea while warming by the fire, is an Irish ritual. Throw a few **tissue travel-packs** in with your skivvies.

If you plan to do a lot of hill-walking or other **outdoor activities,** you might want to bring a pair of **Wellingtons** along with your **hiking boots.** If you don't mind the occasional case of damp feet, however, keep your load light. Umbrellas are nearly useless, as the wind makes the rain seem like it's falling sideways. Be optimistic and pack your **sunglasses.**

Hill-walkers and **cyclists** should also bring the usual compass, flashlight, medical minikit, pocketknife (in your checked luggage), and so forth.

Purchase a **plug adapter** for electronic devices before you leave. (The Irish plug has two horizontal prongs and one vertical.)

Transportation
GETTING THERE
International flights arrive at **Dublin Airport**; the most commonly used carriers from the United States and Canada are Aer Lingus and United Airlines. If you are planning to travel in summertime, book as far in advance as possible for the best fares. Flights from Europe (London, Paris, Amsterdam, et al.) on **budget airlines** like Ryanair can be extremely economical. It's also possible to arrive by **ferry** from England or France.

GETTING AROUND
Dublin's city center is easily **walkable.** The city has an extensive public transportation system that includes **Dublin Bus,** the **Luas light rail,** and the **DART** (Dublin Area Rapid Transit), which is very useful for visitors who want to see more of Counties Dublin and Wicklow.

If you are planning to use a fair bit of public transportation in the Dublin area, consider purchasing a **Leap travel card** (www.leapcard.ie, €19.50), a three-day transit pass valid on the Luas light rail, the DART (within County Dublin), and all Dublin Bus and Airlink buses (excluding day tours). Purchase a Leap ticket at the Dublin airport, either at the information desk or at the Spar grocery shop in the arrivals hall. The card expires 72 hours after the first time you use it.

Day-trip destinations are largely accessible by **public transportation** (Dublin Bus, DART, Bus Éireann, and Irish Rail) and/or **bus tour.** To explore less-traveled areas, rent a **car.** Gas is quite expensive compared to American prices, but competition keeps rental fees surprisingly affordable.

Best of Dublin

Three Days in Dublin

Three days in Dublin is just enough time to hit the highlights (and take an excursion to get a little breather from all the urban hustle and bustle).

Friday

When you arrive Friday morning, refresh yourself with a stroll through **St. Stephen's Green,** pausing for coffee at **Kaph** or at one of the **Powerscourt Townhouse** cafés a block off **Grafton Street** before making your way to **Trinity College Dublin** and the **Book of Kells** exhibition. For lunch, you have your pick of fantastic eateries along Dame and South Great Georges Streets; **The Bank** is perhaps the most atmospheric (and the food is aces), though it may be a little early in the day yet for a cocktail. Pop into the **Market Arcade** on South Great George's Street for a browse through the quirky shop stalls.

In the afternoon, sign up for the guided tour at **Christ Church Cathedral** so you'll be able to climb up to the belfry and ring one of the bells. If you haven't run out of steam yet, head to the **Chester Beatty Library** to view a dazzling collection of manuscripts, engravings, and decorative art pieces from all over the world.

Tonight, buy yourself a pint and settle in for a **traditional music session** at **O'Donoghue's, Hughes',** or the **Stag's Head.**

Saturday

Today, explore Dublin's Northside. After breakfast, stroll up O'Connell Street to the **Garden of Remembrance** and learn everything you ever wanted to know about Joyce, Yeats, Wilde, and Synge across the street at

Christ Church Cathedral

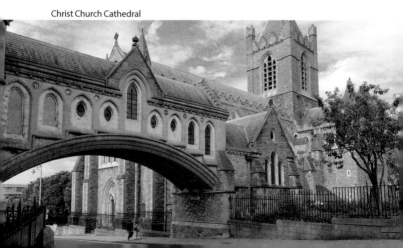

Old Jameson Distillery

the **Dublin Writers Museum.** Then pass a happy hour a few doors down at the **Hugh Lane Gallery,** viewing Harry Clarke's stained-glass scenes from John Keats's poem *The Eve of St. Agnes* up close and personal; then check out Francis Bacon's insanely messy studio to console yourself about the state of your own house!

After lunch at the courtyard café downstairs at the Hugh Lane, take a 15-minute stroll west to **St. Michan's Church** to tour the over-the-top spooky crypts—because who wouldn't want a hardcore spell of *memento mori* while they're on holiday? Now you'll be needing a drink, of course; fortunately the **Old Jameson Distillery** is right around the corner, and the price of admission includes a shot of whiskey.

Take it easy this evening with dinner at **Gallagher's Boxty House** in Temple Bar.

Sunday

It's time for an excursion north of the city! Take the DART to Malahide to stroll the grounds of **Malahide Castle,** popping into the **Avoca food hall** for gourmet souvenirs and an early lunch before joining the hourlong castle tour.

Back in Dublin proper, spend the rest of your afternoon at either the **National Gallery** or the **National Museum of Archaeology and History** (both are centrally located, south of Trinity College between St. Stephen's Green and Merrion Square, and are open on Sunday afternoon). For dinner, treat yourself to a meal you'll remember for decades to come at nearby **Restaurant Patrick Guilbaud** (but be sure to book well ahead!). Then stop for one last pint at an atmospheric **Victorian pub,** like **John Kehoe's, William Ryan's,** or the **Long Hall.**

Sacred Sites and Pilgrimages

Whether your interest is religious or archaeological, this itinerary covering some of the most important cathedrals and monastic ruins in and around Dublin is for you.

Day 1

Fly into **Dublin** and visit **Christ Church Cathedral, St. Patrick's Cathedral,** and **St. Michan's Church,** three Anglican churches (all but the last have pre-Reformation histories, and thus may be of interest to Catholics as well). True pilgrims will want to visit the shrine of St. Valentine at **Our Lady of Mount Carmel.**

Day 2

Make a day trip to County Louth to visit **Mellifont Abbey,** once one of the most prosperous Cistercian abbeys on the island (guided tours available in high season), and **Monasterboice,** which offers scant ecclesiastical ruins and Ireland's two most important high crosses.

Day 3

Quit Dublin for **Glendalough** in the **Wicklow Mountains National Park.** Spend the night here so you can experience the site first thing in the morning, before the arrival of the tour buses. St. Kevin's monastic city is even more memorable when few others are around to share the experience.

Day 4

Rise early and take a walk along Glendalough's **Upper and Lower Lakes.** Head north for the magnificent **Powerscourt House and Gardens** and then back to Dublin.

Glendalough, Ireland's best-known monastic site

Ghosts of Ancient Ireland

Amateur archaeologists can have a field day on the Emerald Isle—pun intended! If you don't have a rental car, you can still do much of this itinerary (Loughcrew being the only place you'll have to skip, as public transportation is nonexistent and taxis unfeasible).

Day 1

Spend your first day in **Dublin** at the **National Museum of Archaeology and History,** which houses the vast majority of the country's treasures from prehistory to the present.

Day 2

Base yourself in County Meath for the next two nights. Visit **Brú na Bóinne** today, Ireland's most important Neolithic site. **Newgrange** is the most famous passage tomb here, though **Knowth** is also accessible by guided tour, and you can take a walk around unexcavated **Dowth.**

Day 3

Visit the **Loughcrew Cairns** for a sense of what Newgrange might have been like before it was excavated and turned into the country's most popular attraction. Head back to Dublin.

the Neolithic burial mound at Newgrange

Dublin

It's not just the world's best (and freshest!) Guinness that brings people to Ireland's capital city. They come to observe the ubiquitous reminders of the city's fascinating, checkered history.

It's a history that traces from Viking origins, through the long centuries of British domination, becoming a nationalist tinderbox during the second decade of the 20th century, and eventually emerging as the capital of a free and independent state in December 1922. The Easter Rising centennial celebrations in 2016 reinvigorated the city's already steady sense of historic pride.

Today Dublin is as fast, modern, and style-conscious as any European capital—and it feels more fast-paced and cosmopolitan every time you visit. Any of the 12 genuine Dublin accents are increasingly rare to hear; the city has become like New York in that most of its 527,000 residents (within the city limits) were born and raised elsewhere. It's also a remarkably youthful place, with more than half its population under the age of 30.

Like other European metropolises, the city has an abundance of neoclassical architecture mixed with fast food places, clothing chains, and souvenir shops—and sometimes exorbitant admission and accommodation prices (though the economic downturn has kept those fees more or less stable ever since). It was perhaps inevitable that the "Celtic Tiger" economic boom of the 1990s and the economic prosperity of the early 2000s would turn the capital city into a mixed bag of excellent gourmet restaurants and Mickey D's, chic nightclubs and tacky tourist traps. But the city is truly what you make of it. Load up on life-altering cultural experiences, spend your afternoon drinking Guinness and talking "sport"—or better yet, do a little bit of both.

Previous: *The Eve of St. Agnes* by Harry Clarke at the Hugh Lane Gallery; the Ha'penny Bridge across the River Liffey.

Look for ★ to find recommended
sights, activities, dining, and lodging.

Highlights

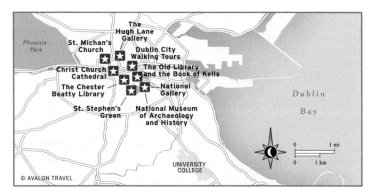

★ **The Old Library and the Book of Kells:** Two pages at a time of Ireland's most famous illuminated manuscript are on display under glass (page 20).

★ **National Gallery:** Check out great paintings by Irish and international artists from the 16th century to the present; Caravaggio's *The Taking of Christ* is the highlight of the European collection (page 21).

★ **National Museum of Archaeology and History:** Once discovered, every Irish treasure from every period in history—including the Tara Brooch, Ardagh Chalice, and Cross of Cong—has found its way into the country's most important museum (page 22).

★ **St. Stephen's Green:** Europe's largest city square features colorful parterres, interesting sculptures and memorials, and many opportunities for people-watching and bird-feeding (page 23).

★ **The Chester Beatty Library:** This well-presented collection of priceless manuscripts is housed on the grounds of Dublin Castle (page 24).

★ **Christ Church Cathedral:** Wander down the central aisle of the city's grandest Gothic edifice, with its precariously tilting columns and strange artifacts (page 25).

★ **The Hugh Lane Gallery:** Revel in a close-up view of Harry Clarke's stained-glass masterpiece, *The Eve of St. Agnes,* and take a peek inside Francis Bacon's infamously chaotic studio (page 28).

★ **St. Michan's Church:** The medieval limestone crypt of this Anglican church offers the city's most macabre sights. Handel used the organ upstairs to practice his *Messiah* for its first performance in 1742 (page 29).

★ **Dublin City Walking Tours:** Whether you're interested in history, ghost stories, or whiskey, the city's various walking tours offer something for you (page 37).

Most of the greater county is made up of sprawling commuter suburbs, though there are a few seaside towns worth an afternoon excursion in fine weather. The fertile plains of Meath to the northwest and the verdant hills and valleys of Wicklow Mountains National Park to the south provide opportunities for unforgettable day trips as well.

Though Dublin originates from the Irish "Dubh Linn" ("Dark Pool"), today its official name in Irish Gaelic is Baile Átha Cliath ("Town of the Hurdles"), the name of an adjoining settlement north of the Liffey.

HISTORY

Actually, the Vikings didn't found Dubh Linn. Ptolemy recorded the existence of a settlement here on his famous map of AD 140; he called it Eblana Civitas. It's said that St. Patrick arrived in 448 and got busy making converts. Then the Vikings came in 841 with the intent of setting up a trading post (trading human cargo, that is) using the existing native Irish settlement. They were driven out by Brian Boru at the Battle of Clontarf in 1014.

But that wasn't the end of the foreign invaders—far from it. The Normans arrived in the 12th century at the plea of the deposed king of Leinster, Diarmuid Mac Murrough. Mac Murrough was only hoping to reclaim his throne, but one imagines he lived to regret his actions when the Normans cast their eyes over the entire island. Henry II, who had sent his troops under the ambitious and opportunistic Strongbow to "aid" the Leinster king, established a court in Dublin to keep an eye on his power-hungry knights—and thus was British domination established. Greater Dublin became known as "the Pale" for its complete subjugation to English government control.

The Norman adventurers settled into their confiscated lands and after a few generations considered themselves Irish—though they still swore loyalty to the British Crown, and those who rebelled swiftly lost their holdings through bloodshed. Still more Plantationers arrived to claim territories allotted by Elizabeth I (the native Irish farmers were forced to work as tenants on what had been their own land). Dublin City was the stronghold of this British Ascendancy, where the Anglo-Irish landowners usually kept townhomes. For them, city artisans—furniture-makers, silversmiths, and architects—kept up a busy practice. Dublin in Georgian times would have been quite an exciting place for all its wealth and prestige.

As a consequence of the failed island-wide rebellion in 1798, the 1801 **Act of Union** stripped Dublin of its independent parliament. A Kerry lawyer, Daniel O'Connell, was sent to London to represent County Clare, and he succeeded in rolling back the Catholic-oppressive Penal Laws in 1829. He was elected the first Catholic Lord Mayor of Dublin in 1841 but died six years later feeling like a failure for having left so much unaccomplished. History would judge him otherwise, but the struggle for civil rights and political independence for Irish Catholics continued.

The city bore the fruits of the **Irish Literary Revival** with the establishment of the **Abbey Theatre,** the world's first English-speaking repertory

Dublin

To Botanic Gardens, Prospect Cemetery, and the Helix Theatre
N2

THE HUGH LANE GALLERY
DUBLIN WRITERS MUSEUM ★
Garden of Remembrance
GATE THEATRE

UPPER DOMINICK ST
MOUNTJOY ST
GRANBY ROW
PARNELL SQUARE WEST
PARNELL SQUARE EAST
HENRIETTA ST
BOLTON ST
KING'S INN ST
LOWER DOMINICK ST
PARNELL ST
MOORE ST
MOORE LN

CHURCH ST UPPER
HENRIETTA PL
LINENHALL TER
COLERAINE ST
LOFTUS LN

BRUNSWICK ST NORTH
KING ST NORTH
HALSTON ST
GREEN ST
JERVIS ST UPR
WOLFE TONE ST
CAPEL ST
MARY ST
HENRY ST

FRIARY AVE
BOW ST
CHURCH ST
BERESFORD ST
LIFFEY ST UPR
ABBEY ST
ABBEY ST UPPER

OLD JAMESON DISTILLERY ★

To National Museum of Decorative Arts & History and Phoenix Park

MARY'S LANE
GREEK ST
ST. MARY'S ABBEY ★

ST. MICHAN'S CHURCH ✝

JERVIS ST LWR
ABBEY ST LWR
LIFFEY ST LWR
LOTTS

CHANCERY ST
GREAT STRAND ST

ARRAN QUAY
USHERS QUAY
ORMOND QUAY LOWER
MILLENNIUM BRIDGE
HA'PENNY BRIDGE
ANGLESEA ST

FATHER MATTHEW BRIDGE
FOUR COURTS ★
ORMOND QUAY UPPER
River Liffey
GRATTAN BRIDGE
WELLINGTON QUAY
TEMPLE BAR

To Guinness Storehouse, Kilmainham Jail, and the Irish Museum of Modern Art

O'DONOVAN ROSSA BRIDGE
ESSEX QUAY
PARLIAMENT ST
PROJECT ARTS CENTRE ★
ESSEX ST
OLYMPIA THEATRE ★
COPE ST
DAME ST

MERCHANTS QUAY
WOOD QUAY
IRISH FILM CENTRE ★
EUSTACE ST
DAME LN

CHRIST CHURCH CATHEDRAL ✝
CITY HALL
CASTLE ST
GEORGE'S ST
EXCHEQUER ST

ST. AUDOEN'S CHURCH ✝
COOK ST
HIGH ST
LORD EDWARD ST
DUBLIN CASTLE

To Vicar Street
AUGUSTINE ST
LAMB ALLEY
THE CHESTER BEATTY LIBRARY ★
LOWER STEPHEN ST
DRURY ST
WILLIAM ST

TIVOLI THEATRE ★
JOHN DILLON ST
NICHOLAS ST
BRIDE ST
GREAT SHIP ST
SOUTH KING ST
LOWER MERCER ST

SWIFT'S ALLEY
FRANCIS ST
HANOVER LN
GLOVERS ALLEY

CARMEN'S HALL
GOLDEN LN
AUNGIER ST
KING ST
YORK ST

N81
ST. PATRICK'S ✝
OUR LADY OF MOUNT CARMEL ★
PETER ROW
PETER ST

DEAN ST
PATRICK ST
KEVIN ST UPPER
NARCISSUS MARSH LIBRARY ★
BISHOP ST

To Rathfarnham Castle and the Pearse Museum

To Whelan's and The Village

0   200 yds
0   200 m

theater, in 1904. Auspiciously enough, the venue on Lower Abbey Street (purchased for the company by Annie Horniman) was on the site of a morgue. Not all Dubliners were open-minded enough to appreciate the efforts of Lady Augusta Gregory and William Butler Yeats; the use of the word "shift" (as in a ladies' undergarment) during a performance of John

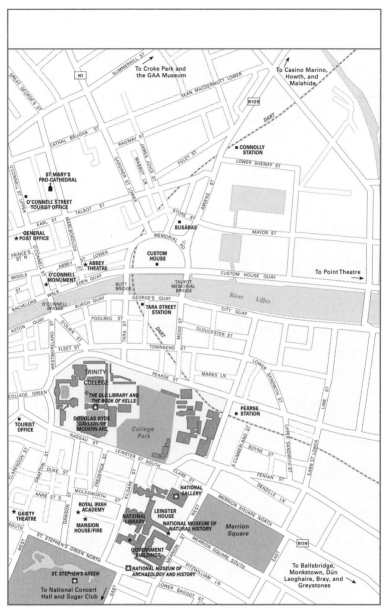

Millington Synge's *The Playboy of the Western World* led to a riot in the theater in January 1907. The original theater burned down in July 1951 and was rebuilt and reopened in 1966. (Despite its ugly new premises, the Abbey is still showcasing the finest in classic and contemporary Irish drama.)

One of the most crucial events in Irish history took place in Dublin on a single day, Easter Sunday 1916, when a nationalist guerrilla group, the Irish Republican Army, took over the General Post Office and declared Ireland a free and independent republic. The British attacked, and citywide chaos and bloodshed ensued. The rebellion was eventually suppressed, and 90 participants (including future Taoiseach and president Eamon de Valera) were sentenced to death. (Only de Valera's American citizenship saved his neck.) Ultimately, 14 of those 90 were executed at Kilmainham Jail, and the nationalist papers declared them martyrs for the cause.

Since the country asserted its freedom from constitutional monarchy in the Republic of Ireland Act of 1949, Dublin's history has been marked by economic stagnation. Membership in the European Economic Community (later European Union) starting in 1973 slowly began to turn things around, and from the mid-1990s to the end of 2008 the city enjoyed an economic boom. The global economic downturn killed the Celtic Tiger for good, however, and Dublin will be handling the consequences of its €85 billion bailout from the E.U. and I.M.F. for years to come.

PLANNING YOUR TIME

As in all European capitals, no amount of time in Dublin will allow you to see everything worth seeing—not even if you stay a month. Rather than exhaust yourself on a one- or two-day visit, be selective in what you choose to see, and spend a bit of time just watching the world go by in a pub, café, or on a park bench in St. Stephen's Green. You'll soak up as much "culture" in those places as you would in the National Museum of Archaeology and History.

Some attractions (especially churches and small museums) close for lunch, so be sure to arrive early enough in the morning to get the most out of your visit. For maximum efficiency, the more ambitious visitor should divide the city into sections and explore one area per day. For instance, plan to visit Kilmainham Jail, the Irish Museum of Modern Art at the Royal Hospital Kilmainham, and the Guinness Storehouse on the same day, since they're all on the western end of the city. Hop-on, hop-off bus tours are a popular means of seeing a lot of places in just a few hours.

As for day trips out of Dublin, there are several possibilities, whether you join in on a bus tour or rent a car. Nestled in the Wicklow Mountains in County Wicklow is Glendalough, one of Ireland's most important monastic sites; Newgrange, part of the Brú na Bóinne funerary complex in County Meath, is one of the most significant Neolithic sites on the whole continent. Other worthwhile excursions include Trim Castle, the largest Anglo-Norman fortress in the country, also in County Meath, and Castletown, Ireland's grandest Palladian manse, in County Kildare, accessible by Dublin Bus. All these places are within an hour and a half of the capital. Or you could just take the DART to one of the county's seaside towns for the afternoon; Killiney south of the city has a great beach, and Howth and Malahide to the north each have several attractions as well.

Sights

Though Dublin sprawls for miles, almost everything you'll want to see is concentrated within an easily walkable area on either side of the River Liffey, wedged between the city's two major train stations (Heuston on the west side and Connolly on the east). North of the Liffey, or "Northside," is a grittier neighborhood, traditionally blue collar and of less interest to tourists; this characterization is becoming somewhat less apt, however, as widespread commercial redevelopment progresses. The Northside's main thoroughfare is O'Connell Street.

South of the river are Temple Bar, Trinity College, St. Stephen's Green, Dublin Castle, Christ Church and St. Patrick's Cathedrals, and many other attractions. Dame Street runs parallel to the river, linking Christ Church with Trinity, and hungry visitors should turn south onto South Great Georges Street for its array of great eateries. Grafton Street, the famous pedestrian shopping strip, links the Trinity College campus to the north with St. Stephen's Green to the south. Wedged between St. Stephen's Green and Merrion Square, a couple of blocks east of Grafton Street, are lots of important buildings within one square block—the National Library, Museum, and Gallery, along with Leinster House (the Irish equivalent of the U.S. Capitol).

SIGHTSEEING PASSES

The Dúchas **Heritage Card** (tel. 01/647-6587, www.heritageireland.ie, €25), available for purchase at all Dúchas sites, will get you into Kilmainham Jail, Phoenix Park Visitor Centre (Ashtown Castle), and the Casino Marino. If you're up for a really ambitious round of sightseeing, though, it's wise to have more than the Heritage Card on hand. The **Dublin Pass** (contact the tourist office for details, tel. 01/605-7700, www.dublinpass.ie, 1/2/3/5-day pass €49/69/79/99, discounts available online) gets you into Dublin Castle, the Dublin Writers Museum, Kilmainham Jail, the Old Jameson Distillery, the Guinness Storehouse, and several other places. (Though it advertises free admission to the Irish Museum of Modern Art, the National Museums, and the Chester Beatty Library, note that there is no charge to these places anyway!) One free Aircoach ride is also included in the pass, though this isn't of much use unless yours is a fly-by-night visit, and there are "special offers" available at many shops and restaurants. Compare a list of the places you want to see with the list of covered attractions on the website, and if the admission charges exceed the price of a pass, pick one up at the tourist office.

TRINITY COLLEGE

Chartered in 1592 by the Virgin Queen for "the planting of learning, the increasing of civility, and the establishment of the true religion"— that's Protestantism—"within the realm," **Trinity College Dublin** (TCD, College Green, at the eastern end of Dame St.) remains the island's most prestigious university. The college was opened in 1594 on the grounds of the Augustinian Priory of All Hallows, which was dissolved under Henry VIII's decree in 1537; the oldest extant buildings date to the early 18th century. Though the college had permitted the admission of Catholics since the late 18th century (provided they converted to Protestantism), it was not until 1970 that the Catholic Church officially permitted it. Now, of course, a majority (roughly 70 percent) of TCD's 12,500 students are Catholic.

The **guided campus tour** (tel. 01/608-1724, departs the main gate every 40 minutes 10:15am-3pm daily mid-May-Sept., ticket €13) is pricey but worthwhile: The tour itself is informative but entertaining, and your ticket includes admission to see the Book of Kells, in the Old Library. Even if you don't have time for the Book of Kells exhibition or a guided campus tour, take 10 or 15 minutes to wander around the perimeter of the immaculate campus green (known as Parliament Square) lined with dignified Georgians (you might even want to duck into the campus chapel, on your left after you pass through the main gate).

★ The Old Library and the Book of Kells

The **Old Library,** which dates to the 1720s, houses the **Book of Kells** (tel. 01/608-2308, www.tcd.ie, 9:30am-5pm Mon.-Sat. all year, 9:30am-4:30pm Sun. June-Sept., noon-4:30pm Sun. Oct.-May, admission without campus tour €11), the best known of all Ireland's illuminated monastic manuscripts. A different two-page spread is on display each day, under thick glass of course; with so much company, you'll be lucky to get a close extended look. Before you get to the viewing room, there's an engaging exhibition, "Turning Darkness into Light," that puts the book into historical and religious context.

The Old Library also houses the Book of Armagh, the Book of Dimma, the Book of Durrow, and the Yellow Book of Lecan, which contains a partial version of the *Táin Bó Cúailnge* ("The Cattle Raid of Cooley"), one of

prestigious Trinity College

don't waste your afternoon in the queue to get in, or spring for the "fast track" option available for purchase online (€14).

Douglas Hyde Gallery of Modern Art

Named for the first president of Ireland, the **Douglas Hyde Gallery of Modern Art** (entrance on Nassau St., tel. 01/608-1116, www.douglashydegallery.com, 11am-6pm Mon.-Fri., until 7pm Thurs., 11am-4:45pm Sat., free) is in the Arts and Social Science Building, south of the Old Library. Two temporary exhibitions are on at a time in separate galleries, and feature paintings, sculpture, and textile arts from an international roster of artists.

SOUTH OF TRINITY

Dublin's political hub, as well as the National Gallery, Library, and Museum, is contained within a single block northeast of St. Stephen's Green, between Kildare and Merrion Streets. One block west, on Dawson Street, is the early Georgian Mansion House, the official home of the Lord Mayor of Dublin since 1715. Dawson Street is lined with other grand old buildings with interesting architectural details; several ground floors have been converted into chic bars and eateries.

Leinster House

Leinster House (entrance on Kildare St., tel. 01/618-3271, www.irlgov.ie/oireachtas, free), once home of the 20th Earl of Kildare (and later Duke of Leinster), now houses the Irish Parliament, the Oireachtas na hÉireann. The Parliament comprises a lower house, the Dáil (pronounced "doll"), and an upper house, the Seanad ("SHAN-add"); meetings (only 90 days out of the year Nov.-May) are open to the public. Tickets are available at the entrance on Kildare Street. Guided tours are also available occasionally; ring for more information.

For a free tour of the Irish **Government Buildings** (Upper Merrion St., tel. 01/645-8813, 10:30am-1:30pm Sat., free), head to the National Gallery lobby first for a ticket. Built between 1904 and 1911 and renovated to the nines in the late 1980s, the Government Buildings house the Taoiseach's offices as well as the Council Chamber (where the cabinet meets) and the Department of Finance. It's a worthwhile stop if you're interested in the Irish government or Edwardian architecture. Another item of interest is the huge stained glass window with nationalist motifs by Evie Hone in the entrance hall, which was commissioned for the New York World Trade Fair in 1939.

★ National Gallery

The **National Gallery of Ireland** (Merrion Sq. W., tel. 01/661-5133, www.nationalgallery.ie, 9:30am-5:30pm Mon.-Sat., until 8:30pm Thurs., noon-5:30pm Sun., free) is well worth a visit for its comprehensive collection of Irish art (plan to linger in the Yeats hall—bet you had no idea the whole family was so talented!) as well as works by Caravaggio, El Greco, Goya, Rembrandt, Vermeer, and Picasso. Other highlights include *The Marriage of Strongbow and Aoife,* a humonguous tableau scene painted by Daniel Maclise in the 1850s, and the Millennium Wing, which houses a permanent collection of contemporary works as well as visiting exhibitions. There's also a quality bookshop and an airy, modern café with pretty good food.

National Library

Check out the main reading room with its coffered dome at the **National Library of Ireland** (Kildare St., tel. 01/603-0200, www.nli.ie, 10am-9pm Mon.-Wed., 10am-5pm Thurs.-Fri., 10am-1pm Sat., free), which usually has a downstairs exhibition featuring scribbled pages from first drafts of beloved works and other interesting tidbits.

National Museum of Natural History

A better official name for the **National Museum of Natural History** (Merrion St., tel. 01/677-7444, www.museum.ie, 10am-5pm Tues.-Sat., 2pm-5pm Sun., free) might just be the Victorian Taxidermy Museum—it's already commonly known as the "Dead Zoo." Most visitors will probably end up skipping this one, but for those with antiquarian taste this quirky museum will provide an hour's diversion.

★ National Museum of Archaeology and History

There's more than one **National Museum,** but this one (Kildare St., tel. 01/677-7444, www.museum.ie, 10am-5pm Tues.-Sat., 2pm-5pm Sun., free) is the one you hear most about, for its phenomenal collection of artifacts from every period in Irish history: prehistoric tools and pottery; stunning gold torcs and other jewelry from the Bronze Age; ornate chalices, crosses, crosiers, bells, and brooches from the early Christian and medieval eras; Viking jewelry and weaponry; 18th- and 19th-century lace, silver, and musical instruments; and clothing and wooden sculptures—even a body!—found preserved in the bogs. The museum's three most important medieval artifacts are the Tara Brooch, an exquisite example of Celtic gold and silver metalwork dating to the beginning of the 8th century; the early 9th-century Ardagh Chalice, made of silver, gold, and bronze, found with other smaller treasures in a Limerick potato field in 1868; and the 12th-century Cross of Cong, an ornate silver reliquary that supposedly houses a splinter of the True Cross. Basically everything of archaeological importance found anywhere in the country is brought here and put under glass (even the bog man, and the effect is disconcerting to say the least). Visiting exhibitions complement a permanent collection of ancient Egyptian, Cypriot, Roman, and Byzantine artifacts.

Dawson Street

The first meeting of the Dáil took place on January 22, 1919, in the early-18th-century **Mansion House,** around the block from Leinster House and signing of the Anglo-Irish Treaty in 1921. The Mansion House is the official residence of the Lord Mayor of Dublin, elected by the city council for a one-year term, and is not open to the public.

Bibliophiles, take note: The **Royal Irish Academy** (19 Dawson St., tel. 01/676-2570, www.ria.ie, 10am-5:30pm Mon.-Thurs., 10am-5pm Fri., free) has a trove of priceless medieval illuminated manuscripts, including *The Cathach,* the oldest Irish psalter (dating to the 6th century, and associated with St. Columba). Generally only one manuscript is on display at a time, though.

★ ST. STEPHEN'S GREEN

Possibly Europe's largest city square, **St. Stephen's Green** is tranquil and immaculately kept. All these verdant walkways, duck ponds, and tidy flowerbeds (nine hectares in all) belie a dark history, however: Before the mid-17th century the area was commonly used for rowdy public executions (including burnings). The space was closed off from "rabble" in 1663 and gradually spiffed up for use by Dublin's elite. In 1877 Arthur Guinness introduced an Act of Parliament to open the green to the public, and this finally happened in 1880. The main entrance is through the **Fusiliers' Arch** at the bottom of Grafton Street; modeled after the Arch of Titus in Rome, it memorializes the 200-plus Royal Dublin Fusiliers killed in the Boer War. The park is dotted with smaller memorials to 1798 rebels Theobald Wolfe Tone and Robert Emmet, William Butler Yeats, Constance Markievicz, nationalist poet and translator James Clarence Mangan, and several other luminaries. The park is perfect for a leisurely stroll at any time of day, or just pick a bench and watch half of Dublin go by on their lunch breaks.

DUBLIN CASTLE AND AROUND

Dublin Castle (Dame St., Cork Hill, tel. 01/677-7129, www.dublincastle.ie, tours 10am-4:45pm Mon.-Fri., 2pm-4:45pm Sat.-Sun. and holidays, €8.50), built by order of King John in 1204, served as the seat of British power in Ireland for more than 700 years. Little of the original castle survives due to many half-hearted refurbishments and a widespread fire in 1689; today you can tour the excavations of the 13th-century foundations (called the "Undercroft," where the old castle joined the city walls), but otherwise it's just the Record Tower, finished in 1258, that remains. Most of the current structure dates from the mid-1700s. Despite its dank and crumbling walls, the castle continued to be used for official balls and banquets into the 20th century. During the Victorian era as many as 15,000 people were entertained there in the five-week period culminating in the annual St. Patrick's Ball (a festivity that, it is safe to say, the holy man would have scarcely approved of). In 1907 the Irish Crown Jewels were purloined from Bedford Tower and never seen again.

Today Dublin Castle is home to many government offices and a neo-Gothic chapel, which was converted to Catholicism in 1943. Guided tours usually include the state apartments, Undercroft, and chapel, but if the state rooms are unavailable due to official business the abridged tour will cost you a euro less.

City Hall

Opposite the castle entrance is **Dublin City Hall** (Dame St., tel. 01/222-2222, www.dublincity.ie, exhibition 10am-5pm Mon.-Sat., 2pm-5pm Sun., free). Built for the Royal Exchange in the 1770s, this neoclassical edifice boasts a gold-leaf dome supported by a dozen fluted columns, as well as plasterwork crafted by one of Dublin's mayors, Charles Thorp. While admission was free at time of writing to celebrate the Easter Rising centennial, there will likely be an admission charge again in 2017. Unless you're in the mood for a history lesson at the exhibition in the downstairs vaults, just pop inside to admire the rotunda with its statue of Daniel O'Connell.

★ The Chester Beatty Library

Bibliophiles and art lovers should put **The Chester Beatty Library** (on the grounds of Dublin Castle, signposted from the car park through the front gates, tel. 01/407-0750, www.cbl.ie, 10am-5pm Mon.-Fri., 11am-5pm Sat., 1pm-5pm Sun., closed Mon. Oct.-Apr., free) at the top of their sightseeing list. Arthur Chester Beatty (1875-1968), a prosperous American businessman living in London, moved his exquisite collection of illuminated manuscripts (and plenty of other treasures) to Dublin in 1950. The shrewd but soft-spoken Beatty spent the remainder of his life here, and he was the first person to be made an honorary Irish citizen. After a 10-minute audiovisual on Beatty's life and times, you make your way up to the galleries to peruse the collections of Chinese snuff bottles and embroidered garments, Japanese inro (lacquered wood containers suspended from a kimono sash), and a wealth of Islamic, Indian, and Asian manuscripts, working your way to the rooms of medieval and Renaissance books and engravings (including several by the late-15th/early-16th-century German master Albrecht Dürer). It's worth lingering in several rooms to watch the demonstration videos on illumination, book-binding, engraving, and other arts. The top-floor exhibits analyze three world religions (Christianity, Islam, and Buddhism) through manuscripts and other sacred objects. Behind glass are fragments of letters written as early as the second century AD, epistles that would eventually be included in the New Testament. There's also a rooftop garden and a classy café on the ground floor. The Beatty collection would be a must-see even if admission weren't free; it's just all the more worthwhile because it is!

TEMPLE BAR

Probably named for a local family in the late 17th century, this area stretches between Dame Street (which turns into Lord Edward Street) and the river, the western and eastern boundaries being Fishamble Street, where Handel first conducted his *Messiah* in 1742, and Trinity College, respectively.

neighborhood"—underwent an ambitious government-sponsored facelift in the 1990s using the designs of several local cutting-edge architectural firms. Today it's a hyper-commercialized hive of pubs, clubs, restaurants, and atmospheric alleyways.

Tucked between Sycamore and Eustace Streets just a couple of blocks south of the river, **Meetinghouse Square** is the hub of the neighborhood, buzzing at all hours with locals and tourists alike. The **Temple Bar Food Market** (tel. 01/671-5717, 10am-4:30pm) transpires here on Saturdays.

You can traverse Temple Bar's alleyways after nightfall without a backward glance, though the proliferation of (albeit harmless) drunken rowdies late at night can sure get on one's nerves. Unless you believe this . . . shall we say, *festive* atmosphere is an integral part of the Dublin experience, you might want to avoid the area after 10pm.

CHRISTCHURCH AND AROUND
★ Christ Church Cathedral

Though the marvelous **Christ Church Cathedral** (Christchurch Place, west end of Lord Edward St., tel. 01/677-8099, www.cccdub.ie, €6, guided tour €4) has its origins in the late 12th and early 13th centuries, much of the building was structurally unsound, and it was almost entirely rebuilt through the generosity of Henry Roe in the 1870s. Roe's chosen architect, George Edmund Street, preserved as much of the original edifice as possible and faithfully replicated the rest in the Romanesque and Early English Gothic styles.

In the yard are the foundations of a 13th-century chapter house, and in the southern aisle you'll spot the tomb of a knight whose nose is worn off; though it is identified as Strongbow's, we know for a fact that his tomb was destroyed when the south wall collapsed in 1562. Cathedral literature states this tomb is a replica of the original, but it's more likely someone else's tomb entirely. A reliquary in the Peace Chapel contains the heart of 12th-century archbishop Laurence O'Toole, patron saint of Dublin. The cathedral offers a few more weird surprises, like the mummified cat-and-rat pair found in a pipe of the church organ and the massive arches on the north side of the aisle leaning at an unnerving angle. Creepy statues of Charles I and II greet you as you enter the crypt, where you can watch a 12-minute audiovisual on the cathedral's history and check out the ornate silver plate presented to the cathedral by William of Orange in celebration of his victory at the Battle of the Boyne.

The cathedral is open daily (9am-6pm weekdays June-Aug., 9:45am-5pm or 6pm weekdays Sept.-May, 10am-4:30pm Sat. and 12:45pm-2:45pm Sun. all year). Evensong, which features music dating to the Reformation period, is performed in the cathedral at 3:30pm Sunday, 6pm Wednesday and Thursday, and 5pm Saturday. Admission to the belfry (where you can ring one of the bells!) is by guided tour only.

Dublin's second Anglican cathedral is **St. Patrick's** (Patrick St., tel. 01/475-4817, www.stpatrickscathedral.ie, €6), built in the Early English Gothic style at the turn of the 13th century near a well where Ireland's patron saint was said to have performed baptisms. St. Patrick's is the largest of Ireland's medieval cathedrals, though it has no crypt because it was built above the trickly River Poddle. Jonathan Swift, who served as Dean from 1713 to 1745, is entombed here beside his mistress, Esther Johnson. Come at the end of the day (weekdays excepting Wednesday) to hear the choir perform evensong; their 18th-century predecessors were the first to sing Handel's *Messiah*. St. Patrick's is open daily (9am-6pm Mon.-Sat. and 9am-11am, 12:45pm-3pm, and 4:15pm-6pm Sun. Mar.-Oct.; 9am-6pm weekdays, 9am-5pm Sat., 10am-11am and 12:45pm-3pm Sun. Nov.-Feb.).

Down the street is the **Narcissus Marsh Library** (St. Patrick's Close, tel. 01/454-3511, www.marshlibrary.ie, 9:30am-5pm Mon. and Wed.-Fri., 10am-5pm Sat., €3). Ireland's first public library was established in 1701 by Narcissus Marsh, who was the Anglican Archbishop of Cashel, Dublin, and Armagh (though not all at once). The archbishop opened the library with 10,000 volumes from his personal collection, and today there are more than 25,000 ancient (and somewhat moldy-looking) tomes arranged carefully on the original shelves in two cathedral-ceilinged galleries. Rotating exhibits under glass feature centuries-old books with hand-painted illustrations, and another case houses Jonathan Swift's death mask. The library staff are very friendly and informative, the volunteers delightfully quirky and garrulous; bibliophiles will find the Marsh library well worth a visit.

Catholics and lovebirds might want to step inside **Our Lady of Mount Carmel** (entrance at 56 Aungier St., tel. 01/475-8821), which houses "some of" the remains of St. Valentine in a niche on your right as you walk up the aisle.

a view of Christ Church Cathedral from the walkway to the belfry, accessible by guided tour

DUBLIN
SIGHTS

St. Audoen's Church

The Anglican **St. Audoen's Church** (Cornmarket, High St., tel. 01/677-0088, 9:30am-5:30pm daily June-Sept., free) is the only remaining medieval parish church in Dublin, flanked by a chunk of the old city wall. St. Audoen's Arch here is the last extant city gate. The Catholic **St. Audoen's** around the corner on High Street is an imposing neoclassical edifice with a huge and hideous Corinthian portico. The two churches form a somewhat amusing study in architectural contrasts. Here too is **St. Mary's Abbey** (Mary's Abbey St., Meetinghouse Ln., off Capel St., tel. 01/833-1618 or 01/647-6587 in winter, 10am-5pm Mon.-Sat. mid-June-mid-Sept., free), once the richest Cistercian monastery in the country. Here "Silken Thomas," Lord of Offaly, had the chutzpah to renounce his allegiance to Henry VIII in 1534, thus sparking a yearlong, nationwide insurrection.

NORTHSIDE

Head north of the Liffey for a glimpse of everyday life in the capital city. The "Northside" neighborhood consists of everything north of the river and south of the M50 motorway skirting the city, and the word is used to refer to a blue-collar attitude as often as it is indicative of urban geography. The "post-code snobbery" of the Dublin elite has eased as developers have erected sparkling new shopping centers, and every just-opened eatery is hipper than the one before it. There is plenty in the way of sightseeing north of the Liffey as well: the Dublin Writers Museum, Old Jameson Distillery, and St. Michan's Church are just a few of the highlights.

O'Connell Street

The Northside's primary thoroughfare, O'Connell Street is a transportation hub where you'll find the General Post Office (headquarters of the ill-fated Easter Rising in 1916) as well as a few decorations of hilariously questionable taste: the "Floozy in the Jacuzzi" (you'll see!), a statue of James Joyce to which locals chain their bicycles, and the "Dublin Spire," a 120-meter light-up metal spoke Dubs know better as the "stiffy by the Liffey."

Erected in 1854 in memory of the "Great Liberator," the **O'Connell Monument** is flanked by four winged figures representing patriotism, fidelity, eloquence, and courage. Farther up O'Connell Street (formerly Sackville), the **General Post Office,** or **GPO** (tel. 01/705-7000, 8am-8pm Mon.-Sat., free), an imposing neoclassical edifice built between 1815 and 1817, served as rebel stronghold during the Easter Rising of 1916. Here Patrick Pearse (also spelled Pádraic or Pádraig) read the Proclamation of the Irish Republic from the front steps, and the shell marks are still visible on the facade.

Just off O'Connell Street is **St. Mary's Pro-Cathedral** (83 Marlborough St., tel. 01/874-5441, www.procathedral.ie, 7:30am-6:45pm Mon.-Fri., 7:30am-7:15pm Sat., 9am-1:45pm and 5:30pm-7:45pm Sun., 10am-1:30pm public holidays, free), the seat of the Catholic Archbishop of Dublin ("pro" indicating the church is an "acting cathedral"; Dublin has two Anglican cathedrals, St. Patrick's and Christ Church, but the Catholic Church still recognizes the latter as its official cathedral because it was designated as such in the 12th century). "The Pro," as locals call it, was designed by amateur architect John Sweetman in 1816 with a Greek revival facade and a richly decorated interior evocative of the great basilicas of Rome.

At the top of O'Connell Street is the **Parnell Monument,** an obelisk pillar topped with a bronze statue by Augustus St. Gaudens.

Parnell Square

At the **Dublin Writers Museum** (18 Parnell Sq., tel. 01/872-2077, www.writersmuseum.com, 10am-5pm Mon.-Sat., 11am-5pm Sun. year-round, closing at 6pm Mon.-Sat. June-Aug., €7.50), you can peruse exhibition boards (presenting Ireland's literary heritage in chronological order, with plenty of biographical details) and glass cases containing typewriters, first editions, original correspondence, and other stuff; an audio guide is included in the admission price. The foyer and upstairs rooms feature portraits and bronze busts of luminaries from Yeats and Beckett to Elizabeth Bowen and Mary Lavin, and there is generally a rotating exhibit upstairs as well.

Across the street is the **Garden of Remembrance** (Parnell Sq. E., tel. 01/874-3074). Opened in 1966 to commemorate the 50th anniversary of the Easter Rising, it features a sculpture by Oisin Kelly depicting the legend of the Children of Lir (who were turned into swans by their sorceress stepmother).

★ The Hugh Lane Gallery

A couple doors down from the Dublin Writers Museum is the **Hugh Lane Municipal Gallery of Modern Art** (22 N. Parnell Sq., tel. 01/874-1903, www.hughlane.ie, 10am-6pm Tues.-Thurs., 10am-5pm Fri.-Sat., 11am-5pm Sun., free), in the erstwhile townhome of the first Earl of Charlemont and designed by William Chambers in the 1760s. The fantastic permanent collection includes works by Monet, Renoir, Degas, Corot, Millais, and Burne-Jones, and native works by Sean Keating, Paul Henry, and Jack B. Yeats, most of which were collected by Sir Hugh Lane before his demise on the *Lusitania* in 1915. The gallery also includes an authentically chaotic re-creation of **Francis Bacon's studio** in London, and Harry Clarke's stained-glass masterpiece, *The Eve of St. Agnes,* is another highlight. The downstairs courtyard café is a very good choice for lunch, with good coffee and friendly service.

Croke Park

Croke Park is Ireland's largest stadium, with 84,000 seats. Those interested in **Gaelic football** and **hurling** should check out the **GAA Museum** (Gaelic Athletic Association, New Stand, Croke Park, Clonliffe Rd., north of the Royal Canal, tel. 01/855-8176, http://museum.gaa.ie) for a high-tech history of the games, including a 15-minute audiovisual. In addition to visiting the museum (9:30am-5pm Mon.-Sat. and noon-5pm Sun. Apr.-Oct.,

10am-5pm Tues.-Sat. and noon-4pm Sun. Nov.-Mar., €6.50), you can take a one-hour stadium tour (€13). The All-Ireland finals take place here every September. To get here, take **Dublin Bus** (#3, #11/A, #16/A, or #123) from O'Connell Street.

Four Courts

Notice that striking (not to mention humongous) green-domed neoclassical structure on the quay? It's the **Four Courts** (Inns Quay, tel. 01/872-5555, 11am-1pm and 2pm-4pm weekdays, free), home of the Irish law courts since 1796; the name comes from the four traditional divisions of the judicial system (Chancery, King's Bench, Exchequer, and Common Pleas). Designed by James Gandon in the 1780s, the building was bombarded by provisional forces and gutted by republican "irregulars" during the Civil War; the restoration work dates to 1932. The public is admitted only when court is in session.

★ St. Michan's Church

Named for a Danish bishop who built the original church on the site of an ancient oak grove, the Anglican **St. Michan's Church** (Church St., tel. 01/872-4154, www.stmichans.com, €6) houses the organ on which Handel practiced the *Messiah* before its first performance at the old Dublin Music Hall on Fishamble Street on April 13, 1742. That's not why teenagers come here in droves, though—it's to see the uncannily preserved remains in the medieval crypt, a phenomenon caused by a combo of methane gas and the limestone foundations, which absorb the moisture in the air. This is, bar none, the most macabre sight in the city, and not for the faint-hearted. Hours vary seasonally (10am-12:45pm and 2pm-4:30pm Mon.-Fri. and 10am-12:45pm Sat. mid-Mar.-Oct., 12:30pm-3:30pm Mon.-Fri. and 10am-12:45pm Sat. Nov.-mid-Mar.).

Access to the crypt is by guided tour, which takes place whenever there

You'll never forget a tour of the vaults at creepy St. Michan's Church.

are enough visitors. Stringy cobwebs dangle from the rough stone ceiling in these dimly lit subterranean vaults, each one belonging to a different aristocratic Dublin family. In the second section, the first cell on your right displays the death mask of Theobald Wolfe Tone as well as the gruesome execution order of John and Henry Sheares, all of whom were patriots in the 1798 rebellion. (The brothers' remains are here too.) You'll pass family vaults on either side, a couple of which have been illuminated to show you how the coffins have been stacked upon those of the previous generation—many of which have collapsed, with undecomposed limbs poking through the splintered wood. You can see the fingernails and everything.

The vault at the end of the first section contains the remains that St. Michan's is known for. You used to be able to touch the hand of the so-called "Crusader," who has been dead for at least 600 years—he was almost two meters tall, and his feet were actually sawn off to fit him in the coffin!—but these days the church caretakers are being more responsible about preserving these formerly human curiosities. The tour guide is still amusingly theatrical, even if he can no longer give you the run of the place.

Old Jameson Distillery

If you have time for only one tipple tour, go for the **Old Jameson Distillery** (Bow St., Smithfield, 1 block north of Arran Quay, tel. 01/807-2355, www. whiskeytours.ie, 9:30am-5:30pm daily, €16, 10% discount online) rather than the Guinness Storehouse; it's a bit less expensive and more engaging, and unlike at Guinness you get a real guided tour (departing every half hour). And of course, a whiskey-tasting is included in the price of admission.

Collins Barracks

The **National Museum of Decorative Arts and History** at the Collins Barracks (Benburb St., one block north of Wolfe Tone Quay, tel. 01/677-7444, 10am-5pm Tues.-Sat., until 8:30pm Thurs., 2pm-5pm Sun., free), opened in 1999, may not be as exciting as the National Museum of Archaeology and History, but it's still worth a visit. Here you'll find collections of silver, coins, period clothing and furniture, ceramics, glassware, and weaponry. There's a special gallery devoted to long-stored items just recently dusted off. On a darker note, the 14 executed Easter rebels were buried on **Arbour Hill** directly behind the barracks.

WEST OF THE CITY CENTER

Guinness Storehouse

Perhaps the biggest tourist trap in Dublin is the **Guinness Storehouse** (St. James' Gate, tel. 01/408-4800, www.guinness-storehouse.com, 9:30am-5pm daily, €16, 20% discount with online booking). It's one thing if you're a devoted stout drinker, but don't feel like you ought to go just because everyone else is. Note that the tour is self-guided—and even cheekier, you have to pay the admission fee even if you just want to have lunch in the

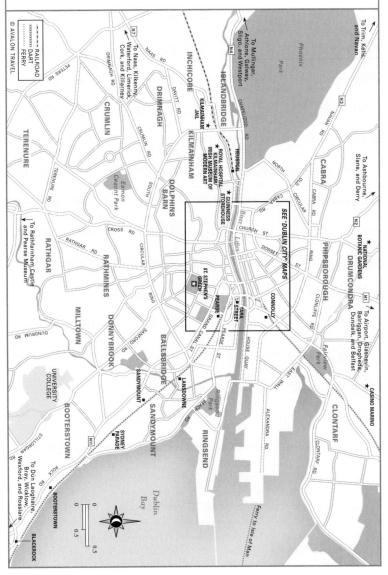

Greater Dublin

© AVALON TRAVEL

RAILROAD
DART
FERRY

To Naas, Kilkenny,
Waterford, Limerick,
Cork, and Killarney

To Mullingar,
Athlone, Galway,
Sligo, and Westport

To Trim, Kells,
and Navan

To Ashbourne,
Slane, and Derry

To Airport, Glasnevin,
Balrigan, Drogheda,
Dundalk, and Belfast

To Rathfarnham Castle
and Pearse Museum

To Dún Laoghaire,
Bray, Wicklow,
Wexford, and Rosslare

Ferry to Isle of Man

Phoenix Park

KILMAINHAM JAIL
ROYAL HOSPITAL KILMAINHAM/ IRISH MUSEUM OF MODERN ART
HEUSTON
GUINNESS STOREHOUSE
NATIONAL BOTANIC GARDENS
CASINO MARINO
ST. STEPHEN'S GREEN
PEARSE
TARA STREET
CONNOLLY

SEE "DUBLIN CITY MAPS"

River Liffey

Dublin Bay

INCHICORE, ISLANDBRIDGE, DRIMNAGH, CRUMLIN, TERENURE, KILMAINHAM, DOLPHINS BARN, CABRA, PHIBSBOROUGH, DRUMCONDRA, CLONTARF, RATHGAR, RATHMINES, MILLTOWN, DONNYBROOK, BALLSBRIDGE, SANDYMOUNT, RINGSEND, BOOTERSTOWN, BLACKROCK, SANDYMOUNT, LANSDOWNE, STYDNEY PARADE

UNIVERSITY COLLEGE

0   0.5
0   0.5

restaurant (which, admittedly, serves up some really good traditional meals like shepherd's pie and Irish stew, all liberally laced with the black stuff). But at least your ticket includes the best pint you'll ever taste in the upstairs, all-glass Gravity Bar with a panoramic city view. The walk is doable (about 15 minutes from Trinity), but you could also take Dublin Bus

The Wraiths of Kilmainham

The long, dark history of Kilmainham Jail—Ireland's largest uninhabited prison—and its tragic association with the Easter rebellion, make ghost stories nearly inevitable. Along with the doomed patriots, the jail housed everyone from common criminals to ordinary citizens who'd fallen on especially hard times. In fact, many victims committed crimes simply because they knew they'd be fed in prison. Even children were incarcerated here. Records indicate that Kilmainham saw approximately 150 executions in its 128-year history, and many of those prisoners were buried in the stone-breakers' yard (where 14 Easter rebels met their deaths). Furthermore, the jail was built on the site of a gallows.

So it comes as no surprise that many folks, visitors and employees alike, will testify that Kilmainham has quite an accumulation of restless spirits. Those volunteers who set about restoring the jail during the 1960s had plenty of chilling stories to share: lights turning on by themselves in remote sections of the building late at night, inexplicable gusts of wind, and heavy phantom footsteps. According to the Paranormal Research Association of Ireland, most of the supernatural activity occurs in the west wing, where you'll find the political prisoners' dark, dank cells.

During the tour your guide will draw your attention to an excerpt of a poem by Patrick Pearse, "The Rebel," scrawled on the wall above a doorway:

> Beware of the thing that is coming, beware of the risen people,
> Who shall take what ye would not give.
> Did ye think to conquer the people,
> Or that law is stronger than life and than men's desire to be free?
> We will try it out with you, ye that have harried and held,
> Ye that have bullied and bribed, tyrants, hypocrites, liars!

Pearse, one of the leaders of the Easter rebellion, was among those executed in May 1916, and his words are as much a contribution to the spooky atmosphere as they are a reminder of Ireland's centuries-old political struggle.

#51B or #78A from Aston Quay or #123 from O'Connell or Dame Street; the trip will take 10 minutes.

Kilmainham Jail

Another very popular attraction, **Kilmainham Jail** (or "Gaol," Inchicore Rd., tel. 01/453-5984, 9:30am-6pm daily Apr.-Sept., 9:30am-5:30pm Mon.-Sat. and 10am-6pm Sun. Oct.-Mar., €7) is a late-18th-century prison that is open to the public essentially to commemorate the 14 nationalists executed in early May 1916 for their leading roles in the Easter Rising. You can enter the stonebreakers' yard where Patrick Pearse, his brother William, and 12 other patriots were shot at daybreak. Over the course of a fascinating (if crowded) hour-long tour, you'll hear plenty of heart-tugging stories. One concerns Joseph Plunkett, who married his longtime sweetheart, Grace Gifford, inside the jail just four hours before his execution on May 4, 1916.

The Easter Rising nearly eclipses the rest of the jail's history, which the guide discusses only briefly; during the Great Famine there were as many as 9,000 people crowded into 188 cells. It's said that people often committed crimes because they knew they'd be fed in prison. You can peep into these cells, many of which are labeled with their most famous occupants. Another highlight of the tour is a trip to the "panopticon," the all-seeing eye, the cavernous open-plan cell block where scenes from several Irish movies (including *Michael Collins* and *In the Name of the Father*) were filmed.

After the tour, head to the upstairs exhibition and look out for a red-lighted side hallway, which is lined with display cases of poignant personal effects of the 14 Easter rebel-martyrs. It's the best part of the visit. To get to the jail, take Dublin Bus #51/B, #78A, or #79 from Aston Quay.

Royal Hospital Kilmainham and the Irish Museum of Modern Art

Just up the road is the **Royal Hospital Kilmainham** (Military Rd., Kilmainham, tel. 01/612-9900, www.rhk.ie, 10am-5:30pm Tues.-Sat. and noon-5:30pm Sun. June-Sept., free), a late 17th-century neoclassical edifice that many at the time grumbled was far too grand for its inhabitants, who were retired soldiers. In summer you can tour the hospital's baroque chapel, great hall, formal gardens, and burial grounds, and concerts are often held here.

On the premises is the **Irish Museum of Modern Art** (tel. 01/612-9900, www.imma.ie, 10am-5:30pm Tues. and Thurs.-Sat., 10:30am-5:30pm Wed., noon-5:30pm Sun., free), with an intriguing collection of works by lesser-known Irish painters, sculptors, and printmakers. Guided tours are available on Wednesday, Friday, and Sunday at 2:30pm. To get here, take Dublin Bus #51/A/B, #78A, or #79 from Aston Quay, #123 from Dame Street or O'Connell Street, or #26 from Wellington Quay.

Phoenix Park

Long before it was Europe's largest enclosed park, **Phoenix Park** served as the largest Viking cemetery outside Scandinavia—surely a fact no one's thinking of while playing or watching any of the soccer, hurling, cricket, or horse racing going on here! The name "Phoenix" has nothing to do with that mythical bird (though it appears on an eponymous monument near the middle of the park); it's just the anglicization of Fionn Uisce, "Clean Water," a reference to a stream running through the park. At seven square kilometers, Phoenix Park is roughly twice the size of Central Park in Manhattan; like Central Park, it has several busy through-roads. Every day as many as 20,000 cars travel through the park, and the Office of Public Works hopes eventually to eliminate all through traffic.

The park's two main entrances are at Parkgate Street (at the southeast corner) and at Castleknock Gate (at the northwest corner), with Chesterfield Avenue being the thoroughfare that bisects the park. Phoenix Park is bordered by North Road to the north and Chapelizod Road to the south.

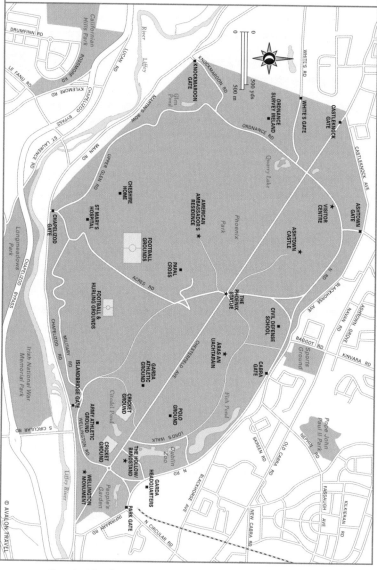

Phoenix Park

Once inside, it's quite easy to orient yourself by a 63-meter obelisk, the **Wellington Monument,** at the southeastern corner. Across Chesterfield Avenue is the **People's Garden,** laid out in 1864, and **The Hollow,** where a bandstand in a natural amphitheater hosts brass and swing bands in the summertime.

On the far side of the park, the **Phoenix Park Visitor Centre** (tel. 01/677-0095, www.phoenixpark.ie, 10am-5pm Wed.-Sun. Nov.-Mar., 10am-5:30pm daily late Mar. and Oct., 10am-6pm daily Apr.-Sept., free) offers a 20-minute audiovisual on the park's history, certainly worthwhile if you've purchased the Dúchas Heritage Card. It's also your point of entry for nearby 17th-century **Ashtown Castle**. This restored tower house is rather small and unfurnished, though, so the half-hour tour is of only moderate interest.

The park holds several official buildings, including the residence of the U.S. ambassador and Garda Síochána headquarters. There's also the home of the Irish president, **Áras an Uachtaráin** (tel. 01/670-9155, hour-long tours 10:30am-4:15pm Sat. summer, 9:30am-3:30pm Sat. winter, free). The "Irish White House" is in the northeastern section of the park, and you can sign up for a visit on a Saturday morning at the visitors center. After an introductory audiovisual presentation, you'll be whisked off to the president's house in a minibus for an hour-long tour of the main state reception rooms and gardens. There are no reservations and spots are limited, so it's wise to arrive when the Phoenix Park Visitor Centre opens at 9:30am to obtain tickets for the first tour at 10:30am. State business can sometimes lead to cancellation of all tours, and note that backpacks and cameras aren't permitted. To get to the visitors center by Dublin Bus, the route that drops you the closest (Ashtown Gate) is #37, which you can board from Lower Abbey Street (Northside).

In the southeast corner is **Dublin Zoo** (tel. 01/677-1425, www.dublinzoo.ie, €17), established in 1830—making it the second-oldest zoo in Europe. Dublin Bus #10 from O'Connell Street will get you here. Hours vary seasonally (9:30am-6pm Mon.-Sat. and 10:30am-6pm Sun. May-Sept., 9:30am-4pm Mon.-Fri., 9:30am-5pm Sat., and 10:30am-5pm Sun. Oct.-Apr.).

GLASNEVIN

An erstwhile suburb three kilometers north of the Liffey, Glasnevin is home to Dublin City University (DCU) as well as two of the city's most important attractions.

National Botanic Gardens

The 19-hectare **National Botanic Gardens** (Botanic Rd., 3.5 km north of Trinity College, tel. 01/837-7596 or 01/837-4388, www.botanicgardens.ie, 9am-6pm Mon.-Sat. and 10am-6pm Sun. in summer, 10am-4:30pm daily in winter, free, guided tour €5) are home to more than 20,000 plant species, 300 of which are endangered and 6 of which are already extinct in the wild. Established in 1795, the gardens feature superb Victorian glasshouses by Richard Turner. It was here in August 1845 that the then-curator, David Moore, first noted the potato blight and correctly predicted its devastating consequences.

To get to the gardens, catch Dublin Bus #13/A from Merrion Square or O'Connell Street, or #19 from O'Connell Street (4/hour daily, 15-minute trip, fare €0.95).

Glasnevin Cemetery

Just west of the botanic gardens is Glasnevin Cemetery, also known as **Prospect Cemetery** (Finglas Rd., 3.5 km north of Trinity College, tel. 01/830-1133, www.glasnevin-cemetery.ie, 9:30am-6pm Mon.-Sat., 9:30am-5pm Sun., closes earlier in winter, free), the largest in the country at 124 acres. Here is the final resting place of many of Ireland's most beloved patriots: Daniel O'Connell (just look for the faux round tower), Charles Stewart Parnell, Michael Collins, Eamon de Valera, Maud Gonne MacBride, Constance Markievicz, Patrick Pearse, and Arthur Griffith. Much of the statuary here bears overt republican and patriotic motifs, apt considering it was established as a Catholic burial ground in 1832, after the Act of Emancipation. Note the watchtowers in the graveyard's southeastern section, which were used to keep an eye out for bodysnatchers. A free 90-minute guided tour departs the main gate at 2:30pm every Wednesday and Friday. Alternatively, there's a map and guide available from the flower shop at the front gate for €3.50.

The cemetery is on Dublin Bus #40 from Parnell Street (5/hour daily, 35-minute trip).

EAST OF THE CITY CENTER

The Dúchas-run **Casino Marino** (Cherrymount Crescent, off the Malahide Rd., 4 km east of the city center, tel. 01/833-1618, 10am-5pm daily May and Oct., 10am-6pm daily June-Sept., noon-4pm weekends Nov.-Mar., noon-5pm weekends Apr., €4) is, in the words of *Irish Times* writer Frank McDonald, "surely our most peculiar national monument. It was designed by an English architect who never set foot in this country for an Irish aristocrat and aesthete who almost went bankrupt trying to recreate Italy in Ireland." These men were William Chambers and James Caulfield (the first Earl of Charlemont), respectively. As a young man, the earl had dragged his Grand Tour of Europe into a nine-year odyssey, and he became good friends with Chambers while both were staying in Rome. He later had Chambers design his "summer home," what is still widely considered one of the best examples of small-scale neoclassical architecture; difficult as it is to picture now, this section of Dublin was still part of the boonies back in the 18th century, and the casino (as in "small house") had a great view of Dublin Bay and the surrounding countryside. Now it's something of an oasis amid the urban sprawl.

Ironically, Chambers never laid eyes on one of his very finest achievements, which is larger and grander than it appears from the exterior. Ingenious touches abound, like chimneys disguised as decorative urns on the roof and rainwater pipes hidden in columns, and the nearly hour-long guided tour offers plenty more interesting historical and architectural tidbits.

The building was taken into state care in 1932, but the 10-year restoration effort commenced only in 1974. To preserve the original flooring, visitors are asked to wear disposable booties over their shoes. To get here, take Dublin Bus #123 from O'Connell Street (4+/hour daily), or ride the DART from Connolly to Clontarf Road (4/hour daily), which is much faster.

SOUTH OF THE CITY CENTER

In the "village" of Rathfarnham is **Rathfarnham Castle** (Rathfarnham bypass, between Rathfarnam Rd. and Grange Rd., Dublin 14, tel. 01/493-9462, 9:30am-5:30pm daily May-Oct., €4), an impressive 16th-century structure with 18th-century interiors by two of England's most prominent architects, William Chambers and James "Athenian" Stuart (he got that moniker after publishing *Antiquities of Athens,* which greatly influenced the neoclassical movement in late-18th-century British architecture). Conservation work is ongoing in the castle itself, where access is by a guided tour of 45 minutes to an hour. Take Dublin Bus #16/A from South Great Georges Street.

Patrick Pearse, one of the Easter rebels executed in May 1916, was a devoted learner and teacher of the Irish language. The nearby **Pearse Museum and St. Enda's National Historic Park** (Grange Rd., Rathfarnham, Dublin 16, tel. 01/493-4208, 10am-1pm and 2pm-5:30pm daily May-Aug., until 5pm Feb.-Apr. and Sept.-Oct., until 4pm Nov.-Jan., free) is housed on the premises of the school he founded in 1909; it features an exhibition on Pearse's life and work with a collection of letters and photographs and a 20-minute audiovisual. The adjacent St. Enda's Park includes a waterfall, walled garden, and self-guiding nature trail. Take bus #16/A to get here.

Activities and Recreation

TOURS

All tours are bookable through Dublin's central **tourist office** (25 Suffolk St., tel. 01/884-7871, www.visitdublin.com, 9am-5:30pm Mon.-Sat., 10:30am-3pm Sun.).

★ Walking Tours

Get some exercise, learn a lot, and maybe even have yourself a tipple on one of Dublin's many excellent guided walking tours. The best known, running since 1988, is the **Dublin Literary Pub Crawl** (tel. 01/670-5602, www.dublinpubcrawl.com, tours at 7:30pm daily and noon Sun. late Mar.-late Nov., Thurs.-Sun. only in low season, 2.25 hours, €12), hosted by local actors who'll perform the work of Ireland's most beloved poets and playwrights at each of the four pubs on the itinerary. The tour starts at The Duke pub on Duke Street off Grafton Street. The performances come between frequent 20-minute beer breaks.

If you love a good old-fashioned ghost story, sign up for a **Haunted History Dublin** walking tour (tel. 085/102-3646, www.hiddendublinwalks.com, runs Mon., Thurs., and Sat. at 8pm, 1.5-2 hours, €13). This company offers both bus and walking tours to several creeptastic destinations, including the infamous Hellfire Club in the Wicklow Mountains. The rendezvous point is opposite Eddie Rocket's on Dame Street.

Want something a little more serious? Then you'll admire your hard-working guides on the **Historical Walking Tour** (tel. 01/878-0227 or 087/688-9412, www.historicalinsights.ie, 11am and 3pm daily Apr.-Sept., noon Fri.-Sat. Oct.-Mar., €12), all postgraduate history students. The two-hour walk departs from the Trinity College entrance. Themed tours, available between May and September, include "Architecture and Society," the "Sexual History of Ireland," and another focusing on the Easter Rising. Another reputable company does an **Easter Rising Walk** (tel. 01/707-2493 or 087/830-3523, www.1916rising.com, 11:30am Mon.-Sat. and 1pm Sun. Apr.-Sept., €13), which departs the International Bar on Wicklow Street and also lasts two hours.

City Bus Tours

Dublin Bus (59 O'Connell St., tel. 01/873-4222, www.dublinsightseeing.ie) offers tours in and around the city. The **Hop-On Hop-Off Tour** (buses every 15 minutes 9:30am-4:30pm daily, €22) is a 90-minute circuit that includes pretty much all the city center attractions, plus Phoenix Park and the Guinness Storehouse, and your ticket entitles you to discounts at several places. The **Ghost Tour** (7pm and 9pm Sat.-Sun., 8pm Tues.-Fri., 2-hour tour €25) offers, among other grisly tidbits, a "crash course in body-snatching." The **Coast and Castles Tour** (10am-2pm daily, 3-hour tour €25) covers the National Botanic Gardens, Casino Marino, Malahide Castle, and Howth Harbour. You can book any of these tours at the Dublin Bus office at 14 Upper O'Connell Street or at the Suffolk Street tourist office, though you can usually get at least a 10 percent discount online; all tours depart the O'Connell Street office.

Boat Tours

One of the most fun and original (if touristy) ways to see more of the city is on a **Viking Splash Tour** (tel. 01/707-6000, www.vikingsplash.com, tours generally every half hour 10am-5pm daily Mar.-Oct., Wed.-Sun. in Feb. and Tues.-Sun. in Nov., €22, €25 June-Aug.). Tours depart 64-65 Patrick Street (near St. Patrick's Cathedral) and St. Stephen's Green North (at Dawson Street). You'll spend the first 50 minutes on this 75-minute tour walking around the city wearing "Viking" hats and behaving outrageously in public at the behest of your guide. In between, of course, you'll learn a lot of historical tidbits. The tour culminates in a 20-minute boat trip on the Grand Canal Basin in a "Duck"—a reconditioned WWII amphibious military vehicle. There is not much "splashing" involved, however.

Day Trips from Dublin

Brú na Bóinne (Newgrange and two other passage tombs), **Powerscourt,** and **Glendalough** in Wicklow Mountains National Park are commonly experienced on a day tour out of the city.

Over the Top Tours (tel. 01/838-6128 or 087/259-3467, freephone tel. for reservations 1800/424-252, www.overthetoptours.com, departs O'Connell St. outside Gresham Hotel at 9:20am and Suffolk St. tourist office at 9:45am daily, returning 5:30pm, ticket €28) offers smallish (max. 14 people) tours of Glendalough and Wicklow Mountains National Park as well as Newgrange and Knowth (€17, same departure points at 8:45am and 9am, admission to site not included).

Game of Thrones fans will definitely want to sign up for a daylong tour (tel. 01/513-3033, www.gameofthronestours.com, €55) of the Winterfell filming locations, which includes two three-kilometer walks in Tollymore forest and Castle Ward Estate in County Down. The tour bus departs Jurys Inn, Custom House Quay at 8am daily.

OTHER ACTIVITIES AND RECREATION

In the City

Be a temporary Dubliner and stretch your legs on the nine-hectare **St. Stephen's Green** (at the bottom of Grafton St., tel. 01/475-7816), or go for a run or longer walk at the seven-square-kilometer **Phoenix Park** (main entrance on Parkgate St., at the southeast corner, tel. 01/677-0095) on the western perimeter of the city center.

Built for the 2003 Special Olympics summer games, the **National Aquatic Centre** (Snugborough Rd., Blanchardstown, Dublin 15, tel. 01/646-4364 or 01/646-4367, www.nac.ie, 9am-8:45pm weekdays, 9am-7:45pm weekends, €7.50-15) features plenty of kiddie delights (slides, wave and surf machines, the works) as well as the official Olympic-size pool. Dublin Bus #38A from Hawkins Street (or Berkeley St., outside St. Joseph's Church) will get you here.

Outside the City

Don't stay in the city center if the weather's fine! There are several sandy beaches in the Dublin burbs; some of them, like **Killiney** (kill-EYE-nee, 16 km south of the city), **Portrane** (24 km north), and **Donabate** (21 km north), have even been awarded the coveted Blue Flag. Killiney is particularly attractive; some say it even has a vaguely Mediterranean vibe on fine summer days. Many Irish celebs (Bono, Enya, and director Neil Jordan, among others) have homes here. Fortunately, you can reach all these beaches via the **DART** (tel. 01/805-4288, www.dart.ie, 2-3/hour daily from Connolly Station, 20-minute trip, get off at Donabate for Portrane as well, single/day return fares €3.80/6.85). **Dollymount,** another Blue Flag beach (and UNESCO Biosphere Reserve, for its web-footed population), is immediately north of Dublin Harbour. The strand is linked to the Dollymount neighborhood by an old wooden bridge. Get here via Dublin Bus #130 from Lower Abbey Street (4-6/hour daily).

For a day tour including Glendalough and Powerscourt in Enniskerry, look into **Walkabout Wicklow** (tel. 087/784-9599, www.walkaboutwickow. com). The base price is €25, €35 if you'd like to add a guided walk, and €75 if you'd like to add a horseback riding excursion. Tours depart the Gresham Hotel on O'Connell Street at 9:20am and the central tourist office on Suffolk Street at 9:35am, returning to Dublin around 5:30pm. Walkabout Wicklow also offers longer guided treks of 3-15 days.

Not many folks can say they've sailed over Ireland in a hot air balloon. Want bragging rights? Contact **Irish Balloon Flights** (80 Cypress Grove Rd., Templeogue, Dublin, tel. 01/408-4777 or 087/933-2622, flight-check line 087/743-7575, www.balloons.ie, 1/2/3 or more passengers €195/190/185 pp). Most flights depart Rathsallagh House in Wicklow (60 km south of Dublin) or Trim Castle in Meath (55 km northwest), though there are other launch locations around the country. The hefty ticket price includes a glass of champagne after a one-hour flight.

Spectator Sports

Catch a **hurling** or **Gaelic football** match at the country's largest stadium, **Croke Park** (Clonliffe Rd., north of the Royal Canal in Drumcondra, tel. 01/836-3222, €25-55), on Sunday afternoons May-September. Except for playoff games (when tickets can be mighty hard to come by), you can purchase admission at the door. For more background on these native sports, check out the **Gaelic Athletic Association** website (www.gaa.ie).

Dublin Bus routes #3, #11/A, #16/A, and #123 frequently link O'Connell Street with Croke Park.

Football (i.e., soccer) and rugby matches are played at **Lansdowne Stadium** (Ballsbridge, tel. 01/668-9300, www.lrsdc.ie) on the south side of the city; capacity is 50,000. Take the DART to the Lansdowne Road Station, a short walk from the park, or ride Dublin Bus #7, #8, #45, or #84.

Food

Whether you want a (relatively) cheap, no-frills meal or a lavish three-course affair, Dublin's eateries run the gamut. So long as you know where to go, you might just end up eating better here than you did in Paris. Plus, finding good-value eats in this city isn't as difficult as you might think.

Some restaurants have started tacking a 10-15 percent "service charge" onto your bill (regardless of the number in your party). If you weren't satisfied with your meal in any way, don't hesitate to ask your server to deduct it.

AROUND GRAFTON STREET

It may be the historic jewel of Grafton Street—Harry Clarke windows, mahogany banisters and all—but unfortunately **Bewley's Oriental Café** (78-79 Grafton St., tel. 01/672-7720, www.bewleys.com) was closed at time of writing. The famous tearooms are supposedly undergoing refurbishments, though the Dublin press has speculated that the exorbitant annual rent of €1.5 million led to the closure. Hopefully it'll be open again by the time you're reading this.

You'll find the best pub grub in the area at **O'Neill's** (2 Suffolk St., tel. 01/679-3656, www.oneillspubdublin.com, food served 3:30pm-9:30pm Mon.-Thurs. and noon-9:30pm Fri.-Sun., €11-14), a commodious, old-fashioned watering hole—open more than three centuries—with excellent carvery lunches that call to mind a Thanksgiving feast (though there's a vegetarian quiche on the menu as well).

You can choose either cafeteria-style or table service at ★ **Cornucopia** (Wicklow St., noon-8pm Mon.-Sat., noon-7pm Sun., €10-14), the city's most beloved vegetarian eatery. The hearty-yet-gourmet fare is so darn good it's a fave lunch spot for omnivores, too—not to mention delicious desserts, many of which are dairy free.

Established as a late-night alternative to the pub scene, **Accents** (23 Stephen St. Lower, tel. 01/416-0040, http://accentslounge.wordpress.com, 10am-11pm Mon.-Fri., 10:30am-11pm Sat., 12:30pm-10pm Sun., under €10) prides itself on being a friendly and relaxing place to while away an evening. There are plenty of couches and bookshelves to peruse. The menu features gluten-free and vegan options along with organic fair-trade coffee and loose-leaf teas—and the hot chocolate gets top marks too.

Looking for a special gourmet meal before you head to the Gate Theatre? The **Trocadero** (3 St. Andrew St., tel. 01/677-5545, www.trocadero.ie, 4:30pm-11pm Mon.-Sat., €16-30) is a romantic Continental eatery lined with red velvet and headshots of legendary Irish actors. The pre-theater menu is something of a Dublin institution. Those who partake of the €27 three-course early-bird special (4:30pm-7pm daily) are expected to "vacate by 7:45pm sharp."

TEMPLE BAR

Don't leave lunch to chance in Tourist Central; far too many pubs here do a bustling business with overpriced, mediocre grub. In fact, avoid eating in any Temple Bar pubs if you can help it. The one must-eat in this neighborhood is **Gallagher's Boxty House** (20-21 Temple Bar, www.boxtyhouse. ie, noon-10:30pm daily, €15-18). Savory boxty pancakes are meant to be a traditional Irish dish, but they aren't too easily found on menus outside of Dublin, and Gallagher's is the best place for them. "The humble spud, made beautiful" is the motto here, and in a swankier setting than you'd expect.

Sinead O'Connor once waited tables at the **Bad Ass Café** (9-11 Crown Alley, tel. 01/671-2596, www.badassdublin.com, noon-11pm daily, until 1:30am Fri.-Sat., lunch €8-10, dinner €12-18), but she's not this cheerfully grungy eatery's only claim to fame: It does a range of super-tasty pizzas, burgers, and Mexican grub, attracting a chilled-out crowd who'd otherwise steer clear of this touristy strip.

SOUTH GREAT GEORGES STREET

You'll find heaps of good restaurants along South Great George's Street, which turns into Aungier Street farther south, and tucked away on its narrow side streets. After browsing for vintage duds or secondhand books at

Dublin Food and Accommodations

To Botanic View and Egan's

N2

To Dublin International Youth Hostel

Garden of Remembrance

CHARLES STEWART

0 200 yds
0 200 m

UPPER DOMINICK ST
MOUNTJOY ST
GRANBY ROW
PARNELL SQUARE WEST
PARNELL SQUARE EAST
GREAT GEORGE'S
O'CONNELL ST UPPER
MOORE ST

HENRIETTA ST PL
HENRIETTA ST
BOLTON ST
KING'S INNS ST
LOWER DOMINICK ST
CHURCH ST

LINENHALL TER
LOFTUS LN
PARNELL ST
MOORE LN
HENRY ST
MOORE ST

BRUNSWICK ST NORTH

KING ST NORTH
GREEN ST
HALSTON ST
BERESFORD ST
CAPEL ST
JERVIS LN UPR
JERVIS ST
WOLFE TONE ST
MARY ST
PRINCE'S ST N

GENERAL POST OFFICE

FRIARY AVE
BOW ST
CHURCH ST

MARY'S LANE
GREEK ST

ST. MICHAN'S CHURCH

HUGHES'

ST. MARY'S ABBEY

THE CHURCH

ABBEY ST MIDDLE
ADELPHI

ABBEY ST UPPER
LIFFEY ST UPR
LOTTS
BACHELORS

GOVINDA'S

CHANCERY ST
BROTHER HUBBARD

PANTIBAR
MORRISON HOTEL/QUAY 14
SIN É

GREAT STRAND ST
ORMOND QUAY LOWER
MILLENNIUM BRIDGE
HA'PENNY BRIDGE

WINDING STAIR CAFÉ

WINDING STAIR
ASTON

GALLAGHER'S BOXTY HOUSE

FOUR COURTS

ARRAN QUAY
FATHER MATTHEW BRIDGE
O'DONOVAN ROSSA BRIDGE
ORMOND QUAY UPPER
River Liffey
GRATTAN BRIDGE
WELLINGTON QUAY

To Four Courts Hostel

USHERS QUAY
MERCHANTS QUAY
ESSEX QUAY
PARLIAMENT ST

ELIZA LODGE

THE CLARENCE

TEMPLE BAR
ANGLESEA ST
COLLEGE

BAD ASS CAFÉ
COPE ST

EUSTACE ST
ESSEX ST
THE CLARENCE

FRONT LOUNGE

BUTTON FACTORY

COOK ST
WOOD QUAY
LORD EDWARD ST

CHRIST CHURCH CATHEDRAL

QUEEN OF TARTS

UMI FALAFEL

DAME ST
DAME LN

ST. AUDOEN'S CHURCH
AUGUSTINE ST
LAMB ALLEY
HIGH ST

KINLAY HOUSE

CASTLE ST

CITY HALL

DUBLIN CASTLE

THE GLOBE
ODESSA
RI-RA
THE GEORGE
FALLON & BYRNE

STAG'S HEAD
TROCADERO
INTERNATIONAL BAR

EXCHEQUER ST

BLAZING SALADS

KAPH

MARKET BAR

POWERSCOURT TOWNHOUSE

BROOKS HOTEL

BEWLEY'S

SWIFT'S ALLEY
CARMEN'S HALL
JOHN DILLON ST
FRANCIS ST
HANOVER LN
NICHOLAS ST
BRIDE ST
GREAT SHIP ST
S GREAT GEORGE'S ST

MARKET ARCADE/
SIMON'S PLACE/YOGISM

THE LONG HALL

L'GUELETON

GOVINDA'S

ACCENTS

LOWER STEPHEN ST
CLARENDON ST
KING ST SOUTH

N81
ST. PATRICK'S CATHEDRAL

GOLDEN LN
PATRICK ST
DEAN ST

OUR LADY OF MOUNT CARMEL

AUNGIER ST
LOWER MERCER ST
GLOVERS ALLEY
YORK ST

PETER ST
PETER ROW
BISHOP ST

To YogaHub

YogaHub

To Rathfarnham Castle and the Pearse Museum

KEVIN ST UPPER
KEVIN ST LOWER
CUFFE ST

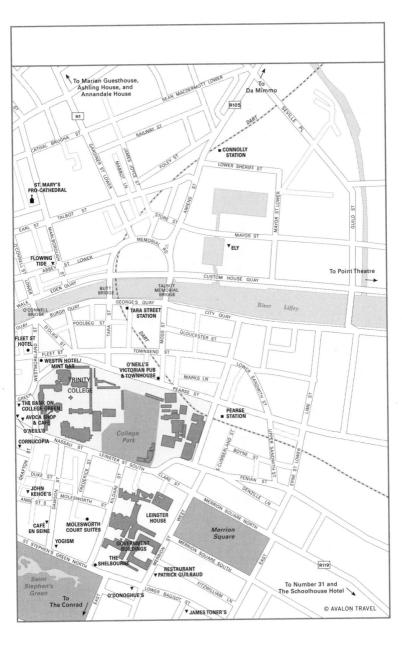

the Market Arcade, pop by the pleasantly hole-in-the-wall **Simon's Place** (S. Great George's St., tel. 01/679-7821, 8:30am-6pm Mon.-Sat., under €8) for a hefty sandwich and a cup of Fair Trade brew.

Another breakfast (or sweet lunch?) option just across the way is **Yogism** (Georges St. Arcade, tel. 01/679-9980, www.yogism.ie, 9am-6:30pm Mon.-Wed. and Sat., 9am-7pm Thurs.-Fri., noon-6pm Sun., €5-9), with gluten-free (buckwheat and flax) pancakes heaped with fresh fruit and dairy or vegan coconut yogurt along with superfood smoothies, not-so-healthy fro-yo cones, and coffee with homemade nut milk options. These guys are doing an awesome job at diet-inclusiveness. There's a second, much smaller location on Dawson Street on the north side of St. Stephen's Green.

Need a spot to duck off the main tourist strip for a quiet cup of coffee? Try **Kaph** (31 Drury St., tel. 01/613-9030, www.kaph.ie, 8:30am-7pm Mon.-Sat., noon-6pm Sun., €5). Their coffee is consistently rated among the best in the city, the baristas are friendly, and the tranquil upstairs seating area is the perfect place to regroup. None of the yummy-looking desserts are vegan, but they do offer a choice of non-dairy milks, and the baristas are totally cool with you bringing something over from all-vegetarian **Blazing Salads** across the street (42 Drury St., tel. 01/671-9552, www.blazingsal-ads.com, 9am-6pm weekdays, 9am-5pm Sat., under €8). Smoothies, salad bowls, pizza by the slice, and freshly baked cakes and breads are on offer here, but for takeaway only.

A bright and airy gourmet food hall, restaurant, and winebar, **Fallon & Byrne** (11-17 Exchequer St., tel. 01/472-1010, www.fallonandbyrne.com, 8am-9pm Mon.-Fri., 9am-9pm Sat., 11am-7pm Sun., lunch €8-17, dinner €18-34) sells mostly organic prepared foods and delectables from all over the world along with fresh coffee and baked goods. While you won't find vegan sweets behind the bakery counter, the restaurant does offer dairy-free dessert options on a separate vegan menu. Best values are the set lunch (2/3 courses €20/25) and the pre-theater dinner menu (2/3 courses €26/30, available 5:30pm-7pm Wed.-Sat., all night Sun.-Tues.), though you might want to book a table online for an evening meal.

For a hefty helping of vegetarian heaven, try cafeteria-style ★ **Govinda's** (4 Aungier St., tel. 01/475-0309, www.govindas.ie, noon-9pm Mon.-Sat., €7-10). Linger at a table by the window watching all of Dublin go by while you dig into your *mattar paneer* curry (or one of many vegan options). Unless the hunger of the world's on you, the "small" lunch portions will keep you going until dinnertime.

Brunch at **Odessa** (13 Dame Ct., off Exchequer St., tel. 01/670-7634, 6pm-late daily, 11:30am-4:30pm Sat.-Sun., €14-22) is a modern legend. It's been so popular for so long that calling Odessa "trendy" doesn't quite fit, but it's still true this loungy eatery attracts a come-to-be-seen crowd (that there's an adjacent "supper club" says something, doesn't it?).

There isn't actually a sign out front at ★ **L'Gueuleton** (1 Fade St., tel. 01/675-3708, www.lgueuleton.com, 12:30pm-4pm and 5:30pm-10pm Mon.-Sat., noon-4pm and 5:30pm-9pm Sun., lunch €11-17, dinner €18-26). This place serves up divine French fare that doesn't take itself too seriously, and in a wonderfully relaxed dining room with exposed brick walls and tasteful yet funky modern art. Lunch is a much better value (the portions are generous), and you don't have to worry about getting a table if you show up around two. Oh, and the token vegetarian dish is excellent as well.

You'd never know it from the entrance off a dingy alleyway, but ★ **Yogahub** (27 Camden Pl., tel. 01/478-9043, www.theyogahub.ie, 7am-9:30pm Mon.-Thurs., 7am-7pm Fri., 9:30am-5pm Sat.-Sun., €6-11) is an urban oasis, with the serene atmosphere you'd expect from a café adjoining a yoga studio. Here you can order the most satisfying full vegan breakfast on the whole island, with chickpea hash, lentil sausages, and sliced avocado and tomato on fresh sourdough. It'll keep you going till dinnertime. The raw gluten-free desserts are scrummy too.

DAME STREET

A sure bet for a pub lunch is **The Stag's Head** (1 Dame Ct., tel. 01/679-3687, food served noon-6pm daily, €8-14), an atmospheric Victorian bar perfect for a leisurely meal (or a meal in a glass).

You'll find some of Dublin's best Middle Eastern grub (plus fresh juices) at the all-vegetarian **Umi Falafel** (13 Dame St., tel. 01/670-6866, noon-10pm daily, €5-8), which offers sit-down service or lightning-fast takeaway with a smile.

It's a shame the **Queen of Tarts** (Dame St. at Parliament St., tel. 01/670-7499, 7:30am-6pm weekdays, 9am-6pm Sat., 9:30am-6pm Sun., €6-9) is in such a tiny space; you can keep passing by, squinting through the window, and noting with disappointment there *still* isn't a table free. This bakery-café is utterly charming and deservedly popular; along with a dazzling array of gourmet desserts, you can order from an extensive breakfast menu, or try a sandwich or savory tart at lunchtime.

MERRION SQUARE

Widely praised as Dublin's best, ★ **Restaurant Patrick Guilbaud** (21 Upper Merion St., tel. 01/676-4192, www.restaurantpatrickguilbaud.ie, 12:30pm-2:15pm and 7:30pm-10:15pm Tues.-Sat., 2/3-course lunch €45/55, 2/3/4-course dinner €90/105/130) has been doing exquisite French fare using local meats and produce for more than 35 years. There's an eight-course "degustation menu" (€185) featuring French twists on traditional Irish dishes like colcannon and braised crubbeens (that's pig's feet, for the uninitiated). And if 25 quid for a chocolate fondant induces a gasp, be assured you'd give your first- *and* secondborn children for it. Reservations are recommended.

NORTHSIDE

There are fewer notable restaurants north of the Liffey, though this is slowly beginning to change. Locals adore **Brother Hubbard** (153 Capel St., tel. 01/441-1112, www.brotherhubbard.ie, 7:30am-9:30pm Mon.-Fri.,

9:30am-5pm Sat.-Sun., lunch €7-12, 2/3-course dinner €25/30) for its home-baked brownies and epic weekend brunches as well as some of the best coffee in the city.

You'll find the other all-vegetarian ★ **Govinda's** (83 Middle Abbey St., tel. 01/872-9861, www.govindas.ie, noon-9pm Mon.-Sat., €8-15) beside Eason Books just off O'Connell Street. Hot tip for shoestring travelers: If you show up just before closing time, say 8:45, they'll be giving full portions away for a euro a pop!

If you want really good Italian food, you have to go to the Italians. The owners of **Da Mimmo** (148 N. Strand Rd., tel. 01/856-1714, 10am-3pm and 5:30pm-10pm Mon.-Fri., 12:30pm-10pm Sat.-Sun., €8-18) hail from Lazio, and as soon as you step in the door you can tell how seriously they take their cuisine, though the atmosphere and prices are super casual. It's well worth the longish walk or taxi ride out here for top-notch pizzas and pastas, and worth waiting a few minutes for a table to open up in this tiny place. It's close to Croke Park, so you might want to eat here before or after a match.

Named after a Yeats poem, the **Winding Stair Café** (40 Lower Ormond Quay, tel. 01/872-7320, www.winding-stair.com, 12:30pm-3:30pm and 6pm-10:30pm daily, €14-24) used to be a cheap-and-cheerful café, a favorite student haunt; now it's an upscale modern Irish restaurant. Gone are the murals and checkered tablecloths, but the food is delicious (if fancy), the wine list is exhaustive, and the waiters are nice. Reservations are a good idea. It's not quite as cool as the original Winding Stair, but better a new, posh version than none at all.

★ **The Church** (Mary St. at Jervis St., tel. 01/828-0102, www.thechurch. ie, bar food served noon-9:30pm Mon.-Wed., noon-10pm Thurs.-Sat., and 12:30pm-8pm Sun., gallery restaurant noon-10pm Mon.-Wed., noon-11pm Thurs.-Sat., and 12:30pm-10pm Sun., bar meals €12, restaurant €12-24) is a fabulously unique bar-cum-restaurant in a converted Methodist church. The fare is relatively traditional—steak, salmon, beef-and-Guinness pie, the usual vegetarian pasta dish—though the cocktails will prove almost as memorable as the setting.

Entertainment and Events

TRADITIONAL PUBS

There're always traditional music sessions on at the chintzy tourist traps of Temple Bar, but you're better off seeking out more low-key venues. Nothing's quite "authentic" in this town—you'll have to go out to the boonies for a session that doesn't have a heavy element of tourist-driven theatricality to it—but some spots are certainly more "authentic" than others. Avoid any place that charges a cover for entry.

Tucked away behind the Four Courts, **Hughes'** (19-20 Chancery St., tel. 01/872-6540) offers live trad nightly into the wee hours and is far less

What's the *Craic*?

You may be wondering why the Irish are always talking about crack—*craic,* that is, an Irish word meaning fun times, news, or enjoyable conversation, though it's one of those special terms that means so much more than its translation. *Craic* can be "mighty," "savage," or "deadly," and it's often (but not always) experienced at the nearest pub. Someone somewhere along the way defined *craic's* essential components by acronym: *ceol* ("kyole," music), *rince* ("RIN-keh," dance), *amhrain* ("OW-rin," songs), *inis scealta* ("IN-ish SHKEEL-tuh," storytelling), and *cainte* ("CAHN-chuh," gossip). At any rate, you'll know great *craic* when you're having it!

touristy than the musical pubs of Temple Bar. Similarly atmospheric is the upstairs bar at **Cobblestones** (N. King St., tel. 01/872-1799, www.cobble-stonepub.ie), where you'll also find trad or folk on a nightly basis. It's a bit more touristy, but that's because **O'Donoghue's** (15 Merrion Row, tel. 01/661-4303, www.odonoghues.ie) offers (arguably) the city's best trad. The walls are covered with pictures of The Dubliners, the '60s folk group that got its start here, and the courtyard/alleyway leading to the entrance is always packed with a youngish crowd more interested in chat than music.

It claims to be Ireland's oldest pub, a hotbed of seditious activity in rebellions gone by, but the **Brazen Head** (Bridge St., tel. 01/677-9549, www.brazenhead.com) is pushing the limits on tourist-kitsch with its silly castellated facade and extremely overpriced drinks (even for Dublin). The nightly session is meant to be traditional, but the guys play a lot of Van Morrison or Thin Lizzy, with only the occasional jig or reel thrown in. Having said all this, there's still a fair bit of *craic* to be found, especially in the spacious courtyard beer garden.

A delightfully "crusty old man's pub" (it used to sell groceries as well), **James Toner's** (Lower Baggot St., tel. 01/676-3090, www.tonerspub.ie) hums with an after-work crowd of all ages. This is believed to be the only pub in Dublin William Butler Yeats ever visited.

A classy yet understated Victorian pub with all the period details, **William Ryan's** (28 Parkgate St., tel. 01/677-6097) is in a residential neighborhood off the tourist circuit, which means the ambience is refreshingly workaday. The same goes for **The Long Hall** (51 S. Great Georges St., tel. 01/475-1590), though weirdly enough, it's smack-dab in the middle of touristville. After a satisfying meal at one of the great restaurants on or near South Great Georges, you can chill out to the strains of Annie Lennox—another nice surprise, in a place like this. Another great Victorian snug-lined pub is **John Kehoe's** (9 S. Anne St., tel. 01/677-8312), where you can have a drink upstairs in the late proprietor's old living room. **The Stag's Head** (1 Dame Ct., tel. 01/679-3687) is another delightful Victorian relic, complete with the requisite hunting trophy above the bar. There's live trad on Fridays and Saturdays starting at 10pm.

Dublin has amassed a reputation for one of the hottest club scenes in Europe, though it's difficult to party properly when even the hippest places close their doors at 3am! Cover charges vary from €5-10 during the week to €15-20 at weekends. Check *inDublin* (www.indublin.ie), a free weekly, for a listing of what's on when that's as comprehensive as it gets. Not into grinding? The city center offers plenty of trendy bars—some you might call "novelty"—where you can kick back with a fancy cocktail and let the night slip by in a whirl of funky lighting and stimulating conversation.

It's within spitting distance of the Trinity College gates, but **The Bank** (20-22 College Green, tel. 01/677-0677, www.bankoncollegegreen.com) is more popular with 20- and 30-something professionals. The stunning Victorian details—polished mahogany, plasterwork, mosaic flooring, open fireplaces, a wrought-iron mezzanine above the horseshoe bar—belie a relaxed atmosphere and down-to-earth staff. Somewhat trendier is the **Market Bar** (14A Fade St., off S. Great Georges St., tel. 01/677-4835, www.marketbar.ie, tapas €4-15), in an old sausage factory. It's an atmospheric space, with tall walls of exposed brick, a ceiling made all of skylights, comfortable seating, and another wall of shelves lined with wooden shoe-trees thrown in for quirky good measure. There are plenty of meaty, cheesy tapas choices along with several tasty vegan plates.

With a breathtaking, impeccably assembled interior, the commodious belle-epoque **Café en Seine** (40 Dawson St., tel. 01/667-4567) draws a youngish, well-heeled crowd of those who don't mind the high drink prices. Get here early, order your cocktails, score a couple of plush armchairs by an ornate period fireplace, and people-watch to your heart's content.

Here's one to write home about: an 18th-century Methodist church converted into a swanky new bar and restaurant, complete with original pipe organ, stained glass windows, and marble wall memorials. Ask the bartender at **The Church** (Mary St. at Jervis St., tel. 01/828-0102, www.thechurch.ie) how the owner achieved this entrepreneurial feat—isn't it sacrilegious, or something?—and the bartender will sagely point out to you that this church was fast plummeting into ruin when John M. Keating purchased the property in the late '90s (and wouldn't the people buried beneath you prefer a swanky bar over a crumbling edifice littered with empty crisp bags?). Millions of euros later, here we are in the coolest, most unusual nightspot on either side of the Liffey. The old crypt has also been converted into a second bar down a long set of stairs, but the main bar is far more atmospheric. You might want to have your dinner up in the organ gallery, a highly unusual feature in ecclesiastical architecture regardless of the denomination.

The swanky **Mint Bar** (Westmoreland St., tel. 01/645-1322, www.westin.com) at the Westin Hotel offers salsa Fridays and "Velvet Lounge" Saturdays, with a mix of lounge, jazz, and swing; the music starts at 10pm both nights, and bar nibbles are available until 10:30. The Morrison Hotel also has a chic bar, **Quay 14** (Lower Ormond Quay, tel. 01/887-2400, www.

morrisonhotel.ie); with a stylish (if at times pretentious) crowd, hip ambience, and titillating cocktail menu, it's perfect for "pre-clubbing."

A hip place to pass the day away with coffee and nibbles, after dark **The Globe** (11 S. Great George's St., tel. 01/671-1220, www.globe.ie) is a perennial pre-club favorite with Dublin's fashion-conscious trend-setters. There's an evening tapas menu, trip hop and acid jazz on the stereo, and a collection of faux-classical marble statues. There's also live jazz on Sunday afternoon. After closing, the Globe becomes part of **Rí-Rá** (Dame Ct., tel. 01/677-4835, www.rira.ie, open at 11:30pm Mon.-Sat., free before midnight during the week, cover €10), possibly the best nightclub in the city for its eclectic crowd, great funk and lounge tunes, and astonishingly friendly bouncers.

Friday nights bring "Salsa Palace" and Saturdays "The Soul Stage" (jazz, soul, hip-hop, and Motown) at the **Gaiety Theatre** (King St. S., tel. 01/677-1717, www.gaietytheatre.com, open at midnight, Fri./Sat. cover €15/20). Both nights feature live bands, four different bars, and old films playing on the main stage until 4am. The motto is "sweets for the sweet" at the classy **Sugar Club** (8 Lower Leeson St., tel. 01/678-7188, www.thesugarclub.com, cover €10/15 before/after 10pm), where a live show prefaces a night of dancing. The lineup is eclectic, from indie rock bands to ska, blues, or Latin. The acoustics are fab, the seats slouchy velour, and the cocktails killer.

LIVE ROCK VENUES

There's something on every night of the week—rock, jazz, blues, trad, you name it—at **Whelan's** (25 Wexford St., tel. 01/478-0766, www.whelanslive. com, €10-23) and at its "sister" venue, the **Village** (26 Wexford St., tel. 01/475-8555, www.thevillagevenue.com). Featuring some high-profile performers (Damien Rice, Rodrigo y Gabriela, and the Flaming Lips just for starters), **Vicar Street** (58-59 Thomas St., tel. 01/454-5533, www.vicarstreet. com, €20-35) is a cozy enough place to catch a show—with its main level dotted with round tables and theater-style balcony, it holds only 1,000.

The city's largest pop/rock venue is the **3Arena** (East Link Bridge, North Wall Quay, tel. 01/819-8888, www.3arena.ie, €40-70), which has hosted Prince, Pearl Jam, Diana Ross, Paul Simon, and many other greats over the years in this converted railway depot that seats up to 8,500.

The **Olympia Theatre** (72 Dame St., tel. 01/677-7744, www.olympia.ie) sometimes offers experimental or unusual drama (like, say, Shakespeare's *Twelfth Night* by a Russian company, in Russian), but it's better known for its eclectic range of concerts at the weekend. The Goo Goo Dolls, Lyle Lovett, Pentatonix, and Sufjan Stevens have all played here.

Another popular space for indie gigs is the **Button Factory** (Curved St., Temple Bar, tel. 01/670-9105, www.buttonfactory.ie), which turns into a nightclub with visiting DJs on Saturday evenings.

If you're not looking for a concert as such, another option is a dimly lit Northside pub, **Sin É** (which means "That's it"; 14-15 Ormond Quay, tel. 01/555-4036), which has live pop/indie/rock music nightly. There's no cover and the bartenders are nice as can be.

Ireland has come a long, long way since homosexuality was legalized in 1993. The positive outcome of the republic's same-sex marriage referendum in November 2015 means that it's easier than ever to be yourself, and not just in the capital city. Dublin is embracing LGBTQ culture like never before. You're spoiled for choice entertainment-wise; May is a great time to be here, for the **Dublin Gay Theatre Festival** (tel. 01/677-8511, www.gaytheatre.ie), when you'll spot Oscar Wilde's mug hanging on banners all over town (though the plays put on are mostly contemporary). Another event worth planning a trip for is the **Gay Pride Parade**, established in 1992; the parade is the culmination of the **Dublin LGBTQ Pride Festival** (www.dublinpride.org), a two-week event toward the end of June. There's also the city's Lesbian and Gay Film Festival, **Gaze** (6 Eustace St., tel. 01/679-3477, www.gaze.ie), for four days in early August, where international flicks are screened at the Irish Film Institute (www.ifi.ie).

There are a couple all-gay clubs in Dublin: **The George** is the oldest (89 S. Great Georges St., tel. 01/478-2983), with something fun on every night of the week. Sunday-night bingo (free admission before 10pm) is still a local favorite. Or catch a drag show at **PantiBar** (7-8 Capel St., tel. 01/874-0710), which is open until 2:30am on Saturdays. Mainstream venues sometimes offer LGBTQ nights, though they don't tend to last for more than a year or two at a stretch. One hopefully safe bet is **Glitz** at Dandelion (130-133 St. Stephen's Green W., tel. 01/476-0870, www.welovedandelion.com, €5 cover) on Tuesday nights.

As for LGBT-friendly hangouts, try **The Front Lounge** (33 Parliament St., tel. 01/670-4112, www.thefrontlounge.ie) for a quiet drink (unless it's karaoke night!), or **Accents** (23 Stephen St. Lower, tel. 01/416-0040, http://accentslounge.wordpress.com) if you're not in the mood to drink. Either way, you'll probably want to plan on an afternoon or evening at **The Boiler House** (12 Crane Ln., tel. 01/677-3130, www.the-boilerhouse.com, noon-5am Mon.-Thurs., noon Fri. to 5am Sun., €22), which has jacuzzi, sauna, and steam rooms along with massage treatments, a coffee bar (sans alcohol), and a "play room." There's a nightclub here one Saturday a month; check the website for details.

Now on to the practical stuff. Stop by the **Outhouse** (105 Capel St., Northside, tel. 01/873-4999, www.outhouse.ie), the city's most established resource center, and peruse the notice boards before having lunch at the café (1pm-9:30pm Mon.-Fri., 1pm-5:30pm Sat.). The **Gay Switchboard Dublin** (tel. 01/872-1055, www.gayswitchboard.ie) also provides advice and information. **Gay Dublin** (www.gaydublin.com) is a decent source of entertainment info, and better yet is the nationwide **Gay Ireland** (www.gay-ireland.com).

OTHER MUSIC VENUES

Venues abound for the listener with more "refined" tastes as well. The National Symphony Orchestra performs nearly every Friday night at the **National Concert Hall** (Earlsfort Terrace, just south of St. Stephen's Green, tel. 01/475-1666, www.nch.ie, 8pm, €10-25), and on other nights there are international bands and orchestras, jazz ensembles, and traditional music performances. Northside, the **Hugh Lane Municipal Gallery of Modern**

Art (22 N. Parnell Sq., tel. 01/874-1903, www.hughlane.ie) also hosts classical concerts.

Serious jazz fans should check out **Jazz on the Terrace** (www.jazzontheterrace.com), which "represents Irish jazz artists abroad and international jazz artists in Ireland." There's a listing of upcoming concerts, gigs, and festivals as well as links to local band websites.

Founded in 1951 in an attempt to preserve the country's musical traditions, **Comhaltas Ceoltóiri Éireann** (32 Belgrave Sq., Monkstown, tel. 01/280-0295, www.comhaltas.com, 9pm Mon.-Thurs. July-Aug., €10) offers a *seisiún* of top-notch singing and dancing along with the jigs, reels, and airs you'd hear in a pub session. Friday nights all year there's a "country set dance" starting at 9pm, where the €8 admission fee basically gets you an informal lesson (and a lot of *craic*). To get here, take the DART from Tara Street in the city center southbound to Seapoint Road.

THEATER AND CINEMA

Ireland's national theater, the **Abbey** (Lower Abbey St., tel. 01/878-7222, www.abbeytheatre.ie, €15-30) commissions new works from Irish playwrights and occasionally revives classic plays by O'Casey, Beckett, Behan, and many lesser-known dramatists. In addition to the rather out-of-date main theater, there's a smaller venue downstairs, **The Peacock.** Afterward, if you feel like chatting about the play with random strangers, the pub to head to is the **Flowing Tide** (9 Lower Abbey St., tel. 01/874-0842).

Other Dublin mainstays include the **Gaiety Theatre** (King St. S., tel. 01/677-1717, www.gaietytheatre.com, €17-55), opened in 1871, which puts on everything from Riverdance to Mother Goose to the more mainstream productions of the annual Dublin Theatre Festival; and the **Gate Theatre** (1 Cavendish Row, tel. 01/874-4045, www.gate-theatre.ie, €15-30), founded by the flamboyant duo of Hilton Edwards and Micheál MacLiammóir in 1928, which offers a range of Irish classics—from Oscar Wilde to Brian Friel—as well as quirkier works along the lines of Harold Pinter.

Dublin has **Bewley's** (www.bewleyscafetheatre.com) to thank for its venerable lunchtime theater tradition, and while the original café is closed for refurbishment the café-theater continues at the **Powerscourt Townhouse** (S. William St., tel. 01/671-7000, www.powerscourttheatre. com). The top-floor townhouse venue will likely continue its own program after Bewley's has reopened. Performances of one-act plays begin at 1pm Monday-Saturday. Tickets are €8-12, with a light lunch of vegetarian soup and brown bread an additional €4.

Opened by President Mary McAleese in 2002, **The Helix** (Collins Ave., Glasnevin, DCU campus, tel. 01/700-7000, www.thehelix.ie, €15-25) sports an art gallery and three separate venues for an eclectic (but fairly mainstream) calendar of plays and concerts. Take Dublin Bus #4, #11/A/B, #13/A, or #19 to Ballymun Road.

If you're more into the experimental side of things, see what's on at the **Tivoli Theatre** (135-136 Francis St., tel. 01/454-4472). The **Project Arts**

Centre (39 E. Essex St., tel. 1850/260-027, www.projectartscentre.ie, €12-20) is another solid venue.

For arthouse and classic film screenings, the place to go is the **Irish Film Centre** (6 Eustace St., tel. 01/679-3477, www.ifi.ie, €9).

COMEDY

One of the best comedy venues in the city is the **Comedy Cellar** at the **International Bar** (23 Wicklow St., tel. 01/677-9250, www.dublincomedy-cellar.com, cover €8), which has shows on Tuesday and Wednesday nights starting at 9pm. As many as 10 jokemeisters will pass the evening, which lasts until closing time.

FESTIVALS AND EVENTS

Naturally, Dublin's **St. Patrick's Festival** (tel. 01/676-3205, www.stpatricks-festival.ie) is Ireland's largest: The parade attracts as many as 1.5 million spectators, and there's everything from concerts to street theater to fireworks over the four days leading up to St. Paddy's Day. If you've come too early in the year for these festivities, there's always **Tradfest** (tel. 01/703-0700, www.templebartrad.com) at the end of January, showcasing the island's best traditional and folk musicians.

The **International Literature Festival Dublin** (tel. 01/222-5455, www.ilfdublin.com) brings an international roster of authors to town toward the end of May. The **Dublin City Soul Festival** (www.dublincitysoulfestival.ie) takes place in Merrion Square around the same time. Admission is by donation, which benefits the Musical Youth Foundation charity for at-risk children. Another fun option this month is the **Dublin Dance Festival** (tel. 01/679-8658, www.dublindancefestival.ie), which features modern and international styles rather than traditional Irish.

One of the biggest and most exciting events on the city's calendar, the **Dublin Theatre Festival** (tel. 01/677-8899, www.dublintheatrefestival.com, €10-35) takes place over the first two weeks in October. Productions are Irish and international, classic and avant-garde, and plays are put on at theaters all over the city. The well-established **Fringe Festival** (tel. 01/872-9016, www.fringefestival.com) offers comedy as well as more experimental work.

And the last weekend in October brings the **Dublin City Marathon** (tel. 01/623-2250, www.dublincitymarathon.ie), established in 1979 and sponsored by Adidas. This race is widely known as the "friendly marathon" for the especially supportive crowds it attracts.

For an exhaustive list of festivals in Dublin and elsewhere, check out **Entertainment.ie** (www.entertainment.ie/festivals).

Shopping

GRAFTON STREET

Though everyone thinks Grafton Street is the best place to shop in Dublin, if you take a walk down the crowded pedestrian street you'll notice that most of the shops are midscale women's clothing boutiques (and the same goes for the huge, glass-domed **St. Stephen's Green Shopping Centre** where Grafton meets the park). You can skip Grafton altogether if you're looking for souvenirs; head for **Powerscourt Townhouse** (59 S. William St., one block west of Grafton St. and signposted, tel. 01/679-4144), which includes several smallish but ultra-classy clothing and jewelry shops along with three quality cafés.

Just around the corner from Grafton Street is a spacious **Avoca Handweavers** shop (11-13 Suffolk St., tel. 01/677-4215, www.avoca.ie), full of delightful gifts—blankets, sweaters (colorful and modern, not the old-fashioned Aran kind), and jewelry, along with household items (aerodynamic spatulas, spice racks, hardcover cookbooks, and so forth) downstairs and a top-floor café, a nice spot for lunch or tea.

Another gem just off Grafton Street is **Ulysses Books** (10 Duke St., tel. 01/671-8676, www.rarebooks.ie), which rightly bills itself as "Ireland's leading antiquarian bookshop." Serious bibliophiles should note that its catalog is available online.

SOUTH GREAT GEORGES STREET

Full of delights is the **Market Arcade** on South Great Georges Street (at Exchequer), with shops and stalls of secondhand books and vintage clothing. Food stalls sell fudge, juices and smoothies, and olives-and-cheese type munchies perfect for picnicking in St. Stephen's Green.

The Grafton Street flower vendors offer a bright note on even the rainiest days.

SOUTH OF TRINITY COLLEGE

There is a wealth of sweater and knickknacky shops along Nassau Street, just east of Grafton Street and south of Trinity, but most of them aren't worth browsing. If it's an Aran sweater you're after, try **Cleo** (18 Kildare St., tel. 01/676-1421, www.cleo-ltd.com), which has an exquisite selection (and, as at those shops selling machine-knit ganseys, you do get what you pay for). Then spend an hour or two at **Kilkenny Design** (5-6 Nassau St., tel. 01/677-7066, www.kilkennydesign.com), an upscale chain store renowned for its stock of cutting-edge Irish fashion, housewares, pottery, silverware, jewelry, sculpture, and framed art. There's also a fantastic upstairs café.

TEMPLE BAR

This area's better known for its tourist-trap pubs, but there are several shops worth an extended browse. The Wilde-inspired **Gutter Bookshop** (Cow's Lane, tel. 01/679-9206, www.gutterbookshop.com) often launches books by local authors (check the website for an events calendar) and stocks a range of classic kids' toys. **Claddagh Records** (2 Cecelia St., tel. 01/677-0262, www.claddaghrecords.com) sells recordings of traditional music.

For funky clothing (new and secondhand), try **Fresh** (1 Crown Alley, tel. 01/671-8423, www.freshtemplebar.com) or **Lucy's Lounge** (11 Fownes St. Upper, tel. 01/677-4779).

Accommodations

Securing clean, relatively good-value accommodations in Dublin can sometimes be a challenge, particularly when there's a festival or other major event going on. Aside from the Irish Tourist Board seal of approval, your best bet is word of mouth (from someone who's stayed at the place in question within the last year). At any rate, be smart and book well in advance.

TEMPLE BAR

It's central, but accommodations in Temple Bar can be noisy. You probably don't want to stay in this neighborhood unless you're planning to be out pubbing and clubbing every night.

Despite an inefficient reception area and a rather inexperienced staff, ★ **Four Courts Hostel** (15-17 Merchants Quay, tel. 01/672-5839, www.fourcourtshostel.com, dorms €16-25, private rooms €28-36 pp) is still one of the best hostels in the city. The location is superb, security is adequate, the rooms are clean and the mattresses comfortable, and there are separate rooms for socializing and quiet pastimes. This place isn't quite as bohemian as it likes to think it is (there are cartoon murals along the staircase spouting random statistics—did you know that lefties live an average of nine years less than right-handers?—and the impossibly buxom blonde carrying a U.S.A. tote bag annoys you more every time you pass her), but the Four Courts still attracts a fun crowd. Basic continental breakfast (i.e., vending-machine coffee is extra) is included in the price.

The top guesthouse/hotel in this neighborhood is the **Eliza Lodge** (23-24 Wellington Quay at Eustace St., tel. 01/671-8044, www.elizalodge.com, rooms €190-228, s €120), You can expect friendly and accommodating staff, mod but comfortable rooms (with in-room safes), and an outstanding breakfast in Elizablues, the downstairs restaurant. Some of the rooms have Jacuzzis and/or balconies overlooking the Liffey and Millennium Bridge.

If you want the convenience of a temporary Temple Bar address without any stress or fuss, the **Fleet Street Hotel** (19-20 Fleet St., tel. 01/670-8124, www.fleethoteltemplebar.com, rooms €120-190, s €70-130) is a safe bet. Rooms are smallish but well appointed, and surprisingly quiet.

Owned by Bono and The Edge, **The Clarence** (6-8 Wellington Quay, tel. 01/407-0800, www.theclarence.ie, rooms €220-370, suites €700-900, penthouse suite €2,500) is unsurprisingly a favorite with celebrities. The individually designed rooms are luxuriously furnished with king-size beds with Egyptian cotton sheets, Shaker-style furniture, a CD and DVD collection, and laptop-sized safes. Check out the website for last-minute deals as low as €179. This hotel is definitely worth maxing out the credit card for.

CHRISTCHURCH

You can see the cathedral out your dorm room window at another of Dublin's most reliable hostels, **Kinlay House** (2/12 Lord Edward St., tel. 01/679-6644, www.kinlaydublin.ie, dorms €17-25, private rooms €30-40 pp). It's big, sure, but not overwhelmingly so. Atmospheric yet well-maintained, Kinlay House has ample kitchen and dining facilities, comfy beds, and professional staff. You can't go wrong booking a bed here.

AROUND TRINITY COLLEGE

Owned and run by the O'Neill family for more than 100 years, **O'Neill's Victorian Pub and Townhouse** (36-37 Pearse St., tel. 01/671-4074, www.oneillsdublin.com, rooms €125-200) offers comfortable new mattresses, hearty breakfasts, and fine period details in both the rooms and the delightful downstairs pub. Street noise from the DART passing nearby can be a problem, so this one is not recommended for light sleepers, and though the location is pretty central, just north of Trinity College, the immediate neighborhood is not especially nice.

Built in 1865 to house the Allied Irish Bank, the five-star **Westin Hotel** (Westmoreland St., tel. 01/645-1000, www.westin.com, rooms €320-600, package deals from €180 pp) retains its Victorian elegance in the reception areas, though the bedrooms are thoroughly modern: in-room massage treatments, laptop safes, minibars, private balconies, and so forth. The Westin is especially known for its trademarked "Heavenly Bed," featuring the most sumptuous bedclothes in all Dublin. Breakfast is extra (€25) unless you've booked a package deal.

You'll pay handsomely for the central location, but the range of top-quality accommodations near and around the green is well worth a splurge. Popular with families, ★ **Molesworth Court Suites** (35 Schoolhouse Ln., off Kildare St., tel. 01/676-4799, www.molesworthcourt.ie, 1/2-bedroom suite €180/200, 2/3-bedroom penthouse suite €260/320) offers swanky, spacious self-catering apartments in a stellar location with the attentive service of a five-star hotel. Each apartment comes equipped with CD and DVD players and a kitchenette.

If you appreciate finding mints on your pillow when you return to your hotel room, try the small, plush, and friendly ★ **Brooks Hotel** (Drury St., tel. 01/670-4000, www.brookshotel.ie, rooms €175-360), where you'll also find plasma TVs in the bedroom—*and* bathroom! The in-room foot spa and pillow menu (from which to select your pillow of choice) are other nice touches. Delicious full breakfasts are cooked to order and included in the room price.

One of Dublin's best guesthouses is **Number 31** (31 Leeson Close, Lower Leeson St., tel. 01/676-5011, www.number31.ie, rooms €200-280), with individually designed bedrooms in two wings: the retro-'50s coach house (with its sunken sitting room and mirrored bar) and the more staid Georgian townhouse. A top-notch breakfast menu, served in the conservatory, features homemade breads and salmon and kippers cooked to order. Top this off with a friendly staff, big comfy beds, and relaxing vibe, and you have a hotel with significant repeat business.

A five-star Hilton hotel, **The Conrad** (Earlsfort Terrace, tel. 01/602-8900, www.conradhotels.com, rooms €360-570) is conveniently located across the street from the National Concert Hall. Rooms are comfortable and well appointed, if a bit on the sterile business-class side, and feature bathrobes and slippers, minibar, HiFi with CD player, ergonomic desk chairs, and converter plugs in case you've forgotten yours.

The Shelbourne (27 St. Stephen's Green, tel. 01/663-4500, www.marriott.co.uk, rooms €330-470) offers incomparably elegant Georgian reception rooms, and the modern bedrooms (featuring down comforters, bathrobes and slippers, minibar, and suchlike) have historically inspired touches. The complimentary on-site parking is a major plus; you won't find this at other city five-star hotels. The full-size swimming pool's kinda nice to have, too.

NORTHSIDE

Accommodations north of the Liffey are generally less expensive. The An Óige **Dublin International Youth Hostel** (61 Mountjoy St., tel. 01/830-1766, www.anoige.ie, dorms €14-21, twins/triples €25-30 pp) is huge and therefore utterly chaotic with so many school groups coming and going, so obviously it isn't your number one choice. That said, the security is tight, the dorms and bathrooms are so clean they're sterile (not a bad thing, considering all the horror stories you hear about the hostels in this city), and continental breakfast in the lovely chapel-turned-dining hall is included in the price. You can also "upgrade" to a reasonably priced fry (€4.50 full Irish or vegetarian, porridge €1 extra).

Good-value budget B&Bs abound along Gardiner Street and Parnell Square, though you may want to choose the room-only option and go for breakfast downtown (especially if you're a vegetarian). These guesthouses are usually well-maintained Georgian townhouses, or a row of them reno-vated into one property. One option is the **Charles Stewart** (5-6 Parnell Sq., tel. 01/878-0350, www.charlesstewart.ie, €55 pp), which offers clean but slightly nondescript en suite rooms with television and hostess tray. The 24-hour reception is handy. Check the website for even better specials, usually at midweek. The rooms are homier at the **Marian Guesthouse** (21 Upper Gardiner St., tel. 01/874-4129, www.marianguesthouse.ie, €25-40 pp, s €35-45), though not all are en suite. The full Irish fry will keep you going till dinnertime.

Another good option is **Adelphi** (67-68 Lower Gardiner St., tel. 01/836-3859, www.adelphidublin.com, €55-80 pp, s €60-230), with friendly staff and super-clean, freshly decorated rooms with large flatscreen TVs. Rates vary considerably based on what's going on in town, so it's a good idea to book well in advance; bedrooms with shared bath are quite a bit less expensive.

The **Morrison Hotel** (Lower Ormond Quay, tel. 01/887-2400, www. morrisonhotel.ie, rooms €325-590, penthouse €1,500) has a great river-side location. Rooms are high-tech, featuring CD players or iPod dock-ing stations, and there's a safe and minibar in every room. Six "studio" rooms have flatscreen Apple computers and sunken bathtubs with leather head- and footrests. The hotel also has one of the most sophisticated bars in the city. The in-house spa offers Turkish baths, seaweed wraps, and aromatherapy.

BALLSBRIDGE

A wonderfully atmospheric hotel with an ever-present sense of history, the oldest section of ★ **The Schoolhouse Hotel** (2-8 Northumberland Rd., tel. 01/667-5014, www.schoolhousehotel.com, rooms €160-230) served as St. Stephen's Parochial School beginning in 1861, and you can see stray bullet holes in the wall of the hotel pub that date to the Easter Rising. The school closed its doors in 1969 and lay empty until 1997, when hotel renovations commenced. The food's fairly good for hotel fare, and the bedrooms are decorated with William Morris reproduction wallpaper to maintain the Victorian flavor. Even if you can't afford to stay here, it's well worth find-ing your way here for a pint in the gorgeously old-fashioned and very cozy bar, with its soaring pitched wooden ceiling, loft seating area, and cheer-ful open fire. The hotel is right by the Grand Canal, a 20-minute walk east of Merrion Square.

OUTSIDE THE CITY CENTER

You'll often find better value for your money outside the city center. Here are a few top guesthouses in Drumcondra and Glasnevin, both a couple kilometers north of town.

A very good budget guesthouse is tidy red-brick **Ashling House** (168 Drumcondra Rd. Upper, tel. 01/837-5432, www.ashlinghouse.ie, €24-45 pp, s €40-74), with clean, modern, no-frills rooms and an add-on continental breakfast option. Ask for a room at the back of the house for a quieter night's sleep. The more upscale **Annandale House** (84 Grace Park Rd., Drumcondra, tel. 01/804-0822, www.annandalebnb.com, €40-60 pp) is recommended for its bright, homey rooms. In fine weather you can take your breakfast (with homemade jam and very good coffee) in the lovely garden out back. These two Drumcondra guesthouses are good options if you're planning on a match at Croke Park, which is only 2.5 kilometers away.

Convenient for a morning stroll through the National Botanic Gardens, **Botanic View** (25 Botanic Ave. at Iona Rd., Glasnevin, tel. 01/860-0195, www.botanicview.com, €40-60 pp, s €50-60) offers immaculate (if a bit pink and frilly) rooms with cable television, a friendly and helpful proprietor, and the full fry at the breakfast table. Take Dublin Bus #13, #19/A, or #83; otherwise it's a brisk 35-minute walk to/from the city center. Nearby **Egan's** (7 Iona Park, Glasnevin, tel. 01/830-3611, www.eganshouse.ie, €50-60 pp, s €75-100) is a bit more upscale, with quaint and tranquil rooms, though the buffet breakfast is an additional €10.

Information and Services

INFORMATION

As you would expect, Dublin's central **tourist office** (25 Suffolk St., tel. 01/884-7871, www.visitdublin.com, 9am-5:30pm Mon.-Sat., 10:30am-3pm Sun.)—which does not accept inquiries by phone—is so busy you could spend all afternoon in line. There is a **secondary office** at 14 Upper O'Connell Street (tel. 01/605-7700, 9am-5pm Mon.-Sat.). You're best off just stopping by to pick up flyers and free listings of upcoming events; *inDublin* (www.indublin.ie) is a great free weekly magazine you can find here or in many hostels and cafés.

Other sources for entertainment info are the twice-monthly *Dublin Event Guide* (www.dublineventguide.com) and the *Evening Herald* (along with its freebie sister paper, the *Herald AM,* www.herald.ie), which is published every day but Sunday.

Dublin's city-center **public library** (Ilac Shopping Centre, Henry St., tel. 01/873-4333, www.dublincitypubliclibraries.ie, 10am-8pm Mon.-Thurs., 10am-5pm Fri.-Sat.) is on the Northside, two blocks west of O'Connell Street.

SERVICES

Banks

Bureaux de change abound in the city center, but the commission charges are lowest at the banks: **Bank of Ireland** (2 College Green or 6 Lower O'Connell St.), **AIB** (40-41 Westmoreland St. or 1-3 Lower Baggot St.), or **Ulster Bank** (33 College Green or George's Quay).

Embassies

The **U.S. Embassy** (42 Elgin Rd., Ballsbridge, tel. 01/668-8777, http://dublin.usembassy.gov) is on Dublin Bus routes #4, #5, #7, #7A, #8, #45, #63, and #84 to Lansdowne Road. The **Canadian Embassy** (65/68 St. Stephen's Green, 4th fl., tel. 01/417-4100, www.dfait-maeci.gc.ca) is more conveniently located. For a complete embassy listing, visit the Irish **Department of Foreign Affairs** online (http://foreignaffairs.gov.ie/embassies).

Emergency and Medical Services

Dial 999 for an emergency. Crime against tourists is relatively rare, though pickpocketing is a problem. Ring the 24-hour **Tourist Victim Support Service** (tel. 01/478-5295 or freephone tel. 1800/661-771) if you need any assistance. The fastest way to reach the Garda (the Irish police) is by dialing 999, which will connect you with the Command and Control center at Harcourt Square (tel. 01/475-5555).

Hospitals in the city center include **St. James'** (James St., tel. 01/453-7941, just south of Heuston Station and the Guinness Storehouse) and **Mater Miserichordiae** (Eccles St., between Berkeley Rd. and Dorset St., north of Parnell Sq., tel. 01/830-1122).

Both branches of **O'Connell's Pharmacy** (21 Grafton St., tel. 01/679-0467, and 55-56 O'Connell St., tel. 01/873-0427) stay open until 10pm daily.

Left Luggage

You can leave that ungainly suitcase in a coin-operated locker at **Busáras** (Store St., 7am-10:30pm daily, €4-10 for 24 hours). Better yet, for around €6, **Connolly** (east side, north of the Liffey at Amiens St., tel. 01/836-6222, 7am-10pm Mon.-Sat., 8am-10pm Sun.) and **Heuston** (west side, Victoria Quay, same phone and hours) train stations also offer locker rooms; a (usually helpful and very chipper) attendant will squeeze your bag into the smallest locker possible to save you a couple bob.

GETTING THERE
Air

Flights depart **Dublin International Airport** (tel. 01/814-1111, www.dublinairport.com) for more than 140 destinations in Europe, Asia, and North America. The most commonly traveled airlines from the United States and Canada are **United Airlines** (tel. 1890/925-252, www.united.com), **Aer Lingus** (tel. 1800/474-7424 from the U.S. and Canada, tel. 01/886-8888 for reservations, tel. 01/886-6705 for departures/arrivals, www.aerlingus.com), **Air Canada** (tel. 1800/709-900, www.aircanada.ca), and **American Airlines** (tel. 01/602-0550, www.aa.com).

An alternative to **British Airways** (tel. 1800/626-747, www.britishairways.com) is the most popular budget airline to Britain and mainland Europe, **Ryanair** (tel. 0818/303-030, www.ryanair.ie), which offers daily service from Berlin (Schonefeld), Birmingham, London (Gatwick, Luton, and Stansted), Edinburgh, Glasgow (Prestwick), Paris (Beauvais), Venice (Treviso), Milan (Orio al Serio), Rome (Ciampino), and other destinations.

Car-rental agencies on the arrivals hall lower level include **Europcar** (tel. 01/812-0410, www.europcar.ie), **Avis** (tel. 01/605-7500, www.avis.ie), and **Budget** (tel. 01/844-5150, www.budget.ie).

A **left luggage service** (tel. 01/814-4633, www.greencaps.ie, 5am-11pm daily) will run you €8-12 per day per item.

Train

Iarnrod Éireann, also known as **Irish Rail** (tel. 01/836-6222, www.irishrail.ie) operates from **Connolly** (east side, north of the Liffey at Amiens St., points north) and **Heuston** (west side, Victoria Quay, points west and south); the stations are linked by the Luas light rail line. Traveling by train is much more expensive than by bus, but the trip is also far more comfortable. Round-trip (or "return") tickets are always a much better value, especially if purchased online.

If you're traveling a lot by train, pick up either a **Trekker Pass** (€110 for four consecutive days) or an **Explorer Pass** (€160 for five days' travel in a 15-day period); these passes are available for purchase only at the ticket desks at Connolly and Heuston Stations.

Bus

Busáras (Store St., tel. 01/836-6111, www.buseireann.ie), the central bus depot, can take you anywhere you need to go via **Bus Éireann.**

This none-too-pleasant station is made even more chaotic by frequent construction work; it's also swarming with pickpockets, so summon all your street smarts. If you plan to do three or more days of bus travel during your holiday, pick up an **Open Road** pass at the central ticket office (3 days' travel over a 6-day period €60, each additional day €16.50).

Boat

Reach Dublin by ferry from Liverpool or Holyhead. For Liverpool, take **P&O Irish Sea Ferries** (tel. 01/407-3434, www.poirishsea.com, 2/day Tues.-Sun., 1/day Mon., crossing 7.5-8 hours, car and driver €150-185, additional passengers €22-37), which does not carry pedestrians. Two meals are included in the fare. The Holyhead-Dublin route is served by **Irish Ferries** (tel. 01/638-3333, www.irishferries.com, 2/day daily, crossing 1.75 hours, car and driver €89, additional adult €25, pedestrians €27). It is also possible to travel between Dublin and the Isle of Man via **Steam Packet** (tel. 1800/805-055, www.steam-packet.com, usually 2/day daily, crossing 2.75 hours, fare €80-260 for car and two passengers, pedestrians €25).

Ferries pull into the **Ferryport Terminal** (Alexandra Rd., tel. 01/855-2222) at North Wall, and there are Bus Éireann shuttles to meet every incoming boat (fare €3). Buses leave Busáras for the ferry terminal 75 minutes before scheduled departures.

GETTING AROUND

The city center is easily walkable, but if you're planning to spend a good bit of time traipsing around the city outskirts, you will probably want to pick up a **Leap visitor card** (www.leapcard.ie, €19.50), a three-day transit pass valid on the Luas light rail, the DART (within County Dublin), and all Dublin Bus and Airlink buses (excluding day tours). Purchase a Leap ticket at the Dublin airport, either at the information desk or at the Spar grocery shop in the arrivals hall. The card expires 72 hours after the first time you use it.

To and from the Airport

The airport is off the M1 12 kilometers north of Dublin, and parking in the short-term lot costs €3/hour.

Dublin Bus (tel. 01/873-4222) operates a frequent **Airlink** service (#748) from the street directly outside the arrivals hall; buy a ticket (single/return €6/10) at the kiosk or on board (with exact change) and look out for the bright green-and-blue double-decker. The bus will take you to O'Connell Street, Busáras, and Connolly and Heuston Stations. The ride is more comfortable on **Aircoach** (tel. 01/844-7118, www.aircoach.ie, departures from O'Connell St. every 15 minutes, every 30 minutes midnight-5am, single/return fare €7/12), which offers 24-hour service.

A taxi to or from the airport will run you €36-40.

Train

Dublin's spiffy light rail system, **Luas** (freephone tel. 1800/300-604, www.luas.ie, departures every 5-10 minutes 7am-10pm, runs until 12:30am Sat. and 11:30pm Sun., fare within city-center zone €1.90), whisks commuters in from the burbs, but it's also useful for tourists looking to get from Heuston to Connolly Station or any point in between (including the

National Museum at Collins Barracks, the Four Courts, Abbey Street, and Busáras). Buy a ticket at the bus stop kiosk before boarding.

For travel outside the city, you'll want to take the **DART,** or Dublin Area Rapid Transit (tel. 01/805-4288, www.dart.ie, fares usually under €10), which is much faster than the bus. There is frequent service (2-3 trains hourly) to Drogheda in County Louth (from Connolly, with other routes to Malahide and Howth), Kildare (from Heuston), or Dun Laoghaire, Killiney, Bray, and Greystones (from Pearse or Connolly).

Bus

For Kilmainham Jail, Phoenix Park, the National Botanic Gardens, and other attractions on the city fringe, take **Dublin Bus** (tel. 01/873-4222, www.dublinbus.ie, single ticket to most destinations under €3). Maps and departure times (generally three or more per hour during the day) are posted at each stop. Exact change is not necessary, though notes are not accepted and if you overpay you won't get change from the driver. You can redeem your passenger change receipt (bring the original ticket as well) at the Dublin Bus office at 59 Upper O'Connell Street.

The Dublin Bus **Airlink** service is the second-least expensive way to get to the airport (#748, fare €6, frequent departures from Ormond Quay, O'Connell St., Busáras, and Connolly and Heuston Stations, 30-minute trip). The least expensive way is to take the local bus (#16A from O'Connell St. or #41 from Lower Abbey St., 3/hour, fare €2.70, 40-minute trip).

Car

It's possible to rent a car without returning to the airport. Rental agencies with city center branches include **Europcar** (Baggot St. Bridge, tel. 01/614-2800, www.europcar.ie), **Dan Dooley** (42 Westland Row, tel. 01/677-2733, www.dan-dooley.ie), and **Hertz** (149 Upper Leeson St., tel. 01/660-2255, www.hertz.ie).

That said, pick up the rental only when you're ready to leave the city, as driving in Dublin can be confusing and stressful even for natives. Pay-and-display parking in the city center will run you €2.90/hour.

Bicycle

With so much traffic and construction work going on, getting around by bike can be pretty risky; don't forget to wear your helmet. It's also pricier to rent a bike (around €20/120 per day/week, plus a €100-200 deposit) than elsewhere in the country. Try **Irish Cycling Safaris** at the Belfield Bike Shop (near the running track on the University College Dublin campus, on Dublin Bus routes #3, #10, and #11B from O'Connell St., tel. 01/716-1697, www.cyclingsafaris.com, until 6pm weekdays and 10am-2pm Sat.), which also offers weeklong themed cycling trips, or **Cycleways** (185-186 Parnell St., tel. 01/873-4748, www.cycleways.com, until 6pm Mon.-Sat., 8pm Thurs.).

There are 79 **taxi ranks** (www.taxi.ie) all over the city, most of which operate 24 hours a day. Between the hours of 8pm and 6am, bus lanes at the following locations also serve as taxi ranks: Dame Street, outside the Bank of Ireland, near Trinity but facing Christchurch; Merrion Row, near St. Stephen's Green; Dawson Street, opposite the Mansion House; and, Northside, on Talbot Street, on the O'Connell Street side of the railway bridge.

Alternatively, ring **National Radio Cabs** (tel. 01/677-2222) or **City Cabs** (tel. 01/872-2688). There are surcharges galore across the board: late-night pickups, phone bookings, luggage handling per bag (even if you load it yourself), and extra passengers.

Vicinity of Dublin City

NORTH OF DUBLIN CITY
Howth

A charming fishing village on a small peninsula north of the city, Howth (rhymes with "both," from the Norse for "headland"; Bínn Eádáir, "Hill of Eadair," after a chieftain of the mythical Tuatha de Danann) makes a fine afternoon excursion, what with its rhododendron gardens and spooky, poorly tended 14th-century abbey ruins overlooking the harbor. There's also a bracing six-kilometer **cliff walk** clearly signposted from the train station, which will take you 1.5-2.5 hours depending on the length of the route you choose.

Howth Castle has remained in the same family, the St. Lawrences and their descendants, for more than 800 years. The current structure dates from 1564 and has been restored and rebuilt many times since then. The

the rhododendron gardens at Howth Castle, north of Dublin City

most interesting story about this castle regards the pirate queen Grace O'Malley, who dropped by for dinner once in 1575 only to be snubbed by Christopher St. Lawrence. O'Malley promptly kidnapped his son and heir and sailed him back to Mayo. (He was eventually returned to his family, but not before the St. Lawrences had much humbled themselves.) Though the castle is not open to the public (they do make exceptions for educational groups), their **cookery school** (www.howthcastlecookeryschool.ie) offers classes. The Howth Castle **gardens** are open in summer (try to go in May or June when the rhododendrons are in bloom), and on the grounds is a pre-historic dolmen known as **Aideen's Grave** (Aideen being the wife of a dead warrior, a little legend attached to the formation much later on). Access to the rhododendron gardens is via the Deer Park Hotel and Golf Course.

To get here, make a right out of the DART station and cross the street, following the main road for about five minutes. Make a left for the Deer Park Hotel entrance (passing the Anglican St. Mary's Church with its small memorial garden), and after another five minutes you'll see the castle on the right (the turnoff is here for a rather ramshackle "transport museum" as well). It's another 10-minute walk straight on for the hotel. Once there, walk along the right side of the building, past the bar, and you'll see a clearly trodden path leading you into the woods (where the rhododendrons are). A short climb up this secret-gardenesque path will afford you a phenomenal view over Dublin Bay. The dolmen is on the wooded path to the fourth tee.

Feeling peckish? Instead of risking the hotel food, try the grub at the dimly lighted, atmospheric **Abbey Tavern** (Abbey St., tel. 01/839-0307, www.abbeytavern.ie, food served 12:30pm-10pm daily, lunch €12-28). Dinner in the upstairs restaurant is overpriced, but the simple, reasonably priced pub lunches hit the spot.

Howth is 16 kilometers northeast of Dublin on the R105, and is served by both **DART** (tel. 01/805-4288, 2/hour daily from Connolly Station, €1.60) and **Dublin Bus** (tel. 01/873-4222, #31, 3/hour daily from Eden Quay, €1.55). The DART will get you there in 20 minutes, but the bus takes nigh an hour.

Malahide

With its pleasant promenade, Blue Flag strand, shady tree-lined avenue, and hip boutiques—not to mention the second-most haunted castle on the island—Malahide (Mullach Íde, "Promontory of St. Ita") makes another pleasant day trip.

With the exception of one lord's temporary eviction at the hands of Cromwell in the 17th century, the Talbot family lived at **Malahide Castle & Gardens** (tel. 01/846-2184, www.malahidecastle.com, 10am-5pm Mon.-Sat. year-round, 10am-6pm Sun. Apr.-Sept., 11am-5pm Sun. Oct.-Mar., €12) from 1174 to 1976. Though most of the present structure dates from the 17th and 18th centuries, Malahide retains the title of oldest inhabited castle. The Talbots converted from Catholicism in 1779, and the exquisitely carved Flemish panels in the Oak Room—depicting various Old Testament tales along with the Coronation of the Virgin—indicate that the room was

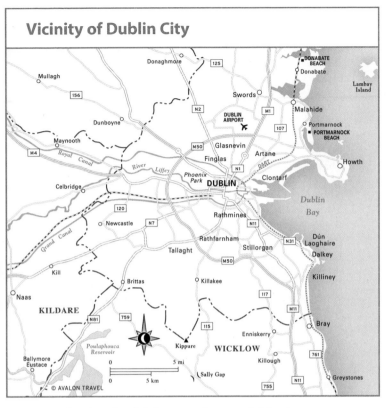

Vicinity of Dublin City

Mullagh • Donaghmore • [125] • DONABATE BEACH • Donabate • Lambay Island

Swords • [156] • [N2] • DUBLIN AIRPORT • [M1] • Malahide • [107] • Portmarnock • PORTMARNOCK BEACH

Dunboyne • Maynooth • [M50] • Glasnevin • Artane • Howth

[M4] • Royal Canal • River Liffey • Finglas • [N1] • DART • Clontarf

Phoenix Park • DUBLIN

Celbridge • Rathmines • Dublin Bay

[120] • Newcastle • [N7] • [N11] • Dún Laoghaire

Grand Canal • Rathfarnham • Stillorgan • Dalkey • [N31]

Tallaght • [M50] • Killiney

Kill • Brittas • Killakee • [117]

Naas • [M11]

KILDARE • [N81] • [759] • [115] • Bray

Poulaphouca Reservoir • Kippure • WICKLOW • Enniskerry • [761]

Ballymore Eustace • Killough • Greystones

0 5 mi
0 5 km

Sally Gap • [N11] • [755]

© AVALON TRAVEL

once used as their chapel. Other rooms feature period furniture, rococo plasterwork, and an extensive portrait collection, and 35-minute guided tours leave every quarter of an hour. Outside, the botanic gardens feature more than 4,500 plant species, many of them exotic; this is a fine spot for a picnic lunch.

The Malahide Historical Society claims the castle houses at least five ghosts (whose sightings are well documented). Some may be the spirits of the 14 Talbot men who breakfasted in the banquet hall on the morning of the Battle of the Boyne—a meal destined to be their last. Another wraith is that of a 15th-century sentry named Puck who fell asleep on duty, thus allowing an enemy to storm the castle, and who hanged himself in shame; he hasn't been spotted in 30 or so years, though. (An alternate version of the story says that Puck fell in love with one of his mistress's lady visitors, and did away with himself out of unrequited love.)

There's a new **Avoca food hall** and mini-mall adjacent to the castle, or you have a choice of eateries on Malahide's main drag. For excellent Greek and Cypriot victuals, try **Cape Greko** (Unit 1, 1st floor, New St., tel. 01/845-6288, www.capegreko.ie, 5pm-11pm Mon., noon-11pm Tues.-Thurs., noon-midnight Fri.-Sat., noon-10pm Sun., lunch €9-15, dinner

€15-25). The service is as quick and polite as the food is delish, and veggie-lovers are well-catered for.

Malahide is 15 kilometers north of Dublin on the R107. Get there via **DART** (tel. 01/805-4288, 2/hour daily from Connolly Station, single/return fare €3.25/6.15). **Dublin Bus** service (tel. 01/873-4222, #32A, 9-11/day daily from Eden Quay, or 3/hour daily on #42 from Lower Abbey St., €3.30) is much slower (the DART journey is 22 minutes, but the bus takes nearly an hour).

SOUTH OF DUBLIN CITY
Dún Laoghaire

Thirteen kilometers south of the city, Dún Laoghaire ("dun LEER-y") is an uneasy mix of seaside resort and industrial harbor. The town has been hyped as a lower-cost alternative regarding food and accommodations, but this seems a little like going to Paris to dine on PB&J. Most folks take the DART down here to visit the **James Joyce Tower & Museum** (1 km east of town in Sandycove, signposted on the R119, tel. 01/280-9265, 10am-5pm Mon.-Sat. and 2pm-6pm Sun. Feb.-Oct., free), housed in a martello tower that features in the opening scene of Joyce's best-known work, *Ulysses*. The 22-year-old Joyce spent just a week here in August 1904 before leaving for Italy to live the life of a literary expat (teaching English, naturally) with future bride Nora Barnacle. On the seaside of the tower is a swimming hole, known as the **Forty Foot Pool** (named not for height, but for the 40th Regiment of the British Army stationed at the tower above). In years gone by the pool was forbidden to women, as men liked to bathe there in the nude. Today, alas, there are few exhibitionists carrying on the tradition.

Another reason to come to Dún Laoghaire is if you're leaving the country by ferry. The **Stena Line** (tel. 01/204-7777 or 01/204-7799 for timetable, www.stenaline.ie, 4/day daily, 2-hour trip, advance reservations

Malahide Castle

recommended, single fare €164-210) links Dún Laoghaire with Holyhead in North Wales. Book online for the best rates.

Dún Laoghaire is 13 kilometers south of Dublin on the R118 coastal road. The **DART** (tel. 01/805-4288, 3-4/hour daily, get off at Sandycove for the Joyce museum, single/daily return €3.25/6.15) can get you down here in 20 minutes or less from Pearse Station.

Around Dublin

Dublin's surrounding counties may be sampled by coach tour easily enough, but these areas are so rich in history—and offer such a lovely respite from the capital's hectic pace—that you'll be glad you decided on an extended exploration.

Wedged between Dublin and Northern Ireland on the east coast, Meath (An Mhí, "The Middle") and Louth (An Lú, "The Least") boast some of the island's most important megalithic and early Christian remains. Newgrange, a Neolithic passage tomb that predates the pyramids at Giza, is arguably the country's most popular tourist attraction, but there are also lesser-known sites (equally worthwhile) in Meath and Louth.

Counties Wicklow (Cill Mhantáin, "Church of Mantáin," a disciple of Patrick) and Kildare (Cill Dara, "Church of the Oak Wood"), on the other hand, are something of a study in contrasts. Half an hour due south of Dublin and you're in another world entirely, verdant hills and winding backroads: That's Wicklow, aptly nicknamed the "Garden of Ireland." Half an hour west and you're in Kildare, marked by a chain of commuter suburbs and flat green pastures—racetrack country.

These counties do, of course, have more than their share of humdrum commuter suburbs. Navan and Dundalk in particular are bulging with anonymous cookie-cutter estates to meet the overwhelming demand for affordable housing within an hour or so of Dublin. Keep on driving, as the few sights in these towns aren't all that worthwhile.

Previous: the Mound of the Hostages at the Hill of Tara; a ruin along the pilgrimage route leading down to Glendalough.

Look for ★ to find recommended
sights, activities, dining, and lodging.

Highlights

© AVALON TRAVEL

cairns are nicknamed the "Hills of the Witch" (page 80).

★ **Trim Castle:** The huge cruciform keep of this mighty Anglo-Norman fortress has been restored with vertiginous catwalks and detailed historical models, but what really makes Trim worth your while is the excellent guided tour (page 85).

★ **Monasterboice:** Along with the remains of a round tower and two small churches, this 6th-century monastic site features the two most magnificent high crosses in all Ireland (page 95).

★ **Powerscourt House and Gardens:** Exquisitely manicured Italianate gardens and statuary, leisurely walking trails, gourmet eats, retail therapy—it's all here (page 100).

★ **The Wicklow Way:** Hike all or part of this 132-kilometer trail from southern Dublin through the Wicklow Mountains and placid green farmlands north of Carlow (page 104).

★ **Glendalough:** Nestled in the gorse-dotted hills of the Wicklow Mountains National Park around two placid lakes, this fantastic 6th-century monastic site was once one of Ireland's most important centers of learning (page 104).

★ **Glenmalure:** The country's longest glacial valley is far removed from the manicured gardens Wicklow is renowned for, but this quiet, utterly remote locale has an appeal all its own (page 108).

★ **Brú na Bóinne:** At this funerary complex, Newgrange, one of Europe's most famous Stone Age monuments, and two other tombs, Knowth and Dowth, attract as many as 200,000 yearly visitors, who admire their astonishing architecture and striking Neolithic art (page 75).

★ **The Hill of Tara:** Go for an outdoor guided tour of the legendary seat of the High Kings of Ireland (page 78).

★ **Loughcrew Cairns:** Set in a stunning hilltop location, these spooky Stone Age

Around Dublin

ARMAGH

Castleblaney

MONAGHAN

Cavan

Ravensdale

CAVAN

Carlingford   Kilkeel

Dundalk

Lough
Sheelin

M1

Ardee

LOUGHCREW
CAIRNS

LOUTH

LOUGHCREW
HISTORIC GARDENS

Kells

MEATH

MONASTERBOICE

Navan

MELLIFONT ABBEY

Drogheda

River Boínne

BRÚ NA BÓINNE

WESTMEATH

The Boyne Valley

Mullingar

BECTIVE
ABBEY

THE HILL OF TARA

Irish

Trim

DUBLIN

Sea

TRIM CASTLE

Dunsany

N4

M4

Maynooth

Donaghmore

M1

OFFALY

Castletown

Dublin

KILDARE

M50

M7

Naas

Newbridge

Blessington

THE WICKLOW
WAY

Enniskerry   Bray

Portlaoise

POWERSCOURT
HOUSE AND GARDENS

Greystones

Wicklow Mountains
National Park

N9

LAOIS

WICKLOW

Roundwood

THE GLEN OF
IMAAL

GLENDALOUGH

Laragh

N8

Baltinglass

Wicklow

GLENMALURE

Rathdrum

Carlow

KILKENNY

Avoca

N11

Brittas Bay

AVOCA
HANDWEAVERS

Kilkenny

CARLOW

Arklow

0   20 mi

0   20 km

Gorey

WEXFORD

© AVALON TRAVEL

Though Ireland has more than 1,200 megalithic tombs (in varying states of preservation, of course), archaeologists have learned the most about everyday life in the Stone Age from the sites of County Meath. From remains at Brú na Bóinne—the megalithic funerary complex of which Newgrange is the centerpiece of sorts—we know plenty more than what they ate (livestock, nuts, wheat, and barley). They "cleaned" their teeth with soot, cleared tracts of forest for growing grain and raising animals brought over from England, and decorated their pottery and tomb walls with elegant tri-spiraling motifs. And the population stats are downright horrifying: The average life expectancy was 26 years for women and 29 for men, and the infant mortality rate was as high as 75 percent.

In pre-Christian times the high king of Ireland had his royal court at Tara in Meath. There is more legend than fact associated with the Hill of Tara, however; this broad grassy mound with its unimpressive ruins is more a national symbol than anything else, since it was Tara where St. Patrick sought permission to preach the new religion on this island. St. Buite, a disciple of Patrick, founded a monastery at Monasterboice near the River Boyne in the early 6th century. "Boyne" is actually a corruption of his name. The Hill of Slane is also associated with Patrick, who according to legend lit a paschal fire here in view of King Laoghaire's palace on the hill of Tara. After a spiritual duel of sorts between Patrick and the king's druidic advisors, the enraged king reluctantly converted to Christianity.

Wicklow and Kildare were hives of early Christian activity as well. The early 6th-century St. Brigid is the unofficial patron of Kildare, though the county had strong pre-Christian ties to a goddess of the same name (leading many to speculate that a "Saint Brigid" never actually existed). Yet another Patrick legend has the saint, at the beginning of his evangelist mission, desiring to land on a beach just south of Wicklow Town. The locals were less than friendly, and in a scuffle on the beach one of his disciples, Mantáin, lost a few teeth. For this reason the county's Irish name, Cill Mhantáin, can be more loosely translated as "Church of the Toothless One." ("Wicklow" is Anglo-Norman, and has no such story to explain it.) The region's most important monastic site, Glendalough, was founded in the 6th century as well, by the hermit St. Kevin.

These counties' proximity to the capital meant that English forces were omnipresent throughout the darkest periods in Irish history; the Penal Laws and other anti-Catholic legislation were easiest to enforce by simple geography. One of the darkest epochs came in 1690, the failed Jacobite revolution, when the forces of the deposed Catholic king of England, James II, assembled along the Boyne to fight the Parliament's choice of monarch, the Protestant William of Orange (James's son-in-law). It is not an exaggeration to state that the fate of Ireland hung in the balance, and the English victory enabled hundreds of years of further social and political oppression.

Newgrange, Meath's principal attraction, is most often done as a day trip out of Dublin, though there's more here—the Loughcrew Cairns and Trim Castle especially—to warrant at least an overnight stay in the Boyne Valley. It is perhaps most efficient to experience Louth's sights—nearly all of which are in or near Drogheda, and can be visited in the span of a day—while en route to Belfast. Kildare's attractions can be visited in passing from Dublin to any points west or south, but you will certainly want to linger in Wicklow. The county's most important (and most popular) sight, Glendalough, can be done in a day trip from Dublin, but it's better to spend the night; ideally you should spend two or three, since there are great hiking opportunities in the national park. If you don't have time for an overnight visit, make a day trip here, to Powerscourt House and Gardens, or to the slightly shabby seaside town of Bray for an exhilarating cliffside walk. Those walking the whole Wicklow Way should bank on a week and a half.

Meath

Meath is often referred to as "The Royal County," since the pre-Christian seat of the high kings was here, on the Hill of Tara. Originally there were five Irish provinces—Leinster, Munster, Connaught, Ulster, and Meath—but the fifth and smallest was subsumed into Leinster by an Act of Parliament under Henry VIII in 1543, which formed two new counties, Meath and Westmeath.

Newgrange and the other Boyne Valley sights can be done in a day tour out of Dublin, but it's far better to base yourself in Trim or Slane and take your time. And if you're interested in the archaeology but can't stand crowds (you'll find 'em at Newgrange even in winter), consider visiting the spooky, yet-to-be-excavated Loughcrew Cairns instead of Brú na Bóinne. The views from those "hills of the witch" will literally take your breath away.

THE BOYNE VALLEY

From superstitious Stone Age farming communities to the seat of royal power, home of saints and scholars and a bloody battle for the English throne: The history of the Boyne River valley is even richer than the soil. A day tour out of Dublin, such as the one offered by **Mary Gibbons Tours** (tel. 01/283-9973, www.newgrangetours.com, departs the Dublin tourist office on Suffolk St. at 10:15am Mon.-Sat., returning at 4:30pm, €35, includes admission fees), will take you to Brú na Bóinne, the Hill of Tara, and the Battle of the Boyne site. **Bus Éireann** also offers a **Newgrange and Boyne Valley tour,** though it doesn't run daily (Busáras, Store St., tel. 01/836-6111, www.buseireann.ie, departs bus station 10am on Thurs. and Sat. and returns at 5:45pm, €29, includes admission fees).

Meath and Louth

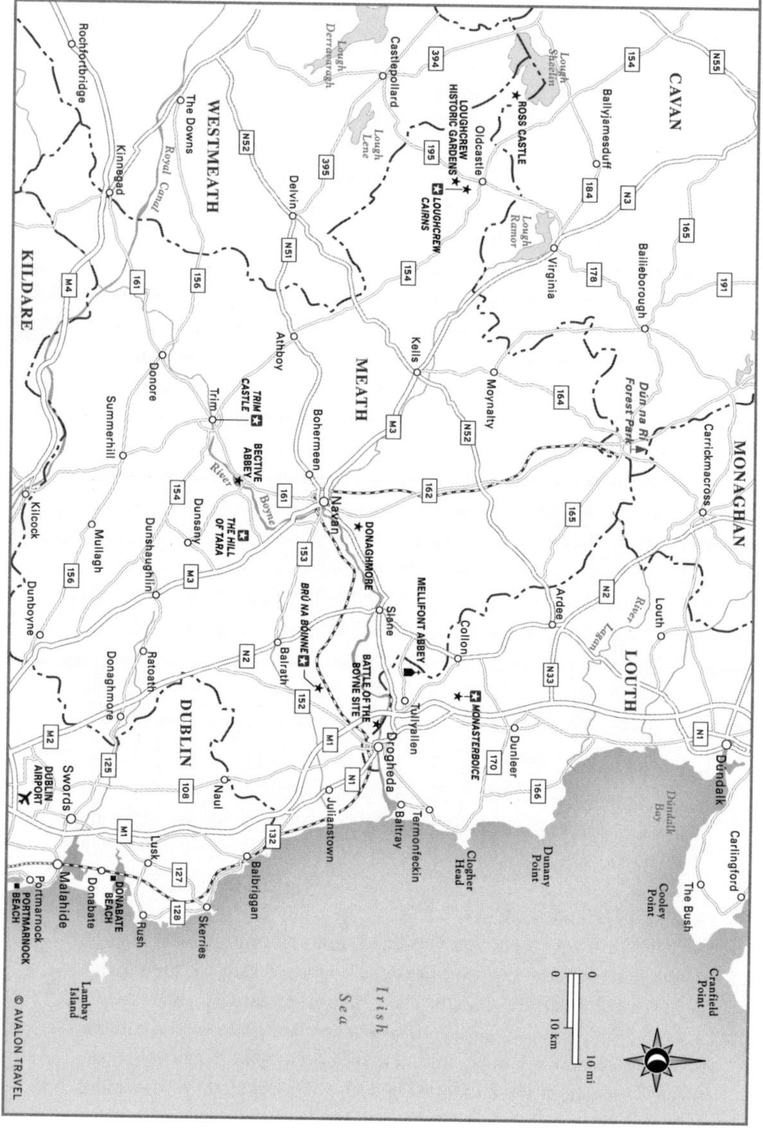

Locally, the village of Slane makes a very pleasant base for visiting the Boyne Valley sights, though Trim and Drogheda are good options as well.

★ Brú na Bóinne

Opened in 1997, the very informative **Brú na Bóinne Visitor Centre** (2 km west of Donore on Staleen Rd., clearly signposted from Drogheda/M1 and Slane/N2, tel. 041/988-0300, www.worldheritageireland.ie or www. newgrange.com, €3 exhibition only, €6 with Newgrange, €5 with Knowth, €11 combo ticket) is your access point (via quick shuttle bus ride) for three of Europe's most important prehistoric burial chambers: Newgrange, the best-known and most-visited, as well as Knowth and Dowth, the latter of which has yet to be excavated. (It's also the only monument you can check out without going through the visitors center.) Newgrange and the interpretive center are open year-round (9:30am-5:30pm daily Mar.-Apr. and Oct., 9am-6:30pm daily in May, 9am-7pm daily June-Sept., 9:30am-5pm Nov.-Feb.); Knowth is open the same hours but only late March through October. On this UNESCO World Heritage Site there are more than 90 monuments and earthworks in all.

You need only to look at the lush river valley around you to understand why the first Neolithic farmers chose to settle here between 3800 and 3400 BC. The Boyne provided rich soil, fish, drinking water, and a means of transport, and the surrounding forests provided plenty of timber. The river attained spiritual significance as well, a symbol in their pagan religion of the sometimes-hazy boundary between the "real" and "other" worlds.

These elaborately constructed megalithic passage tombs were the product of that belief, and the 40 burial mounds at Brú na Bóinne are the first signs of human activity in this region. **Newgrange** (Sí an Bhrú) was built between 3300 and 2900 BC, making it 500 years older than the Giza pyramids and a thousand years older than Stonehenge. This type of megalithic tomb was built all over western and northern Europe during the fourth millennium BC, however, and it's somewhat ironic that the architects and laborers who spent at least 15 years erecting Newgrange would never be entombed there themselves. Yes, even in Neolithic times a rigid social hierarchy was firmly in place.

You may be startled at first by the tomb's spiffy white quartz facade, a reconstruction based on the findings of University College Cork (UCC) archaeologist Michael J. O'Kelly. The entry stone is carved with exquisite triple spirals, the most common interpretation being that this motif symbolizes the cycles of nature. The mound alone weighs 200,000 tons and covers a full acre; grooved channels in the upper surfaces of the roof stones siphon off the rainwater, keeping the chamber dry. Clearly, this monument, a marvel of Stone Age technology, was built to last.

Dr. O'Kelly's discoveries between 1962 and 1975 included the cremated remains of five bodies in the niches around the cruciform central chamber, though they were not cremated inside the tomb (no soot was found on the walls). Dearly departed members of the Neolithic upper crust were probably deposited here until the next winter solstice, when the dawning light streaming through the roof box would have, so they believed, transported their spirits to the afterlife. After the solstice these remains would have been transferred to other graves nearby, though probably not beneath the myriad "satellite tombs" around each of the three primary monuments; these would have been reserved for families lower on the social ladder.

Dr. O'Kelly also alighted—pun intended—on the roof box above the doorway and was the first person in modern times to witness the solstice illuminate the burial chamber. Today you can view a simulated version toward the end of the tour, and once back in the visitors center you can enter your name into a drawing to see it for real come December 20. Before you go, though, spend a few minutes deciphering the eerie early-19th-century graffiti.

The guided tour of Newgrange is not for claustrophobics, as the passageway is very low and narrow and the central chamber is too small for the number of visitors per group.

Knowth (Cnóbha), roughly the same size as Newgrange, is accessible by a second shuttle bus. Excavated by George Eogan from Trinity College Dublin in 1967 and 1968, this passage tomb is encircled by 127 large curbstones, and the two chambers within see the light of the spring equinox. Knowth alone contains 45 percent of Irish tomb art, and more than 25 percent of the tomb art in all Europe, so it's a real disappointment that you can't actually enter either of its two passages (you can only take a peek inside). According to UCC archaeologist Elizabeth Shee Twohig, many motifs in megalithic art were probably "derived from altered states of consciousness." A replica of a carefully carved phallic stone found at Knowth is on display in the exhibition; whatever their intention in building such monuments, clearly these Stone Agers were having their fun.

Though **Dowth** (Dubhadh)—with its 115 curbstones and two westward-facing tombs—is comparable in size to Newgrange and Knowth, it has never been properly excavated. Archaeologists believe that, like Knowth, this site was still a hive of activity in early Christian times. The crater at the center of the mound is the result of excavations in the 1840s; like Newgrange, Dowth's west face was quarried by local builders. You can walk around the site, though entrance to the mound is not possible.

The **Brú na Bóinne interpretive center** is kid-friendly without being dumbed down, featuring replicas of Neolithic clothing, tools, and tchotchkes. Birdcalls play on a speaker above a full-scale model of a circular thatched hut, a speculative reconstruction based on the post holes and foundation trenches uncovered during the excavation. There's also a seven-minute audiovisual inside an ersatz planetarium, and a low stone doorway on the far side leads into a full-scale model of the inner chamber at Newgrange. Along with the usual tearoom and gift shop, the center also houses a full-fledged tourist office.

Brú na Bóinne is one of Ireland's top tourist attractions, which means you need to be strategic in planning your visit. In high season it's wise to arrive at opening to beat most of the coach tours and school groups. Come in the afternoon and you may not be able to visit the sites at all—spaces on the tours fill up extremely quickly. Purchase a combo ticket for the interpretive center and both monuments, and consider buying the Dúchas Heritage Card if you'll be visiting other OPW (Office of Public Works) sites on your trip.

Brú na Bóinne is 55 kilometers northwest of Dublin off the N2, and the site is also clearly signposted from Slane and Drogheda on the N51. Those not driving can do Brú na Bóinne as a day tour out of Dublin.

But if you'd like to spend the night, there is accommodation just across the road at **Newgrange Lodge** (Staleen Rd., tel. 041/988-2478, www.newgrangelodge.com, dorm beds €21, private rooms €25-30). This hostel-slash-guesthouse is large, clean, and well-appointed (with kitchens for self catering), but its size makes it very popular with groups, who can be a bit overwhelming if you are hoping for a quiet evening. That said, you may be interested in kayaking, archery, paintball, or guided hikes at the adjoining activity center (www.activitynation.ie).

Bective Abbey

The substantial ruins of **Bective Abbey** (on the L4010 7 km north of Trim, signposted off the Navan road/R161, always accessible, free) are well worth seeking out. This is Ireland's second Cistercian monastery, founded in 1147 as a "daughter house" of Mellifont Abbey in County Louth and converted into a mansion after minions of Henry VIII forcibly dissolved it. Romantically labyrinthine, the abbey's highlight is a lovely arcaded cloister—and if it seems familiar, it may be because one of the scenes in *Braveheart* (with Sophie Marceau and Jeanne Marine) was filmed here. What a perfect spot for a picnic!

If you'd like to spend the night in these lovely pastoral surroundings, eco-conscious **Bective Mill** (signposted on the L4010 opposite Bective

the romantic ruins of Bective Abbey

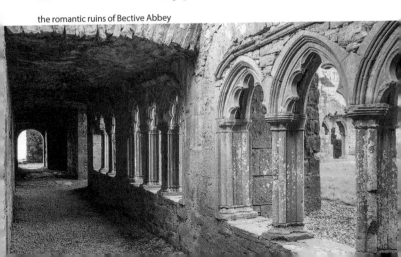

Abbey, 100m down a local road, tel. 087/396-2399, www.bectivemill. com, €40 pp, s €50) is a cozy, well-kept B&B with its own duck eggs on the breakfast menu. This waterside guesthouse is a particularly good choice for anglers, who have access to three kilometers along the River Boyne. For dinner, try **The Station House** (Kilmessan, 3.5 km southeast of Bective Abbey on the L4010, tel. 046/902-5239, www.stationhousehotel.ie, food served 12:30pm-10pm daily, €17-28, B&B rooms €80-180), a converted railway station that has happily retained much of its 19th-century charm.

★ The Hill of Tara

As with Rome, all roads once led to the **Hill of Tara** (12 km south of Navan off the M3, tel. 046/902-6222, visitors center 10am-6pm daily late May-mid-Sept., exhibition €4), legendary seat of the high kings of Ireland from the 3rd through the 10th century AD—and fortunately, the M3 motorway hasn't destroyed the site's tranquility, as many locals feared it would. Here St. Patrick obtained permission from King Laoghaire to preach Christianity on the island after explaining the concept of the Holy Trinity using a shamrock plucked from the grass. For this reason the site is often called the **Ráth of the Synods** (a synod being, essentially, a religious assembly). The 20-minute guided tour takes you by the **Mound of the Hostages,** a Bronze Age passage tomb built between 2500 and 2000 BC; remains of several ring forts and earthenworks, including a "banquet hall" (more likely used as another burial site) and the **Fort of King Laoghaire,** supposedly entombed standing up and in full armor; and the **Lia Fáil,** the overtly phallic "Stone of Destiny," where the kings were crowned—suspiciously Arthurian, eh? The tour, coupled with a 20-minute audiovisual at the visitors center (housed in a deconsecrated church), will give you a sense of the historic importance around this sheep-dotted hill. The site is fairly popular with locals (some walking their dogs) any time of year, and you don't have to pay a fee just to walk around.

In more recent history, Tara was the site of an Irish defeat in the rebellion of 1798, and in 1843 the "Great Liberator," Daniel O'Connell, held a mass rally on this hill. It's said as many as a million people turned up to hear his call for the repeal of the Act of Union. Even if that figure is exaggerated, most agree at least half a million people were there that day—still a stunning statistic, considering the pre-famine population was somewhere in the neighborhood of eight million.

Once you've taken a wander around the site, pop into **Maguire's** (tel. 046/902-5534, 9:30am-6pm daily) for coffee and a sandwich. Bibliophiles should budget at least half an hour at **The Old Book Shop,** a veritable trove of wonders. This tourist complex, such as it is, is refreshingly untouristy!

To get to Tara from Dublin (40 km), head north for Cavan on the M3. The **Bus Éireann** (tel. 01/836-6111) Dublin-Navan route (#109, at least one departure per hour daily) can leave you off at Tara Cross within easy walking distance of the site, if requested.

The Battle of the Boyne

The largest battle in Irish history was fought on July 1, 1690, between supporters of William of Orange and the Jacobites, who sought to restore the Catholic king he had deposed. There were more than 61,000 troops amassed on the **Battle of the Boyne site** (Oldbridge Estate, 6 km west of Drogheda via the L16014, tel. 041/980-9950, www.battleoftheboyne.ie, 9:30am-4:30pm daily Mar.-Apr., 10am-5pm daily May-Sept., 9am-4pm daily Oct.-Feb., €4) on that fateful morning. The date of the battle is still seared on the Irish national psyche, especially in the north, where Protestant schoolboys continue to celebrate the "marching season" with truly frightening zeal.

As at the Hill of Tara, you really need some context (provided by a 13-minute audiovisual and weaponry displays in the exhibition center) to get anything out of a visit to the battle site; otherwise it's just an ironically peaceful riverside stroll. To get here, take the N51 west from Drogheda (5 km) or east from Slane (13 km), or take the N2 or M1 motorway out of Dublin; the site is clearly signposted from the N51. If you're relying on public transport, the **Bus Éireann** route out of Drogheda (#163, 6/day Mon.-Sat., 5/day Sun.) stops in the nearby village of Donore. From Dublin, take the #110 bus (6/day Mon.-Sat., 5/day Sun.) and transfer in Drogheda. It's much more efficient to take one of the Boyne Valley day tours, however.

Loughcrew Historic Gardens

The complex at **Loughcrew Historic Gardens** (Loughcrew House, 5 km south of the village of Oldcastle, signposted off the R195/Mullingar road, tel. 049/854-1060, www.loughcrew.com, 9:30pm-5:30pm Mon.-Fri. and 11am-5:30pm Sat.-Sun. mid-Mar.-Oct., 11am-4pm Sat.-Sun. and upon request Nov.-Mar., €6) is yet another example of 21st-century big-house enterprise: You can wander through the restored 17th- and 19th-century gardens (which include the ruin of St. Oliver Plunkett's family church), go ziplining or tree-climbing at the **adventure center** (tel. 049/854-1356, half/full day of activities €32/52), and have lunch in the adjoining café. The neoclassical **Loughcrew House** used to offer B&B, but caters primarily to wedding and stag/hen parties now. The estate mounts a music and opera festival on a circular stage in the garden (€35), and a weekend **jazz festival** (€60) attracts some pretty high-profile performers. Visit the website for more details on both events, which take place in the month of June.

If you're visiting in low season, you'll need to pick up the key here if you wish to venture inside one of the Neolithic passage tombs at the Loughcrew Cairns.

Loughcrew House is 106 kilometers northwest of Dublin. To get to the house, garden, and cairns, take the M3 from Dublin to Kells and pick up the westbound Oldcastle road, the R154, and follow the signs for Loughcrew Gardens from the village.

Unfortunately, Bus Éireann's Drogheda-Oldcastle service is too infrequent and convoluted to be of any use to the tourist. Consider renting a car if Loughcrew is at the top of your destination list.

If the prospect of elbowing through the crowds at Newgrange in summer gets you seriously queasy, consider a visit to the relatively quiet (and "undeveloped") necropolis of the **Loughcrew Cairns** (Corstown, 3 km east of Oldcastle off the R154, tel. 049/854-2009 or 041/988-0300 for off-season inquiries, 10am-6pm mid-June-mid-Sept., free), constructed around 3000 BC. These 30 megalithic tombs (scattered on three neighboring hills) are known as the Hills of the Witch, for legend claims a beldam jumped from one hill to the next, dropping stones from her pocket to form them. Sliabh na Caillighe (meaning "Hill of the Witch") is the highest at 280 meters, and supposedly provides a view of 17 counties. The other two hills are known as Carnbane East (195 meters) and Carnbane West (205 meters). (You don't need to be a mountaineer to scale these hills, but for heaven's sake, put on sensible footwear!) The Neolithics decorated the largest tomb, Cairn T (on Carnbane East), with their trademark stone carvings; as at Newgrange (which was erected around the same time), New Agers flock here on the equinoxes to watch the morning light stream inside. If you'll be visiting around the spring or fall equinox (March 19-21 or September 19-21), you may want to take part in the **Loughcrew Equinox Festival** (www.facebook.com/carnbane), organized by the Oldcastle Tourism Group.

There are guides on-site during official opening hours, from whom you can obtain the key to Cairn L (on Carnbane West). Otherwise, to borrow the key to Cairn T from the Loughcrew Gardens visitors center, you are required to leave your passport or driver's license, a laundry list of contact details, and/or a €50 deposit. Contact **Loughcrew House** directly (tel. 049/854-1356, info@loughcrew.com) should you wish to borrow the key outside visitors center opening hours (key available 10am-4pm only). Bring a flashlight!

To get to the cairns, take the M3 from Dublin to Kells and pick up the westbound Oldcastle road, the R154; follow the signs for Loughcrew

Climb up to the Loughcrew Cairns for gorgeous green views over County Meath.

Gardens from the village. You'll have to double back on that road once you've picked up the Cairn T key (though you can still wander around the site without it, of course).

Backpackers will definitely want to crash at **Loughcrew Megalithic Centre** (tel. 086/736-1948 or 087/397-4295, www.loughcrewmegalithiccentre.com, dorm beds €23), which includes a 16-bed hostel and campsites, a pleasant tearoom, and **Maggie Heaney's Cottage,** restored to its humble 18th-century roots. If you're busing it from Dublin (#109), the hostel offers pickup service from Kells. If you're driving, take the R163 west from Kells; the center is liberally signposted because the way there is very twisty-turny on potholed local roads.

Note that the café at Loughcrew Megalithic Centre is not to be confused with the Loughcrew House tearoom, where you can obtain the key to the Loughcrew cairns (although the owners are hoping to obtain their own key at some point). There is a route from here up to the top of the hill, and if you're here in the summer there'll be an OPW employee on site who can let you in.

LOUGH SHEELIN

Tucked away in the quiet western corner of County Meath, Lough Sheelin makes for a relaxing stopover once you've explored Newgrange, Tara, and Loughcrew by car. If you're charmed by the idea of staying in a castle without signing away your firstborn child, ★ **Ross Castle** (5.5 km southwest of the village of Mount Nugent on the L7081, turnoff is signposted on the right, tel. 087/125-0911, www.ross-castle.com, rooms €120-200) is the place for you. This 16th-century tower house overlooking Lough Sheelin comes with its very own Romeo-and-Juliet-style ghost story—it's said the maiden of the castle still wanders the grounds at night searching for her lost love. On a more practical note, this B&B is absolutely first rate, from the warm welcome and tranquil lake views to the beautiful (but not too stuffy) antique furniture, including four-poster beds and the full-sized suit of armor greeting you in the entryway. Nothing's too much trouble for caretaker Jackie Moran—breakfasts are bountiful and the coffee is delish. The original tower rooms are positively oozing with medieval atmosphere, so much so that some folks will be more comfortable staying in one of the more modern rooms in the ground-floor annex.

You'll definitely want to eat dinner at the castle (three-course meal €30), but in low season your best option is the lakeside **Crover House Hotel** (signposted off the R154 west of Mount Nugent, tel. 049/854-0206, www.croverhousehotel.ie, food served 12:30pm-9pm daily, €12-24), which is just over the border in County Cavan. The atmosphere is reminiscent of an American golf club, but the fare is above average and the staff are friendly. To get here, drive back to Mount Nugent and turn left onto the R154; the hotel is signposted on the left about two kilometers down the road, and it's another two kilometers or so from there.

DONAGHMORE

The small graveyard and 11th- or 12th-century round tower at **Donaghmore** (Domhnach Mór, "Big Church," 3km northeast of Navan on the N51 en route to Slane, always accessible, free) are worth a stop for the eerie 16th-century church ruin: There's only one wall left, and the doorway and two bell arches above look disconcertingly like a screaming face. There's also a collection of finely carved 18th- and early-19th-century headstones. It's nice to see an old Irish burial ground so exceptionally well cared for. The monastic community was founded in the 5th century by St. Cassán, a disciple of St. Patrick.

SLANE

If you're planning to do the Newgrange-Tara-Battle of the Boyne circuit, **Slane** (Baile Shláine) is far and away the most pleasant base—it's only 9 kilometers northwest, 24 kilometers northeast, and 12 kilometers west of those respective sites. Despite the occasional high-profile concert at Slane Castle, the village is delightfully quiet, friendly, and down-to-earth, priding itself on its illustrious sons: the early 20th-century poet Francis Ledwidge and John Boyle O'Reilly, a Fenian who became editor of a Boston newspaper, the *Pilot,* after escaping an Australian penal colony in the late 1880s.

Sights

Slane Castle (on the N51 just west of the village, tel. 041/988-4400, www.slanecastle.ie, noon-5pm Sun.-Thurs. May-July, €7), on whose grounds a natural amphitheater is now the country's coolest concert venue, was built in the 1780s using several prominent British and Anglo-Irish architects. Today you can tour several of the drawing rooms and bedrooms, among them the chamber in which King George IV enjoyed the occasional rendezvous with the lady of the house. The current Lord Conyngham, an enterprising chap, seems to be squeezing a profit out of his ancestral home in every manner feasible.

The **Hill of Slane,** where St. Patrick lit his paschal fire in a sort of religious competition with the druids at Tara in 433, is crowned with the atmospheric ruins of the 15th-century **Slane Abbey.** Above a gorgeous mullioned window rises a dramatic belfry—look up and you'll find you can see up all the way to the roof. To get here, take Chapel Street away from the river (past George's Patisserie) to the signpost on your left, just beyond the modern Celtic cross that serves as a 1798 monument. The road winds gently uphill for another kilometer, and at the crest you'll find lovely panoramic views of the Boyne River valley.

Francis Ledwidge, a tremendously promising poet who grew up just outside Slane, was killed in the first World War. He was just shy of 30. The **Ledwidge Museum** (Janeville, Slane, tel. 041/982-4544, www.francisledwidge.com, 10am-5pm daily mid-Mar.-Oct., 10am-3:30pm Nov.-Mar., €3) commemorates Ledwidge's life and poetry in a small exhibition and garden.

The Táin Trail and the Cattle Raid of Cooley

The Táin Trail cycling route is 504 kilometers long, a loop that extends from Roscommon to Carlingford on the Cooley Peninsula—hitting Longford, Athlone, Trim, Slane, and Kells, and plenty of sleepy midland villages along the way. County Louth includes 150 kilometers of this route, which hits the various settings of the medieval epic *Táin Bó Cúailnge* (literally "The Driving-Off of Cows of Cooley," but the anglicized title is *The Cattle Raid of Cooley*).

The epic follows the exploits of the teenage Ulster warrior Cuchulainn and his nemesis, Maeve (queen of Connaught). In an attempt to best her husband's wealth, Maeve (also spelled "Medb") plots to steal the finest bull in Ulster, and because the rest of the Ulster army is incapacitated by a mysterious curse, Cuchulainn is the only one who can stop her. Drawn-out battles ensue, some pitting Cuchulainn against his own loved ones.

If you're planning to cycle the Táin Trail, contact **Táin Tours** (Carlingford, tel. 087/239-7467, kmckeybushire@gmail.com) for bike rental (€15/80 per day/week). Bicycles are delivered to your accommodation and they'll give you all the maps and resources you need. More information is available through the **East Coast & Midlands Tourism** office (tel. 044/934-8761, www.discoverireland.ie).

A two-hour **Slane historical walking tour,** led by Mick Kelly (tel. 087/937-7040), departs the Conyngham Arms every evening at 7pm.

Activities and Recreation

Slane is on the **Táin Trail** cycling route. Since there's no bike shop in the village proper, pedaling to Newgrange isn't really an option unless you've brought one with you. Climbing the **Hill of Slane** (it's a leisurely kilometer) is a nice way to pass an afternoon, as both the monastic ruins and the view at the top are eminently picture-worthy; alternatively, head over the bridge (just south of the square) and pick up the path along the Boyne. Otherwise, there's always the **Stackallen Tennis and Pitch and Putt Club** (Stackallen, Pig Hill, 2 km from Slane on the Navan-bound N51, tel. 041/982-4279 or 087/977-3213, info@stackallen.com).

Food and Entertainment

Savor a *pain au chocolat* and a *café au lait* at **George's Patisserie** (Chapel St., tel. 041/982-4493, www.georgespatisserie.com, 9am-6pm daily, €6). The ornate three-tier cakes on display conjure daydreams of a grand old-fashioned wedding. Though the café offers only sweet things, there's a delicatessen on the premises featuring local meats and cheeses, and the freshly baked breads (including gluten-free options) make for good picnic fixings.

The old-style tearoom is no more, but the dark, spacious, comfortable **Boyle's** (Main St., tel. 041/982-4195, www.boylesofslane.ie) is still the best spot in town for an afternoon drink. The friendly bartenders show plenty of traditional Irish hospitality, too. **The Village Inn** (Main St., tel.

041/982-4230) has a fun collection of pictures and posters from castle concerts gone by. There's also good *craic* to be found at the old-school pub at the Conyngham Arms.

The **Conyngham Arms** (Main St., tel. 041/988-4444, food served noon-8pm daily, €15-25) does pub grub as well as more formal meals in the restaurant; your other option in the village is **The Poet's Rest** (Chapel St., tel. 041/982-0738, 12:30pm-9:30pm Mon., 5pm-9:30pm Thurs.-Fri., 12:30pm-9:30pm Sat., 12:30pm-8:30pm Sun., €12-20), which will get the job done with smiling service. But if your budget allows, try the **Brabazon** (Rathkenny, 7 km north of Slane on the N51, tel. 041/ 982-4621, www.tankardstown.ie, 6pm-8:30pm Wed.-Thurs., 6pm-9:30pm Fri.-Sun., also 12:30pm-3:30pm Sun., vegetarian/omnivore's fixed-price dinner €55/70), part of the swanky 18th-century Tankardstown House.

Accommodations

Whether you're looking for budget beds or charming self-catering digs, head on over to the IHH **Slane Farm Hostel and Cottages** (Harlinstown, 2 km from the village on the Kells road, the R163, tel. 041/988-4985, www. slanefarmhostel.ie, Mar.-Nov., dorms €18, doubles €25 pp, singles €30, cottages €80/350 per night/week), a converted 18th-century stablehouse all done up in cheerful green trim. The kitchen, sitting room, and dormitories are amazingly clean and homey, stocked and decorated with far more care than most people give their own living spaces. Breakfast is €5 and includes eggs from the resident hens and produce from the vegetable garden.

B&Bs in and around Slane are strangely sparse. As far as hotels go, the **Conyngham Arms Hotel** (Main St., tel. 041/988-4444, www.conynghamarms.com, rooms €115-150) is about as old-fashioned as it gets, with cathedral ceilings, four-poster beds (not in every room, though), and that certain air of faded gentility. The restaurant fare is far better than average, too—but don't plan on an early night, as the noise from the pub can be heard even on the top floor. The finest accommodation in the area is a restored Georgian manor, **Tankardstown House** (Rathkenny, 7 km north of Slane on the N51, tel. 041/ 982-4621, www.tankardstown.ie, B&B €100-200 pp). Book online for a package including dinner, spa treatments, high tea, and/or sightseeing excursions.

Information and Services

You'll find the local **tourist office** (Main St., tel. 041/982-4010, www. meathtourism.ie, 9:30am-5pm Mon., Thurs., and Sat.) across the street from the Conyngham Arms Hotel.

There's an ATM in the Londis supermarket on the Collon road (the N2). Pick up cough drops at **Breen's Pharmacy** (Main St., tel. 041/982-4222).

Getting There

Slane is 15 kilometers west of Drogheda on the N51 and 48 kilometers northwest of Dublin on the N2. **Bus Éireann** passes through Slane on

(#33, 3-4/day daily), Portrush (#36, 3-4/day daily), and Clones in County
Monaghan (#177, 6/day daily). There is also direct service from Drogheda
(#183 or #188, at least 6/day Mon.-Sat.).

Getting Around

Newgrange Bike Hire (Drumree, tel. 086/069-5771, kevinohand@eircom.
net, ring for rates) is 300 meters from the Brú na Bóinne visitors center.

For a taxi in the Slane area, ring **M&L Cabs** (tel. 087/214-3088 for a cab,
tel. 086/360-1338 for a minibus).

TRIM

Dominated by the fascinating ruins of an Anglo-Norman castle, **Trim** (Baile
Átha Troim) is a tidy little town on the River Boyne 40 minutes northwest
of Dublin. It's a quiet place—some may find it a bit too quiet, especially
after dark—but its medieval attractions and a couple of delightfully scruffy
pubs make Trim a pleasant spot to spend the night.

Between the humongous castle and the town's smallish size, orienting
yourself is fairly easy. The street that hugs the castle ruins changes names
from the New Dublin Road to Castle Street to Bridge Street—here crossing the Boyne—to High Street to Navan Gate Street as it curves north-
ward. Most of the town's amenities are on Market Street, which shoots
westward off the main drag where Castle meets Bridge Street. Turn off
the west end of Market Street onto Emmet Street, home to several pubs
offering live trad.

★ Trim Castle

Granted the land by Henry II, Hugh de Lacy and his son Walter built a
motte-and-timber tower in 1172 on the site of the Boyne-side **Trim Castle**
(tel. 046/943-8619, 10am-6pm daily Apr.-Oct., 10am-5pm weekends Nov.-
Mar., admission with/excluding the keep €4/2), only to burn it down the
following year to prevent the Irish from taking it by force. They rebuilt
the castle over the following three decades, and it was—and remains—the
largest Anglo-Norman castle in the country. Before its restoration in the
late 1990s, Trim was partially rebuilt (and filled with various livestock and
ragamuffin extras) for the filming of *Braveheart,* and you can flip through
a photo album available from the admission desk.

Only the service tower is missing from the imposing, three-story, cruciform keep, accessible by guided tour only; it's an informative-but-interest-
ing 45 minutes. On the ground level, three large and wonderfully detailed
models of the castle at three different periods in its history highlight many
notable architectural features, like the "roof scars" that are all that remain
of a double A-framed, red-tiled roof, or the squinches that still lend struc-
tural support. Metal catwalks allow visitors to peruse the upper levels, and
the view from the parapet is worth the vertigo on the spiral stairs.

Elsewhere on the castle grounds, the Barbican Gate has five parallel murder holes (there are also two in the town gate, from which you enter the grounds), and the jail features an oubliette.

Other Sights

Just across the Boyne are the **yellow steeple,** once the bell tower of the Augustinian Abbey of St. Mary (its present ruined state thanks, yet again, to Cromwell), and the **Sheep's Gate,** the only extant gate from the old town walls. The early-15th-century **Talbot Castle** (High St.) incorporates a portion of the old abbey and was once owned by Jonathan Swift (he lived there for only one year, though his mistress spent much more time there). The Millennium Bridge at the end of Castle Street connects the medieval ruins on either side of the river.

Newtown Abbey (Lackanash Rd., 1.5 km east of town, always accessible, free) contains the ruins of the **Cathedral of Saints Peter and Paul,** remarkable for its well-worn double tomb effigy of a knight and his wife. The sword that separates them has inspired locals to refer to them as "the jealous man and woman." The rainwater that collects in the carvings is said to have curative properties—for warts, that is—and the space between the effigies is littered with rusted safety pins. To get here, take the New Road/Navan exit at the roundabout at the end of New Dublin Road (just east of the castle), cross the Boyne, and make the first right onto Lackanash Road, a residential street. It's a 20-minute walk or a 3-minute drive from town.

Trim is also a viable base for the Boyne Valley's prime attractions (Tara is 23 km, Newgrange 34 km). Need a break from driving, or don't have wheels? Contact Anne Leavy at **Tours na Mí** (tel. 046/943-2523, abirdyleavy@iol.ie).

Activities and Recreation

Tee off at the **County Meath Golf Club** (Newtonmoynagh, 1.5 km outside town, tel. 046/943-1463, www.trimgolf.net), which has an 18-hole parkland course.

You have a choice among equestrian centers in the area (no more than a 10-minute drive): There's the **Kilcarty Horse Riding Centre** (Kilcarty, Dunsany, tel. 046/902-5877 or 086/088-7841), the **Pelletstown Riding Centre** (Pelletstown, Drumree, tel. 01/825-9435, www.pelletstownriding-centre.com), or the **Moy Riding Centre** (Summerhill, Enfield, tel. 04/055-8115, www.moyridingcentre.com).

Food

You don't have a ton of choice here, but there are a few decent eateries. For breakfast (a bagel sandwich or the full fry) or lunch (lasagna and such), try **Java Juice** (1 Haggard Court, Haggard St., across the river from the castle, tel. 046/943-8771, 9am-5pm Mon.-Sat., 10am-5pm Sun., under €10), which boasts the best coffee in town.

For dinner, Trim's top eatery is the family-run **Stock House** (Emmet House, Finnegan's Way, tel. 046/943-7388, www.stockhouserestaurant.ie,

5pm-9pm Tues.-Thurs., 5pm-10pm Fri.-Sat., 1pm-8:30pm Sun., €16-23). Though steak is (unsurprisingly) the specialty here, there are several veg and seafood options, and the service is first rate. If you can't get a table at the Stock House, try **Franzini's** (5 French's Lane, tel. 046/943-1002, www. franzinis.com, 6:30pm-10pm Mon.-Sat., 5pm-9pm Sun., €12-26). The menu is strangely eclectic: You can order a burger, pasta . . . or duck glazed in peach sauce! You have a choice of fun cocktails too. This place is overpriced, however—the food is good, but by no means exceptional.

Entertainment and Events

You can't leave Trim without taking a pint at **Marcie Regan's,** a.k.a. **David's Lad** (Lackanash Rd., Newtown, tel. 046/943-6103, open at 9pm Thurs.-Tues.), which claims to be Ireland's second-oldest pub. Granted, with the rough stone walls, grungy chairs, and cement floors it feels like drinking in your uncle's basement, but the fact that everybody knows everyone here makes for an authentically Irish night out. The half dozen snow-haired gents who play traditional music here on Friday nights (starting a bit after 10:30) have been jamming together longer than you've been alive. To get here, take the New Road/Navan exit at the roundabout at the end of New Dublin Road (just east of the castle), cross the Boyne, and make the first right onto Lackanash Road, a residential street. The pub is directly across the road from Newtown Abbey.

Another delightfully old-fashioned pub is **James Griffin's** (21 High St., tel. 046/943-1295, www.jamesgriffinpub.ie), but if it's more trad you want, check out **The Emmet Tavern** (Emmet St., tel. 046/943-1378), with sessions Thursday-Saturday; **The Olde Stand** (Emmet St., tel. 046/943-1286) Friday-Sunday; or **The Steps** (Emmet St., tel. 046/943-7575) on Thursday. The **Castle Arch Hotel** (Summerhill Rd., tel. 046/943-1516, www.castlearch-hotel.com) offers trad every Saturday night.

Accommodations

Built in 1810, the marvelous **Highfield House** (Maudlins Rd., tel. 046/943-6386, www.highfieldguesthouse.com, €45 pp) was once a maternity hospital. The house is situated on a hill a couple minutes' walk from the castle, and its imposing stone facade, with bright flowers tumbling from the window boxes, matches the amazingly authentic decor. Gilded mirrors, cathedral ceilings and ornate plasterwork, high windows and sumptuous curtains, original oil paintings of young ladies in powdered wigs—it might sound on the stuffy side, but the rooms are actually quite comfortable (with new showers). Just keep in mind you're staying here for the atmosphere, not the breakfast. For the full fry done up right, try **Tigh Cathain** (Longwood Rd., 1 km from town on the R160, tel. 046/943-1996, www.tighcathain-bnb.com, €35-38 pp, s €50), a Tudor-style bungalow surrounded by carefully tended gardens, or **Crannmór Country House** (Dunderry Rd., 1.5 km northeast of the town center, tel. 046/943-1635, www.crannmor.com, €35-40 pp), a spacious, ivy-clad farmhouse in equally tranquil surroundings.

Trim's swankiest beds are found at the **Castle Arch Hotel** (Summerhill Rd., on the southern end of town, tel. 046/943-1516, www.castlearchhotel. com, €75-100 pp). Formerly known as Wellington Court (there's a monument to the duke of Waterloo fame nearby, on the corner of Emmet St. and Patrick St.), the town's only hotel often has terrific weekend packages up for grabs, so check the website before you go. Alternatively, you might be able to book a last-minute B&B for as little as €43 per person sharing.

Information and Services

The **tourist office and heritage center** (Mill St., tel. 046/943-7111 or 046/943-7227, www.meathtourism.ie, 9:30am-5:30pm Mon.-Sat., noon-5:30pm Sun. May-Sept., 9am-5pm Mon.-Sat. Oct.-Apr., exhibit €3.20) offers a 20-minute audiovisual show on Trim's medieval history (unfortunately, not included in the castle admission price).

The **AIB** (Market St., tel. 046/943-6444), **Bank of Ireland** (Market St., tel. 046/943-1230), and **Ulster Bank** (High St., tel. 046/943-1233) all have ATMs. There are two pharmacies on Market Street, **Kelly's** (tel. 046/943-1279) and **Farrell's** (tel. 046/943-6600).

Getting There and Around

Trim is 56 kilometers northwest of Dublin off the M3, picking up the R154 in the hamlet of Black Bull 26 kilometers outside the city. **Bus Éireann** (tel. 01/836-6111) operates a local service from Dublin (#111, 9/day Mon.-Fri., 8/day Sat., 4/day Sun.), though to get here from anywhere else by bus, you'll have to head back to Dublin first.

If you need a taxi, ring **Donal Quinn** (tel. 046/943-6009 or 087/222-7333), who offers 24-hour service.

Louth

Considering it's the smallest county on either side of the border, Louth has quite a fair bit to offer the visitor, including the truly magnificent high crosses of Monasterboice and the remains of once-powerful Mellifont Abbey with its unusual octagonal lavabo. Pass through the county's principal town, Dundalk, to reach the Cooley Peninsula, with its thoroughly lovely medieval heritage town of Carlingford. This is the setting for the 8th-century epic *The Cattle Raid of Cooley*, an oral tradition finally set to paper by the monks of Clonmacnoise and Noughaval (in Wexford) in the 12th and 14th centuries. Thomas Kinsella's 1969 translation is the definitive one.

Base yourself in Carlingford or in far less touristy Drogheda, a pleasantly workaday place in the throes of citywide redevelopment.

DROGHEDA

A gritty-but-lively industrial town about an hour's drive north of Dublin, Drogheda ("DROH-heh-duh," Droichead Átha, "Bridge of the Ford") is

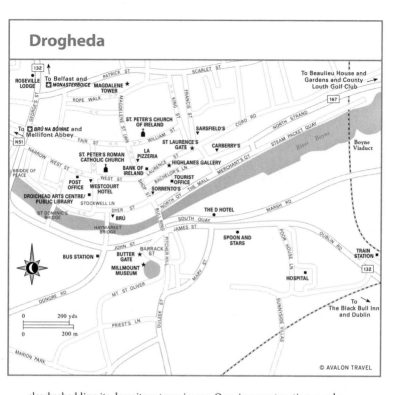

Drogheda

slowly shedding its dormitory town image. Ongoing construction may be unsightly, but it definitely adds to the sense that this is a city on the upswing. It's delightfully untouristy, and your best choice for a base if you want to sample the local nightlife after a day at Newgrange and all the other Boyne Valley attractions. There are plenty of sights in Drogheda proper as well, including a folk and archaeology museum and craft complex, and a liberal sprinkling of vivid historical reminders—after all, Drogheda was one of Ireland's most important medieval walled towns 600 years back. The city was devastated more than any other by the advent of Oliver Cromwell in 1649; his forces slaughtered more than 2,700 members of the town's garrison on September 11 of that year. Sir Arthur Aston, commander of the resistance, was beaten to death with his own wooden leg by Cromwell's henchmen.

Sights

Drogheda's medieval heritage allows for a full day of sightseeing. Seven hundred years ago the town wall was a mile and a half long, and the area enclosed was twice that of medieval Dublin. There were eight defense gates, of which the 13th-century **Butter Gate** (Barrack St., just north of Millmount) and **St. Laurence's Gate** (between Laurence St. and Cord Rd. at Francis St.) remain (though the Butter Gate is nearly a century older). An even more dramatic sight is the Magdalene Tower (on the northern end of town, at the end of Magdalene St.), which is said to be haunted by the spirit of a nun—though there is very little left to haunt! The belfry is all that remains of a 13th-century Dominican friary, though the tower itself probably dates from the following century: downright precarious, and downright eerie. But wait, there's more—excavations unearthed a skeleton of a woman who must have stood seven feet tall!

The town's primary tourist attraction is the Millmount Museum (Millmount, on the southern end of town, clearly signposted from town center, tel. 041/983-3097, www.millmount.net, 10am-6pm Mon.-Sat., 2:30pm-5:30pm Sun., admission to museum/tower/combo €3.50/3/5.50), housed within an early-18th-century military complex that also includes a martello tower (offering a nice panoramic view of the river valley). The museum itself is a motley assortment of religious artifacts, rare rocks, and cottage industry antiques, and the pre-1800 guild banners are supposedly the only ones left in the country.

On the site of a Franciscan monastery and center of learning founded in the early 15th century, the Highlanes Gallery (56-57 West St., tel. 041/983-7869, www.highlanes.ie, 10:30am-5pm Mon.-Sat., suggested donation €2) now houses Drogheda's civic art collection as well as traveling exhibitions from Ireland and abroad. The building itself dates from 1829.

Before the construction of the Boyne Viaduct in the 1850s, northbound passengers had to disembark at Drogheda and secure alternative transportation to the next station 10 kilometers away. No wonder the architect, a Louth man named John Mac Neill, was considered a genius in his day. At 427 meters long, with 18 arches each 18 meters wide, this bridge spanning the river on the eastern side of town is still a formidable sight.

St. Peter's Roman Catholic Church (West St.) is the final resting place of St. Oliver Plunkett's head. Tried for "treason" (having allegedly taken part in the "Irish Popish plot") and martyred in 1681, Plunkett's noggin was "rescued" and brought to Drogheda by a group of French nuns. What remains is now on display—a truly frightening sight—in a tall, ornate brass-and-glass case. Another glass reliquary nearby holds three of the saint's ribs, a scapula, and other carefully labeled bones. This is the most morbid attraction in Louth, if not the entire eastern seaboard.

Still more morbid attractions are to be found at the mid-18th-century St. Peter's Church of Ireland (William St.). In the churchyard you will find a relatively rare cadaver tomb (depicting the departed in a decayed state, something of a fad in the century or so after the bubonic plague). Furthermore, the previous edifice had a wooden steeple, where as many as 100 people took refuge during Cromwell's rampage in 1649. Cromwell set fire to the tower, and no one survived.

Take in Plunkett's head along with a load of other historical sights—the old town walls, St. Mary's Catholic and Protestant churches, Millmount, and more—on the Medieval Drogheda walking tour (tel. 041/983-7070, departs the tourist office on Mayoralty St. at 11am and 2pm Tues.-Fri., €3). The tour lasts about an hour, and pre-booking is essential.

Activities and Recreation

In fine summer weather, there's no better diversion than a leisurely garden stroll. **Beaulieu House and Gardens** (Beaulieu, Drogheda, 5 km east of town on the Baltray road, signposted off the R167, tel. 041/983-8557, www. beaulieu.ie, 11am-5pm Mon.-Fri. May-mid-Sept., garden €5, house and garden €12) was erected on the site of a Plunkett castle in the 17th century. The admission price includes a guided tour (departing on the hour) of the big house in all its Georgian splendor. The walled garden dates from 1732, and there's also an early-19th-century church on the grounds that features some spooky tomb effigies. June and July are the best times to visit, as the roses are in full bloom.

Established in 1892, the **County Louth Golf Club** (Baltray, 7 km east of Drogheda on the R167, tel. 041/988-1530, www.countylouthgolfclub.com) is rated in the top six courses on either side of the border.

The more ambitious can cycle to nearby attractions—Mellifont Abbey and Monasterboice (both about 8 km), the Battle of the Boyne site (5.5 km), or Brú na Bóinne (11.5 km).

Food

Drogheda has never enjoyed a reputation for fine dining, though fortunately that's beginning to change with all the ongoing hubbub of "urban renewal." The pub at the **Westcourt Hotel** (West St., tel. 041/983-0965, www.westcourt.ie, food served noon-9pm daily, 3 tapas plates for €11.50) used to be old school, but they've recently remade it into **West 29,** a stylin' spot for tapas and cocktails.

For something a bit more traditional, head to the **Black Bull Inn** (1 km outside the city center on the Dublin road, tel. 041/983-7139, www.black-bullinn.ie, food served noon-10pm daily, €10-14), which is on every local's list of favorites. Asian-inspired dishes are a specialty, and all the burgers are made with local beef.

Two of the most popular eateries in town are Italian: **La Pizzeria** (15 St. Peter's St., www.pizzeriadrogheda.ie, 12:30pm-10pm or later daily, €10-15) and the more upscale **Sorrento's** (41 Shop St., tel. 041/984-5734, 6:30pm-11pm Tues.-Sun., €12-20). As with most Italian eateries in this country, keep low expectations and you may be pleasantly surprised!

With a great location right on the Boyne, ★ **Brú** (The Haymarket, Unit 8, North Bank, tel. 041/987-2784, www.bru.ie, 1pm-10pm or later daily, lunch €7-10, dinner €12-23, 3-course meal €24) would get the business even if the food were only half as nice as the view (and the floor-to-ceiling panoramic windows take full advantage). The Continental fare is excellent, however, and the sticky toffee pudding's the best in the county. Perhaps surprisingly for a place this chic, the waitstaff let you linger for as long as you like. All in all, no one would disagree with the owners that "a new era in urban dining has arrived in Drogheda."

Entertainment and Events

Drogheda has a pretty happenin' arts scene, the prime venue being the **Droichead Arts Centre** (Stockwell St., tel. 041/983-3946, www.droichead. com, €7-20). This is the place for film screenings, plays, concerts, and art exhibitions. The city hosts a few festivals throughout the year, the most popular being the **Drogheda Arts Festival** (tel. 041/987-6100) in April. The arts fest is a feast for the eyes and ears, with plenty of street theater, concerts, comedy acts, film screenings, dance performances, and visual art and crafts exhibits. (The Drogheda Samba Festival in July was another event locals got really excited for, though its future is uncertain since the 2015 festival was cancelled due to lack of funding.) There's also the **Irish Steel Guitar Festival** (tel. 041/984-5684, www.steelguitarireland.com), which attracts musicians from Nashville and the United Kingdom, in October.

Many of Drogheda's hip young things can be found at **Brú** (The Haymarket, Unit 8, North Bank, tel. 041/987-2784), a posh riverside bistro, which has a DJ on Friday and Saturday nights. Another hot spot is the chic bar at **The d Hotel** (Scotch Hall, tel. 041/987-7700), which also has a DJ on the weekends.

Not into "hot spots"? Fair enough. Far and away the best pub in town is **Tí Chairbre,** better known as **Carberry's** (North Strand, tel. 041/983-7409). With a fire burning brightly in the grate, layer upon layer of concert posters pasted to the walls and ceiling, and scratchy old recordings of American "Memphis blues" on the stereo, the atmosphere here is second to none—all in all, one gets the impression that very little has changed here since even your granddaddy was in diapers (or "nappies," as the Irish call them). The drinks are relatively cheap, the bartender's friendly, and the trad sessions are wonderful (*sean nós* Tuesday night, traditional music Wednesday, and another trad session on Sunday afternoon around 2pm-4pm). Come even if it isn't a music night—the locals are great fun.

If you're not in the mood for trad, you can catch an outdoor jazz session starting at 4pm on Sunday at the **Black Bull Inn** (Dublin Rd., tel. 041/983-7139, blackbullinn@eircom.net). Another worthwhile watering hole is the family-run **Sarsfield's** (Cord Rd., near St. Laurence's Gate, tel. 041/983-8032, www.sarsfieldsbar.com), which sponsors several local sports teams. In decades past several Drogheda pubs would open at 7:30am so dock and factory workers could have a pint before work, and until quite recently Sarsfield's was continuing that tradition.

Shopping

The best place for high-quality gifts is the **Millmount Design Store** (Millmount Craft Centre, tel. 041/984-1960, elainejewel-design@eircom. net), featuring work coming out of the Millmount Centre craft studios: knitwear, quilts, ceramics, silver, glassware, and suchlike.

Budget travelers' only option is **Spoon and the Stars** (13 Dublin Rd., tel. 087/970-9767, www.spoonandthestars.com, large dorms €18, private rooms €30 pp), but it's a good one. The management is easygoing and helpful and the proximity to the train station is a definite plus, though being on such a busy road doesn't make for a quiet night.

There aren't many bed-and-breakfasts in the area, but one to try is **Roseville Lodge** (Georges St., tel. 041/983-4046, www.rosevillelodge.com, €40 pp), an ivy-clad Victorian with genuinely welcoming proprietors a few minutes' walk northwest of the center of town. Coming from points south, you'll continue on the R132 to the right as it crosses the River Boyne, and the bed-and-breakfast is several blocks up this road on the left.

For an even more central location, try the **Westcourt Hotel** (West St., tel. 041/983-0965, www.westcourt.ie, €60 pp, s €65, weekend discounts available). The rooms and atmosphere are standard business class, though the staff are friendly and the bar food is a pretty good value for all its fanciness. On the weekends this hotel isn't a good choice for the early-to-bed set, as the bar and nightclub noise seeps up into most of the bedrooms.

With all the trimmings of a four-star cosmopolitan establishment, **The d Hotel** (Scotch Hall, south of the Boyne, tel. 041/987-7700, www.thedhotel.com, €95-130 pp) offers mod-yet-comfy bedrooms, a trendy bar with plenty of fun cocktails to choose from, complimentary laundry service, friendly staff, and an awesome breakfast menu. The d Hotel is part of a slick shopping complex, Scotch Hall—all of which exemplifies the city's mostly admirable push for redevelopment and renewal. Check the website for special deals.

Information and Services

The very helpful **tourist office** (Mayoralty St., tel. 041/983-7070, www.drogheda.ie, 9am-5:30pm Mon.-Sat.) is just off the North Quay, behind the Sound Shop.

You'll find plenty of ATMs and bureaux de change along Drogheda's main drags: **Bank of Ireland** (14 St. Laurence St., tel. 041/983-7653), **Ulster Bank** (104 West St., tel. 041/983-6458), or **AIB** (Dyer St., tel. 041/983-6523). **Hickey's Pharmacy** (10-11 West St., tel. 041/983-8651) is open Sundays and holidays.

Getting There

Drogheda is on Ireland's east coast between Dublin (50 km south) and Belfast (120 km north), reachable by the M1 motorway (which becomes the A1 in the U.K.) linking those two cities.

Drogheda is on the main Belfast-Dublin bus route (#1, 7/day Mon.-Sat. from both cities, 6/day Sun.). The Dublin-Dundalk route (#100 or #101, departures from Drogheda every 30 minutes), popular with commuters, is the quickest way to get back to Dublin. Other direct routes include Athlone and Galway (#70, departing Galway 12:30pm Mon.-Sat., and Fri. and Sun.

at 6pm), and Slane (#188, 6/day Mon.-Sat.). You can also reach Drogheda from Kells (#188, 3/day Mon.-Sat., transfer at Navan). Beware that the **Bus Éireann** station (John St. and Donore Rd., tel. 041/983-5023) is popular with pickpockets.

If you haven't purchased a Rover pass, however, you might want to take a slightly less expensive coach service: **Matthews Coaches** buses (tel. 042/937-8188, www.matthews.ie, single/return ticket €10/15) depart Parnell Street in Dublin 22 times a day Monday-Friday, 10 times on Saturday, and 9 times on Sunday, with equally frequent return service.

Drogheda is also on the Belfast-Dublin **Irish Rail** line (Dublin Rd., about half a kilometer east of the city center, tel. 041/983-8749, at least 5 express departures daily, frequent local service), which is perhaps the country's most popular commuter service.

Getting Around

Drogheda is small enough to walk everywhere; if driving, prepare yourself for considerable congestion and pay-and-display parking. There are taxi ranks on West Street at Duke Street and just opposite St. Laurence's Gate. Or ring **East Coast Cabs** (tel. 041/981-1198 or 086/838-4444).

For bike rental, contact **Quay Cycles** (11 N. Quay, tel. 041/983-4526, €14/day) or **P.J. O'Carolan** (77 Trinity St., tel. 041/983-8242, €15/day).

MELLIFONT ABBEY

Ireland's first Cistercian monastery, **Mellifont Abbey** (from *mellifons,* Latin for "honey fountain"; Tullyallen, 1.5 km off the R168, the main Drogheda-Collon road, tel. 041/982-6459 or 041/988-0300 for info in winter, www.heritageireland.ie, 10am-6pm daily May-Oct., €4, accessible without charge in winter) was established in 1142 by St. Malachy, the Archbishop of Armagh. Malachy planned with St. Bernard of Clairvaux to open a stricter, more rigorous religious order, a community made up of both French and native monks. Though the French and Irish failed to gel, the Cistercian ideology (and architecture) caught on in this country, and Mellifont became the "mother house" for many smaller monasteries.

The abbey's most unusual feature is its lavabo, an octagonal building used as a communal washing-place before meals, which was completed in 1157 (or nearer to the year 1200, depending on whom you ask). Otherwise, stumps of arches are most of what remains here, but never fear—if you can't restore this place in your imagination, there are several artists' renderings that can do it for you.

The focus of the visitors center is an exhibition on medieval masonry, but otherwise it's a bit short on the features one expects from Dúchas sites (no audiovisual, and no tearoom). Visit Mellifont before Monasterboice, because the abbey ruins aren't all that impressive compared to the exquisite high crosses at the latter site. Also note that in low season there won't be anyone to charge you an admission fee (but then again, you won't get the guided tour).

Unfortunately, there is no public transportation to Mellifont, but it's worth hiring a taxi from Drogheda to take you to both monastic sites. Biking it is also an option.

★ MONASTERBOICE

Established in the 6th century by St. Buite, a disciple of Patrick, Monasterboice (Mainistir Bhuithe, signposted off the M1 10 km north of Drogheda, tel. 041/982-6459, always accessible, free) is the only Irish monastery to bear the name of its founder. This secluded site in lovely pastoral surroundings consists of an incomplete round tower (now 33.5 meters high), two small churches (built in the 14th or 15th century), and, most important, a group of absolutely breathtaking 10th-century high crosses. These were no doubt used to teach the Gospel at a time when only scholars and holy men could read.

The 5.5-meter-high Muiredach's Cross, named for an abbot who died in the year 923, is widely considered the finest high cross in all Ireland, and it features both Old and New Testament scenes. It must have been carved before his death, however, as an inscription on the base reads, "a prayer for Muiredach, under whose auspices the cross was made." On the eastern face, the Last Judgment is the central panel, with St. Michael weighing souls toward the bottom and St. Paul on the smaller panel above. On the shaft are the Adoration of the Magi, Moses striking the rock (to bring water to the Israelites), David and Goliath, Cain and Abel, and Adam and Eve. The central scene on the western face is of the Resurrection, with Moses and Aaron on the smaller panel above; Christ's mission to the apostles, doubting Thomas, and Christ's arrest are on the shaft. Though the carvings on the base are more difficult to discern, they are probably the signs of the zodiac. The cross is topped with a miniature church, the scenes with St. Paul and Moses comprising its sides.

The carvings on the other two high crosses, designated North and West, were surely just as magnificent at one time, but these two have suffered the weather more acutely. Of the 50 panels on the West Cross, only a dozen are still discernible. In the lee of the tower, the West Cross is one of the tallest in the country at 6.5 meters high (some say it's as tall as 7 meters), and its central panels also depict the Crucifixion and Last Judgment. Flanking this Crucifixion scene, however, are two small scenes showing sheep-shearing and -milking—allusions to Christ's traditional role as the "Good Shepherd." The shaft's eastern face depicts scenes from the Old Testament (David killing a lion, the sacrifice of Isaac, David with the head of Goliath, and David and Samuel), just as the western face is devoted to scenes from the Gospels (Christ's baptism, the ear-cutting scene in the garden of Gethsemane, and the kiss of Judas); like the Muiredach Cross, the West Cross also has a "house cap" on top.

Damaged by Cromwell's troops, the North Cross isn't quite as remarkable as the others; it features another Crucifixion scene on the western face and an abstract geometric design on the eastern face.

Monasterboice is about a 10-minute drive north of Drogheda. If you don't have a car, the best thing to do is to hire a taxi, as there is no public transportation to the site.

CARLINGFORD

The substantial seaside village of Carlingford (Cairlinn), a listed medieval heritage town in the shadow of Slieve Foy (a.k.a. Carlingford Mountain), is the focal point of the Cooley Peninsula in northern Louth. The locals take tremendous pride in the romantic stone ruins that make a ramble down the main streets so enjoyably atmospheric, and ongoing development on the outskirts of town hasn't so far diminished that laid-back medieval vibe. Various seafood, music, and sporting festivals transform this quiet place during the summer, but the fun is thoroughly infectious—even if you don't like oysters.

Most of Carlingford's shops, pubs, and eateries are on the Market Square and the Dundalk road on its southern side. Walking past the 15th-century, weed-dappled Taaffe's Castle from the tourist office and bus stop by the water will bring you to Newry Street; turn right at the Carlingford Arms pub and you've found the square. To your left is the atmospheric Tholsel Street, and through the arch in the gate tower you'll come to the old Holy Trinity Church, now the town's heritage center.

Sights

Carlingford's medieval architecture is unsurpassed in any other Irish town of its size. On the aptly named Tholsel Street you'll find the **Tholsel,** the gate tower, which was used by customs officials to monitor the influx of goods in medieval times. Just up that cobblestoned lane is **The Mint,** established in the mid-15th century by royal charter (though no coins ever came out of it). Pause to check out the small but elegant ogee arches flanked by intricately carved Celtic motifs.

The town center is dominated by the 15th-century **Taaffe's Castle,** a tower house chock-full of interesting architectural features: Note the murder holes, crenellated battlements, and slit windows used by archers all those centuries ago.

As far as monastic ruins go, the early-14th-century Dominican **Carlingford Friary** (Dundalk Rd., signposted from the heritage center) isn't terribly remarkable. The OPW takes good care of these ruins, but the graffiti and mold-speckled masonry create an air of neglect that will attract the romantically inclined.

On a rocky cliff overlooking the harbor on the western end of town, the eerie and imposing early Norman **King John's Castle** is so named for the king's visit to Carlingford in 1210—though building had commenced about 20 years before that, under the auspices of Hugh de Lacy (who, rather ironically, King John was heading off to fight at Carrickfergus Castle in Antrim). The castle's interior is closed off because it's no longer structurally sound, though hopefully conservation work will commence soon. In the meantime it's still worth climbing the steps for a brief walk-around and a peek through the barred doors.

Go for a one-hour walking tour covering Carlingford's medieval history, a worthwhile alternative to wandering around the town's ruined castles and monastery learning only what's on the OPW signposts; call **Carlingford Walks** (tel. 086/352-2732, tours at 11am, 2pm, and 5pm Wed., Thurs., and Sat., 11am and 2pm Fri. and bank holidays, 2pm and 5pm Sun. Apr.-Sept., appointments available Oct.-Mar., 4-person minimum, €5).

If you're interested in learning more on Carlingford's medieval history but can't make the walking tour, head to the **Holy Trinity Heritage Centre** (tel. 042/937-3454, www.carlingfordheritagecentre.com, 10am-12:30pm and 1:30pm-4:30pm Mon.-Fri., noon-4:30pm weekends, free).

Activities and Recreation

The 40-kilometer **Táin Way** walking route encircles the peninsula and the Cooley mountains, including plenty of scenic forest paths. Pick up an OS map at the tourist office before you leave. There's also a more adventurous 500-kilometer cycling route, the **Táin Trail,** which takes you through five counties, taking in all the legendary sites mentioned in *Táin Bó Cúailnge* ("The Cattle Raid of Cooley").

The **Carlingford Adventure Centre** (Tholsel St., tel. 042/937-3100, www.carlingfordadventure.com) offers a dizzying variety of day and weekend activities for all age groups—rock-climbing, archery, sailing, kayaking, volleyball, and plenty more—and packages include meals and housing in the center's hostel.

If you've ever wanted to learn how to sail, contact the **Carlingford Sail Training Centre** (tel. 042/937-3879, www.carlingfordsailtrainingcentre. com). The **Carlingford Sailing Club** (tel. 042/937-3238, www.carling-fordsailingclub.net) also offers sailing lessons and boat hire on weekends March-November. But if you feel like kicking back and watching it all go by, you can take an hourlong cruise on the lough with County Down-based **Castle Cruises** (tel. 028/4175-3425, daily departures June-Aug. subject to weather, €15).

Or would you rather be playing golf? The **Greenore Golf Club** (signposted off the R175, tel. 042/937-3212) is an 18-hole championship course five kilometers east of Carlingford, on the northern tip of the peninsula.

Food

Your best option for lunch or tea is **Dan's Stonewall Café** (The Square, tel. 042/938-3797, 9am-6pm daily, €8-15). The menu is on the pricey side for a small-town coffee shop, but at least the waitstaff are friendly.

Carlingford is darn near heaven for seafood lovers. Tucked at the back of a charming courtyard in an old stone edifice off the Dundalk road, **Kingfisher Bistro** (McGees Court, tel. 042/937-3716, www.kingfisherbistro.com, 6:30pm-9pm Tues.-Fri., 6:30pm-late Sat., 5:30pm-8:30pm Sun., €15-29) offers the most adventurous menu in town and is also the best choice for vegetarians. But ask a random local for a recommendation, and more often than not you'll be told to go to **Magee's Bistro** (Tholsel St., tel. 042/937-3751, www.mageesbistro.com, 10am-4pm and 6pm-9pm weekdays, 6:30pm-9pm or later Sat., noon-4pm and 6:30pm-9pm or later Sun., €16-25, 2/3-course Sun. lunch €18/22 12:30pm-3:30pm). You can't beat the medieval ambience on the patio out front when the weather's good. Ring for a reservation on summer weekends.

If neither of these eateries is open (hours can be irregular in low season), try the pub food at the **Carlingford Arms** (Newry St., just off Market Sq., tel. 042/937-3418, food served noon-9pm daily, €14-24)—it's pretty good, if pricey. The portions are generous, however, and the barstaff are quite pleasant. Another option in the dead of winter is the restaurant at **McKevitt's Village Hotel** (Market Sq., tel. 042/937-3116, www.mckevitts. ie, food served noon-9pm daily), which usually has a three-course €25 menu on offer 7pm-9pm.

Entertainment and Events

The **Carlingford Arms** (Newry St., tel. 042/937-3418) and **McKevitt's** (Market Sq., tel. 042/937-3116) are both sure bets for live music in summer. Otherwise, pop in for a pint at the delightfully old-fashioned **P.J. O'Hare's** (Tholsel St., the Square, tel. 042/937-3106).

The **Oyster Festival** (mid- to late August, ring the tourist office for details) is the biggest event on the Carlingford social calendar: live bands, oyster-tastings, kiddie amusements, and plenty more. Needless to say, book your accommodations well in advance. The **Carlingford Maritime Festival** in June is another big draw, with a regatta and boat races, walking tours, and seafood cookery demonstrations. Contact the tourist office or the **Carlingford Marina** (North Commons, tel. 042/937-3073, www. carlingfordmarina.ie) for more information.

Accommodations

Since the IHH **Carlingford Adventure Centre and Holiday Hostel** (Tholsel St., tel. 042/937-3100, www.carlingfordadventure.com, dorms €17-22, private rooms €30-35 pp) exists primarily to house people going windsurfing and whatnot, you may feel out of the loop if you aren't participating. You can expect clean dorms and en suite private rooms.

There are several rather posh bed-and-breakfasts along Ghan Road (in full view of Carlingford Lough and County Down beyond), but the stylishly designed and lavishly landscaped ★ **Shalom** (Ghan Rd., signposted on the R173 opposite the tourist office, tel. 042/937-3151, www.jackiewoods. com, €40-45 pp, s €55) is recommended for its accommodating proprietor and electric heating pads. All in all, it's a good value even if you're traveling on your own. Self-catering apartments are also available in the adjacent building.

With lots of Georgian character, a picturesque setting, and a top-notch restaurant and cookery school, 18th-century **Ghan House** (tel.

042/937-3682, www.ghanhouse.com, €75-125 pp, 4-course evening meal €45) is arguably Carlingford's classiest accommodation. Just be forewarned that the housekeeping isn't always on par with the food. Book a B&B-plus-dinner package online for the best value.

There's also the **Four Seasons Hotel and Leisure Club** (just east of the village on the R173, tel. 042/937-3530, www.4seasonshotelcarlingford.ie, rooms €180-220), startlingly out of place in a town with such a low-key medieval character. It's your typical hotel, right on down to the overpriced bar and restaurant food, though the pool, sauna, and other leisure facilities are certainly a plus.

Information and Services

For pointers, postcards, and plenty more, head to the **Cooley Peninsula Tourist Office** (Old Dispensary, on the water, tel. 042/937-3033, www.carlingford.ie, 10am-5pm Thurs.-Mon. Nov.-Mar., 10am-5:30pm Mon.-Sat. and 11am-5:30pm Sun. Apr.-Oct.).

There's an **AIB** ATM on Newry Street, directly opposite the Carlingford Arms pub and restaurant, but no bank as such. Get cough drops at **Bradley's Pharmacy** (Market Sq., tel. 042/937-3259).

Getting There and Around

Carlingford is 24 kilometers east of Dundalk on the R173, just 10 kilometers southeast of the border with County Down in Northern Ireland and 108 kilometers north of Dublin. **Bus Éireann** offers a Monday-Saturday service on the Dundalk-Newry route (#161), with five departures from Dundalk but only two from Newry. For departure times, ring the bus station in Dundalk (tel. 042/933-4075) or Newry (tel. 028/3062-3531).

Need a lift? Call **Carlingford Taxis** (tel. 086/332-2256).

RAVENSDALE

Inland, the Cooley Peninsula is surprisingly developed, and the hamlet of Ravensdale (on a minor road, signposted off the R173 about 10 kilometers east of Dundalk) isn't a real tourist attraction as such. Ravensdale is on the **Táin Way** walking route, and there are a couple of other diversions to note. The grounds of the mansion of the Earl of Clermont are now part of the lovely **Ravensdale Forest Park,** the "big house" in question having burned like so many others in the Irish Civil War. Those interested in going horseback riding through these woods should contact **Ravensdale Lodge Equestrian & Trekking Centre** (Ravensdale, signposted off the N1, tel. 042/937-1034, www.ravensdalelodge.com).

There's something for everyone in County Wicklow (www.visitwicklow.ie), especially outdoor enthusiasts. The **Wicklow Way** is the most popular walking trail in the country, so there are plenty of accommodation and dining options along the route. You'll not have to sacrifice comfy mattresses and scrummy steak dinners for this weeklong adventure! Even the less-athletic visitor will enjoy a stroll through the gardens at Powerscourt, Kilruddery, or Avondale. Idyllic Glendalough, one of the country's most important monastic sites (just behind Clonmacnoise, in fact), offers at least nine different trails, whether you're out for a casual ramble or an all-day mountain climb.

ENNISKERRY

Just 18 kilometers south of Dublin, **Enniskerry** (Áth na Sceire, "Ford of the Reef") is a charming planned village, a perennial favorite with Dublin day-trippers for one reason: the magnificent **Powerscourt House and Gardens.** This tiny, tidy town—essentially just the one central square, marked with a small clock tower and lined with houses and a smattering of shops—was designed by the Earl of Powerscourt in the mid-18th century to house his staff. Most visitors just pop by for the afternoon, but several fine accommodation options make it worth an overnight stay, especially if you're planning on heading farther south into the vales of Wicklow.

★ Powerscourt House and Gardens

No one could argue that **Powerscourt House and Gardens** (signposted from the village, tel. 01/204-6000, www.powerscourt.com, 9:30am-5:30pm daily, €9.50) isn't the finest estate in the country. The 19 hectares include a breathtaking Italianate garden designed in the early 19th century; the terraces were laid in the 1840s using granite and pebbles from the beach at Bray, and took more than 100 men a dozen years to complete. Lovely mid-19th-century garden sculptures—Apollo, Diana, cherubs, and so forth—bear obvious Italian and French influence. Indeed, it's easy to forget you aren't taking a ramble through some Florentine villa; only the temperature and Great Sugarloaf Mountain (501 meters) looming beyond remind you that the Mediterranean is a plane ride away. Beyond the terrace is a large lake guarded by a pair of fantastic winged horses cast from zinc in 1869.

There's more: a Japanese garden teased out of old boglands; winding paths flanked by rhododendrons and towering trees of North American origin; a tower shaped like a pepper urn, built in 1911 in anticipation of a royal visit, which you can climb for a fairly panoramic view; a huge walled garden with resplendent gates and an ivy-covered memorial to the seventh Viscountess of Powerscourt, which incorporates busts of four Renaissance masters; and a pet cemetery including some strangely poignant epitaphs ("faithful beyond human fidelity").

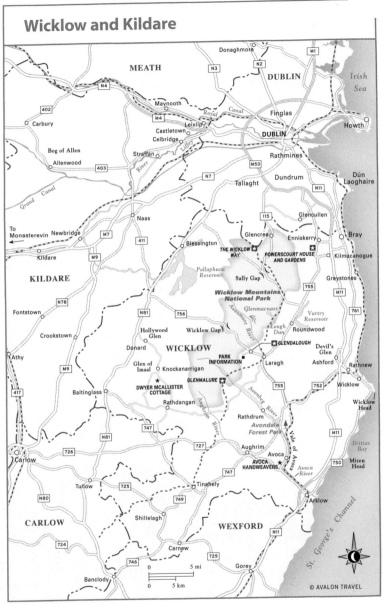

Wicklow and Kildare

The house itself has been transformed into the classiest sort of mall: There's an Avoca shop (including delectable, if pricey, foodstuffs for take-away), an interior design gallery, and a huge conservatory offering more practical souvenirs in addition to the usual potted plants. And of course, you can have lunch here, too—on a patio overlooking the Italian garden.

The famous **waterfall** (9:30am-7pm in summer, 10:30am-dusk in winter, €6) is five kilometers away (signposted from the Enniskerry square), and, cheekily enough, the €9.50 ticket doesn't cover your admission. The cascade was created in 1821 for King George IV's visit to Powerscourt, but it was a lucky thing he never made it out of the house to see it; the bridge built to view it was washed away as soon as the waterfall was "turned on." Even today it's the highest waterfall in the country at 121 meters.

Powerscourt House and Gardens is one of the most popular tourist attractions in the country, so you'd better skip it if you prefer to keep off the beaten track—Secret Garden, this isn't. And gorgeous as they are, the only things Irish about these gardens are the labor and rain that nurture them daily.

Powerscourt also has a **golf club** (signposted from the house and gardens entrance, tel. 01/204-6033) with two different courses, both of them ultra-scenic.

Food and Accommodations

The **Terrace Café** (tel. 01/204-6070, 10am-5pm daily, €10-16) on the mansion's ground floor offers a fantastic view and sophisticated, high-quality lunch fare—quiches, salads, and the like. Alternatively, you can head back into the village for an equally tasty (and somewhat less expensive) meal at **Poppies Country Cooking** (The Square, tel. 01/282-8869, www.poppies.ie, 8am-6pm daily, €7-10), a warm, always-bustling café with hearty portions and friendly staff. Enniskerry's evening dining options are surprisingly not-awesome given Powerscourt's popularity; make lunch your big meal of the day and go for a simple pub dinner at **The Old Forge** (Churchill, on the R760, tel. 01/286-8333, food served 3pm-9pm daily, €11-16).

The **Knockree Hostel** (Lacken House, 7 km west of Enniskerry on the road to the hamlet of Glencree, signposted from Enniskerry, tel. 01/286-4036 for info, tel. 01/830-4555 to book, www.anoige.ie, dorms €18-22) has

the Italianate gardens at Powerscourt House, elegant and precise

lovely pastoral and mountain views. Unlike other An Óige hostels in remote locations, this one doesn't do evening meals, so stock up on groceries at the village store on the main square. For accommodations in the village proper, try **Ferndale** (The Square, tel. 01/286-3518, www.ferndalehouse. com, Apr.-Oct., €40 pp, singles charged at double rate), a cheerful, immaculately maintained Victorian townhouse.

For something much grander, book a room at the **Summerhill House Hotel** (half a km south of the village, signposted off the N11, tel. 01/286-7928, www.summerhillhousehotel.com, rooms €90-175), with extensive and perfectly manicured grounds in the shadow of Sugarloaf Mountain. There's a posh "cocoon spa" here too.

Information and Services

Enniskerry doesn't have a tourist office, but the Powerscourt staff can answer any questions on the surrounding area. Check out the helpful community website (www.enniskerry.ie) before you go.

There is an **ATM** (but no bank) on the square.

Getting There and Around

Enniskerry is 18 kilometers south of Dublin. Traveling by car, take the M11 out of the city and take the Enniskerry exit onto the R117; both house and waterfall are clearly signposted from the square.

Day excursions to Powerscourt as well as Glendalough are available through **Bus Éireann** (tel. 01/703-2574, departing Busáras 10:30am daily mid-Mar.-Oct., returning 5:45pm, €27.50, including admission fees). This tour doesn't include the waterfall, so if you'd like to see everything, spring for a tour with **Norman Dowling** (tel. 01/451-7877, www.dowlingcoach-drive.com, €33, includes all entry fees). This tour includes Glendalough, Avoca, and Mount Usher Gardens as well as Powerscourt, and you can arrange for pickup from your accommodation in Dublin.

From the Bray DART station, you can also reach Enniskerry via Dublin Bus #184 or #185 (3/hour daily). A slower but less convoluted way to go (to the house and gardens only) is a 60-minute ride on **Dublin Bus** (tel. 01/873-4222, www.dublinbus.ie, 3/hour) #44 or #44C from Townsend Street in Dublin.

WICKLOW MOUNTAINS NATIONAL PARK

Much of northern Wicklow has been designated a national park, approximately 20,000 hectares (or 200 square kilometers)—that's 10 percent of the county in all. The park is a delight whether you're walking the **Wicklow Way** or just driving through, with a load of astonishingly isolated glens and hollows; the views from the Sally Gap, the lofty intersection of the R759 and Military Road (the R115), are splendid, as is the view from the road that bends around the Glenmacnass Waterfall on the Military Road just north of Glendalough. These gorse-dappled hills also include sizable tracts of mountain blanket bog and a wealth of indigenous flora, fauna, and

★ The Wicklow Way

The country's most popular walking route, the 132-kilometer **Wicklow Way,** begins in Marlay Park in suburban Dublin and winds south into Wicklow Mountains National Park, passing through Glendalough and down the western flank of the monster-mountain Lugnaquilla in Glenmalure, and ending just over the Wicklow-Carlow border in Clonegal. The Wicklow Way walking trail info site (www.wicklowway.com) is by far the best resource in planning your hike: scope out the route, book accommodations and evening meals, arrange luggage transfer, and plan for appropriate clothing and equipment.

The way is dotted with original An Óige hostels (www.anoige.ie), some of which have been around since the 1940s, and plenty of B&Bs that cater especially to walkers. The route is less frequently traveled south to north, so if you're planning to walk it in high season it's worth considering starting off in Carlow instead of Dublin. In general, expect plenty of company if you're walking it in June, July, or August. Those who only have time to walk part of it generally start in Roundwood and walk south to Glendalough, a distance of approximately 12 kilometers. **St. Kevin's Bus Service** (tel. 01/281-8119, www.glendaloughbus.com) can get you back to Dublin from either place.

To get to Marlay Park (also known as Marley Grange) in Dublin, take the Ballinteer-bound **Dublin Bus** (tel. 01/873-4222, www.dublinbus.ie, #16, 3/hour) from O'Connell Street. If starting in Carlow, take the Dublin-Waterford **Bus Éireann** (tel. 01/836-6111, #5, 2/day Mon.-Sat. at 9am and 5:30pm, 3/day Sun. at 11am, 4:30pm, and 6pm) to Kildavin (3 km southwest of Clonegal on a local road, request stop) or, if you need to do any last-minute shopping, the larger town of Bunclody (5 km south of Clonegal on the R746); there is no bus service to Clonegal.

birdlife. Though **Glendalough** is the best-known hamlet within the park, there are other villages in which you could base yourself: **Laragh** is just a kilometer and a half east of Glendalough, and there's also **Roundwood** 11 kilometers up the road. Also inside the park, **Glenmalure** is popular with hikers on the Wicklow Way.

For tidbits on local geography and botany as well as navigational advice, head to the national park **information office** (Bolger's Cottage, tel. 0404/45656, tel. 0404/45425 for guided walks, off-season tel. 0404/45338, www.wicklowmountainsnationalpark.ie, 10am-6pm daily May-Aug., weekends in Apr. and Sept., free), which is at Glendalough, 100 meters west of the Upper Lake car park and two kilometers west of the Glendalough Visitor Centre. The info office hosts a summer lecture program and "sensory garden" as well.

★ GLENDALOUGH

Perhaps Ireland's most famous monastic site, **Glendalough** (Gleann dá loch, "Glen of the Two Lakes") is an utterly enchanting spot—no less so, miraculously enough, for all the coach buses and cheesy food and souvenir stands clustered outside the stone gateway to the old monastery and modern graveyard. This is a lush, glacier-carved valley dotted in yellow gorse, with walking trails skirting two placid lakes and the substantial remains of a holy community founded by St. Kevin in the 6th century: a 10th- or 11th-century **round tower,** one of the tallest in the country at 30 meters, with a cap rebuilt from fallen stones in 1876; a badly weathered high cross; and the ruins of seven churches. By the 9th century Glendalough was second in size and prestige only to Clonmacnoise in County Offaly. (There are several illuminated manuscripts associated with Glendalough housed at Oxford and the British Library. Most interesting is the passage in the 11th-century Book of Glendalough that tells of a UFO sighting in unequivocal terms.)

One of Ireland's most beloved saints (after Patrick and Brigid, of course), Kevin's life is shrouded in intriguing (and sometimes dark) legends. It's said that after Kevin cured the high king's pet goose, he asked for the land under the bird's flight path as a reward. Many stories tell of his love of animals: Once, while he was praying with arms outstretched, a bird laid an egg in his open palm, and Kevin remained stock-still until it hatched. Another legend claims a local woman became smitten with Kevin and visited him in his cliff-top cave, known as **St. Kevin's Bed;** angered by her advances, he pushed her off the ledge and she drowned in the lake below. (That place is now known, rather inaccurately it seems, as **Lady's Leap.**) This much is true, however: Once word got around of an extraordinary hermit in an idyllic situation, other monks were joining him in droves, and a community was formed.

You can take in most of the monastic ruins (aside from **Temple na Skellig** on a ledge over the Upper Lake, accessible only by boat—though you can't hire one!) on a leisurely walk along the south shore of the Lower Lake. The old monastery grounds hold a small priest's house in the shadow of the round tower, the **Cathedral of Saints Peter and Paul** (dating from the 10th and 12th centuries), and the 12th-century **St. Kevin's Church**—this one is quite unusual, having its original stone roof. The miniature round tower in the west gable resembles a chimney, which is why it's better known as "Kevin's Kitchen."

A visit to the Dúchas-run **Glendalough Visitor Centre** and **tourist office** (tel. 0404/45325, www.glendalough.ie, 9:30am-6pm daily mid-Mar.-mid-Oct., 9:30am-5pm mid-Oct.-mid-Mar., €4) isn't tremendously informative if you've been to other monastic sites, since the exhibit (including the 15-minute audiovisual) covers early Irish monasteries in general—the construction and function of round towers, manuscript illumination, everyday life, and so forth. There's not a lot of info about St. Kevin, and the legends told in an automated storytelling nook for the kiddies are 100 percent sanitized. That said, it's a worthwhile stop if the weather's bad, especially if you've purchased the Dúchas Heritage Card. The exhibit also includes a collection of early grave slabs and a bullaun stone, a primitive crucible carved out of a larger rock. (Initially used for crushing grain and herbs, later folklore claimed rainwater collected in the bullaun had curative properties—warts, of course.)

St. Kevin's Church in Glendalough

Go for a long ramble through the isolated Glenmalure Valley.

You can also pick up a scale map of the nine Glendalough **walking trails** (2-11 kilometers in length, from easy strolls to hill walks requiring navigational skills) for 50 cents. A walk in any direction is glorious, though the path along the Upper Lake at sunrise or sunset offers the most breathtaking views of all (and you'll enjoy them in utter solitude). An easy climb to **Poulanass Waterfall** begins at the national park information office on the eastern shore of Upper Lake, as does a far more strenuous hike up **Spinc Mountain** (490 meters). Alternatively, the fit and adventurous can scale **Camaderry Mountain** (700 meters) on the northern side of Upper Lake; the path begins at the Upper Lake car park. The **Wicklow Way** also skirts the eastern flank of Spinc Mountain.

For more information on outdoor activities and other topics, check out the Glendalough community website (www.glendalough.connect.ie).

Accommodations

You'll find more accommodation options in nearby Laragh than around Glendalough proper, though if you're of a romantic persuasion, consider spending the night at the hostel or hotel (which are right on the edge of the park) and taking a moonlit ramble through the ruins.

It's big enough to attract a lot of school groups, but the **Glendalough International Youth Hostel** (The Lodge, on the Upper Lake road, signposted off the R756, tel. 01/882-2563, www.anoige.ie, dorms €16-21) is still adequate for the backpacking set. All the rooms are en suite. As for bed-and-breakfast, you'll find a gorgeous view from the bedrooms at **Pinewood Lodge** (signposted on the Upper Lake road, tel. 0404/45437, www.pinewoodlodge.ie, €40-50 pp, s €60). You can rent bikes through the B&B and chill out in the garden after a long day's pedal.

It's on the stodgy side, and the food won't wow you, but the family-run **Glendalough Hotel** (tel. 0404/45135 or 0404/45391, www.glendaloughhotel.com, €65-95 pp) is situated right outside the old monastery gate.

Between the location and the size (with 44 rooms, it's on the large side for a rural inn), it's a very popular wedding venue, so consider yourself warned. (If you stay here, consider walking down the road to Laragh to eat at the Wicklow Heather.)

Getting There

Glendalough is 60 kilometers south of Dublin; you can take the M11/N11 out of the city as far as Ashford before turning away from the coast (onto the R763), though the route south from Enniskerry (on the R755), passing Great Sugar Loaf to the east, is far more scenic. **St. Kevin's Bus Service** (tel. 01/281-8119, www.glendaloughbus.com, single/return €13/20) operates a daily bus service from Dublin to Glendalough via Bray and Roundwood, departing St. Stephen's Green North (at Dawson St., opposite Mansion House, at 11:30am and 6pm Mon.-Sat. and 11:30am and 7pm Sun. Sept.-June, 11:30am and 6pm Mon.-Fri. and 11:30am and 7pm Sat.-Sun. July-Aug.). There are at least two daily return buses from Glendalough (three on weekdays in July and Aug.).

LARAGH

A hamlet less than two kilometers east of Glendalough, Laragh is a vital stop for eats (whether dining out or stocking up on groceries) and gas (but no ATM). There are a few bed-and-breakfasts in and around the village, but the views just can't measure up to those in Glendalough proper. One to try is the relatively new **Trooperstown Wood Lodge** (on the R755, the Roundwood/Annamoe road, 2.5 km north of the village, tel. 0404/45312 or 086/263-1732, www.trooperstownwoodlodge.com, €40 pp). While the rooms are fairly standard, you can expect an old-fashioned welcome in the form of a tea-and-biscuit tray, and the owners (who also run the grocery-slash-gas station in the village) will be a big help in getting your bearings in the area.

Pilgrims may want to stay in one of the self-catering *cillíns* (small churches) at the **Glendalough Hermitage** (signposted from the R756 just west of Laragh village, tel. 0404/45777, www.glendaloughhermitage.ie, twin room €40 pp, s €50), a prayer retreat run by St. Kevin's Parish Church. Each cottage (the architecture inspired by the Glendalough church ruins) has its own kitchenette, bathroom, sitting area, and open fireplace.

Open for breakfast, lunch, and dinner, the ★ **Wicklow Heather** (on the main road, the R756, tel. 0404/45157, 8am-10pm daily, dinner €16-24) serves up a refreshingly eclectic menu (and good coffee) in a romantic, if slightly quirky, dining room (the pitched wood roof with head-bangingly low crossbeams is decked out in white lights and bric-a-brac: kettles, farm implements, even lacrosse sticks). The service is pleasant, too—and you might even get a free half shot of Bailey's with your check. There's also nice-if-standard bed-and-breakfast available a couple doors down at **Heather House** (tel. 0404/45236, www.heatherhouse.ie, €40 pp), with breakfast served at the restaurant.

St. Kevin's Bus Service (tel. 01/281-8119, www.glendaloughbus.com, single/return €13/20) passes through Laragh en route to Glendalough. For a taxi, ring John Preston (tel. 087/972-9452).

ROUNDWOOD

There's not a whole lot going on in Roundwood, which advertises itself as the highest village in the county. The Wicklow Way passes less than two kilometers west (by the shore of Lough Dan, which unfortunately is surrounded by private land), accounting for most of the buzz in this sleepy one-street village on summer afternoons. Tired walkers doff their boots at the Wicklow Way Lodge (4 km southwest of the village off the R755, tel. 01/281-8489, www.wicklowwaylodge.com, Feb.-Nov., €50-55 pp). The walking route passes right in front of the B&B, and while no evening meals are provided, the owners will happily drive you into the village.

A unique fusion of Irish and German cuisine makes the Roundwood Inn (Main St., tel. 01/281-8107, bar food served noon-8:45pm daily, €12-20) a favorite with locals, and it should be your top choice for dinner if you're spending the night in Glendalough (though the Wicklow Heather in Laragh comes a very close second). Reservations are required at the adjoining restaurant (tel. 01/281-8107, 7:30pm-9:30pm Fri.-Sat., 1pm-2pm Sun., €15-25), though fortunately the full menu is available in the pub. Meat-lovers are expertly catered to here—enjoy your venison, local lamb, or suckling pig with a bottle of obscure German wine—though the quality of the seafood dishes can be a bit inconsistent. (Vegetarians are better off dining at the Wicklow Heather.) The inn dates from the 1750s, and the decor is an odd mix of hunting lodge and mock Tudor.

Roundwood is nine kilometers north of Laragh on the R755 and is clearly signposted from the eastern end of the village. It's also a stop on the St. Kevin's Bus Service Dublin-Glendalough route (tel. 01/281-8119, www.glendaloughbus.com).

★ GLENMALURE

Ireland's longest glacial valley, Glenmalure will probably remind Pennsylvanians of the Poconos. Between the hills clad in evergreens and yellow gorse, the nonexistent cell-phone service, the horse-drawn caravans on shady backroads, and the mobile library in the parking lot of the Glenmalure Lodge, you might be forgiven for thinking you've entered a time warp (in the very best sense). Glenmalure Lodge (11 km west of Rathdrum on a local road, tel. 0404/46188, glenmalurelodge@yahoo.com, food served noon-9pm, meals €10-20, B&B €35-40 pp, s €40-55) was established in 1801 and has a really cozy, amiable vibe; even if you're just passing through, do stop by for a pint at one of the picnic tables out front. (Too bad that time warp doesn't cover the drink prices.)

Pass the lodge, and after five or six kilometers the road terminates at a car park beside the River Avonbeg, where you'll find a modern monument to those patriots who perished in the 1798 rebellion. Just cross the small cement bridge and take off in either direction for a scenic ramble. The more ambitious can climb **Lugnaquilla,** the tallest mountain outside County Kerry at 924 meters. Approaching the mountain from Glenmalure (on the eastern side) is the easiest route; provided you're in good shape, the return trip will take about six hours. Glenmalure is also halfway along the **Wicklow Way.**

Public transport is nonexistent in this area, and even getting here by car can be tricky; the winding, pothole-riddled local roads aren't as well signposted as they could be. The surest way to reach the Glenmalure Valley is via Rathdrum, which is 11 kilometers east. From Laragh, the village just east of Glendalough, take the R755 south to Rathdrum (also 11 kilometers), or take the M11/N11 south out of Dublin and pick up the Rathdrum road (the R752) from the town of Rathnew. Then from Rathdrum, Glenmalure is clearly (and correctly) signposted at a T junction beside the town square.

THE GLEN OF IMAAL

The **Glen of Imaal** (Gleann Ó Máil), named after the brother of a 2nd-century high king, is the prettiest part of western Wicklow—though the area doesn't attract many visitors because the northeastern section is blighted by a (however clearly marked) military firing range. Unfortunately, since the closing of the An Óige hostel five kilometers south of the village of Donard in 2006, backpackers have no place to spend the night (and after all, who in their right mind would open a B&B near an artillery range?). If by chance you find yourself driving down a shady backroad west of Glenmalure, however, you might want to stop at the Dúchas-run **Dwyer McAllister Cottage** (Derrynamuck, on the local Knockanarrigan-Rathdangan road, signposted from Knockanarrigan, tel. 0404/45325, 2pm-6pm daily mid-June-mid-Sept., free), a small folk museum in a thatched cottage of historical importance. During the 1798 rebellion several Irish leaders were surrounded in this cottage by British troops, and one of them, Samuel McAllister, burst out of the cottage to meet his death so his comrade Michael Dwyer could escape out the back.

AVOCA

A darling little village just beyond the southeastern border of the national park, **Avoca** (Abhóca) was put on the map by the popular BBC television series *Ballykissangel,* which ran six seasons between 1996 and 2001.

Based on writer and creator Kieran Prendiville's childhood memories of holidays in County Kerry, pretty much all of "Bally-K" was filmed here in real-life shops and pubs (well, *pub*). Just north of the village, the **Meeting of the Waters** is a verdant spot immemorialized in a sentimental poem by Thomas Moore. Here the Avonbeg and the Avonmore merge to form the River Avoca, making it a popular hangout for local anglers.

Avoca Handweavers

"Bally-K" aside, most visitors are here for **Avoca Handweavers** (Old Mill, up Main St. just beyond the village, tel. 0402/35105, www.avoca.ie, 9:30am–6pm daily), a craft complex that includes Ireland's oldest working mill (opened in 1723). This is where the Avoca mohair-tweed-and-gourmet-goodies empire began—or began again, to be more precise—in the 1970s, when a couple of Dublin businesspeople reinvested and reopened the mill. Today you can still pop into the weaving shed and watch the artisans at their looms. The shop isn't as spacious as you would expect, but the prices are a bit better than in the gift shops, and there's also an upstairs bargain room worth checking out. You can expect a gourmet meal at the ★ **café** (mains €10-13)—savory tarts, Guinness pie, and some of the most delicious brown bread you'll find anywhere to go along with your vegetable soup. Indeed, it's by far the best lunch spot in the area.

Food

Get your fill of traditional pub grub (shepherd's pie, fried cod, and suchlike) at **Fitzgerald's** (Main St., tel. 0402/35108, food served noon-8:30pm daily, €10-15), where the two televisions alternate between sport and soap. (There's a decent vegetarian option, too.) The *Ballykissangel* pub scenes were filmed here; check out the cast photos on the walls. There's live folk and trad on weekends year-round. Another option for hearty lunch or dinner grub, and live trad on Friday and Saturday nights in the summer, is **The Meetings** (4 km north of Avoca on the R752, tel. 0402/35226, www.themeetings.ie, food served noon-9pm daily, €12-18), a mock-Tudor pub so named for its location at the Meeting of the Waters. April-October you might also find an outdoor ceilidh—a rollickin' music and dance session—on Sunday afternoons starting around 4pm.

Accommodations

At ★ **Ashdene** (Knockanree Lower, less than 1 km from the village past the Avoca Handweavers shop, tel. 0402/35327, www.ashdeneavoca.com,

Avoca

Apr.-Oct., €38-40 pp, s €40-45), proprietor Jackie Burns greets you with tea and apple pie with fresh cream. This B&B is exceptionally homey, with plenty of pink and tranquil, unspoiled views of the surrounding hills and forest, along with thoughtful touches like Q-tips in the bathroom and herbal teas on the hostess tray. The breakfast is as outstanding as the welcome: real brewed coffee, freshly squeezed orange juice, deluxe fruit salad, and Nutella for your toast (ah, heaven!). Another option is **Rockfield** (2.5 km southeast of Avoca, signposted off the R754, tel. 0402/35273, www.accommodationavoca.com, €38-43 pp, s €55), which also has lovely views of the surrounding countryside.

The Old Coach House (Meeting of the Waters, 4 km north of Avoca on the R752/Rathdrum road, tel. 0402/35408, www.avocacoachhouse.com, €35-40 pp, s €45-60), built in 1840 to accommodate coaches traveling from Dublin to Wexford, is a two-minute drive, is open year-round, and provides excellent value across the board.

Information and Services

You'll find the library and tourist office in one teeny building: the **Avoca I.T. Centre** (Main St., tel. 0402/35022, www.avoca.com, 9am-1:30pm and 2pm-5pm Mon.-Fri., 10am-2pm Sat.).

Getting There and Around

Avoca is 65 kilometers south of Dublin, with various possible routes; you could take the M11/N11 and turn off for Avoca at Rathnew, though the routes through the national park (the R115 or the R755) are, of course, much more scenic. Avoca is 23 kilometers south of Glendalough on the R755 (picking up the R752 in Rathdrum). The Dublin-Arklow route (#133) of **Bus Éireann** (tel. 01/836-6111) stops in Avoca as well as the Meeting of the Waters twice a day (once on Sunday), the two departures being at 9am and 5:30pm Monday-Saturday (arriving 11:05am and 7:35pm) and 2pm on Sunday (arriving 4:20pm). Note that this bus departs the Connolly Luas station on the eastern side of the city center during the week, and from Busáras on Sunday. Return buses pass through Avoca at 8:15am and 1:15pm Monday-Saturday and 5:45pm Sunday.

THE WICKLOW COAST

The gardens and mountains of Wicklow generally attract more attention than the county's beaches. There's little to bring the visitor to **Wicklow Town** (the beach is rocky and littered with broken beer bottles), though the tourist office tries its darnedest with the Wicklow Gaol; the exhibition is downright cheesy, and not worth your time. The coastal walk from Bray to Greystones and the pristine strand at Brittas Bay are well worth stopping for.

Bray

Though this seaside town 20 kilometers south of Dublin has certainly spiffed itself up in recent years, Bray's ongoing shortage of quality cafés, restaurants, and accommodations puts a damper on any plans for an overnight visit. If, when walking the streets here, you get the sense that this isn't the best the east coast has to offer, you'd be hitting the nail on the head.

Having said all this, the **coastal walk** from the Bray promenade eight kilometers south to Greystones is a deservedly popular activity with Dublin day-trippers, and it's easy as pie to get down here on the DART, walk the route, and then return on the DART from Greystones. Bray itself is small enough to get the hang of in a few minutes; Strand Road hugs the promenade (or "esplanade," as it's locally known), to which Main Street runs briefly parallel; continuing down the main drag will eventually get you to Glendalough (30 km southwest). Turning off the northern end of Main Street onto Sea Point Road or Quinsborough Road will get you to the seafront the quickest.

Bray has its share of cultural attractions, namely **Kilruddery House & Gardens** (3 km south of town on the Greystones road/R761, tel. 01/286-3405, www.killruddery.com, gardens 1pm-5pm Sat.-Sun. in Apr., 1pm-5pm daily May-Sept., house 1pm-5pm May, June, and Sept., gardens/combined €7.50/16), a late-17th-century manor with a stunning domed greenhouse and Elizabethan-style architectural detail (all of which was added in the 19th century). The estate has been in the family of the earls of Meath since 1618, and the formal garden, laid out in the 1680s, is one of the oldest in the country. There's also an aquarium on the waterfront, **National Sealife** (Strand Rd., tel. 01/286-6939, www.visitsealife.com/bray, 9:30am-6pm Mon.-Sat., €12), which places as great an emphasis on marine conservation as it does on entertaining the kiddies. Book online for discounted tickets.

The town's best pub, for live music and general *craic,* is the **Harbour Bar** (Seapoint Rd., tucked away on a side road just north of the promenade, tel. 01/286-2274). This pub-cum-lounge is popular with all sorts, from hardcore sea anglers to the town's small "alternative" population. It's also worth stopping by the **Mermaid Arts Centre** (Main St., tel. 01/272-4030, art gallery 10am-6pm Mon.-Sat.) to see what's playing in its theater and art house cinema.

FOOD AND ACCOMMODATIONS

The menu at the ever-busy **Box Burger** (7 Strand Rd., tel. 01/538-1000, www.boxburger.ie, 5pm-10pm Wed.-Thurs., 5pm-11pm Fri., noon-11pm Sat., noon-10pm Sun., €8-12) includes a very tasty seitan burger with vegan cheese, and folks on a gluten-free diet can get their burger on a deluxe quinoa or avocado salad—so there really is something for everyone. You'll find this restaurant inside a Victorian railway building just down the street from the DART station. Next door is **Platform Pizza** (7 Strand Rd., tel. 01/538-4000, www.platformpizzabar.ie, noon-10pm Sun.-Wed., noon-11pm Thurs.-Sat., €8-22), owned by the same couple. Both eateries are local favorites.

Bray's B&Bs have a time-warp feel to them—clean, tidy, and otherwise adequate, but depressingly in need of an interior facelift. If you're determined to spend the night here, it's worth springing for a hotel. Try The Martello (Strand Rd., tel. 01/286-8000, www.themartello.ie, rooms €100-120, s €90), which also has one of the town's most popular nightclubs Friday through Sunday nights (until 2:30am).

PRACTICALITIES

The **tourist office** (Main St. at Seapoint Rd., tel. 01/286-7128, www.bray. ie, 9:30am-1pm and 2pm-5pm Mon.-Sat. June-Sept., 2pm-4:30pm Mon.-Sat. Oct.-May) is in the town's old courthouse.

Getting to Bray from Dublin is easy, with frequent service from Pearse and Connolly Stations on the DART. The **Irish Rail** station (tel. 01/236-3333, trains every 5 minutes at peak, 2-3 off-peak departures/hour, single/return ticket €3.80/6.85) is off Quinsborough Road, about 500 meters east of Main Street. If driving, you have a choice between the M11 motorway and the coastal road, the R119, though both get congested at peak periods.

Greystones

The eight-kilometer Bray coastal walk will leave you off in Greystones, another fishing village-turned-resort town-turned-commuter suburb. After that windswept jaunt, reward yourself with lunch at ★ **The Happy Pear** (Church Rd., less than a two-minute walk up the main street from the DART station, tel. 01/287-3655, http://thehappypear.ie, 9am-6pm Mon.-Sat., 10am-6pm Sun., €8-12). Everything about this vegetarian café is a delight, from the hearty hot meals and fresh salads (served with a genuine smile) to the pay-it-forward coffee option (at time of writing there were 45 coffees purchased for anyone in need, whether they forgot their wallet or are just having a bad day). Enjoy your mushroom chowder and coconut cappuccino upstairs in the bright and relaxed seating area, then pick up a snack for later in the small whole-foods grocery downstairs. Dinner service is available on Friday and Saturday evenings 6-10pm.

Though Greystones boasts a Blue Flag beach, there's not a whole lot going on otherwise, so you're best off heading back to Dublin on the **Irish Rail** (Church Rd., tel. 01/888-0343, 2-3 departures/hour, single/day return €5.90/10.80) suburban service.

Brittas Bay

A pristine five-kilometer Blue Flag strand, Brittas is the county's nicest beach. Located 18.5 kilometers south of Wicklow Town on the R750, it's predictably popular with Dublin day-trippers. There isn't anyplace to stay or eat in the area, though, strangely enough, so it makes the most sense to pack a picnic lunch. Oh yes—and beware that cheeky €4 parking fee!

Traveling through County Kildare feels a bit like walking a treadmill in purgatory. The landscape is flat and uninteresting (and presently tree-less, despite the name Kildare, which means "Church of the Oak Wood"), dominated by sprawling suburban commuter estates. Kildare is also the center of Ireland's horse industry.

Flat fertile farmland aside, Kildare's principal geographical features are an enormous peat bog (950 square kilometers) in the county's northern reaches, known as the **Bog of Allen,** which spreads into Counties Laois, Offaly, and Westmeath; the bog surrounds the **Hill of Allen** (200 meters), a scenic viewpoint topped by a lookout tower and rich in folklore (it's said the Irish hero Fionn mac Cumhaill lived here and buried his trea-sure somewhere along its slopes). In recent years the hill has been badly scarred by quarrying and pollution. Two canals cross the Bog of Allen: The 212-kilometer **Grand Canal,** used to transport both cargo and pas-sengers from Dublin to points west, is still open for recreational vessels; and the less commercially successful **Royal Canal,** closed in 1961, never-theless traces a 144-kilometer walking route known as the **Royal Canal Way** (www.irishtrails.ie).

CASTLETOWN

Yet another ho-hum commuter suburb, **Celbridge** is on the map for Ireland's largest, most glorious Palladian country house: the unimagi-natively named **Castletown** (tel. 01/628-8252, www.castletown.ie, 10am-6pm Mon.-Fri., 1pm-6pm weekends Easter-Sept., 10am-5pm Mon.-Fri. and 1pm-5pm Sun. in Oct., €7). It was built in the 1720s for William Conolly, Speaker of the Irish House of Commons, a Donegal man of humble beginnings who was eventually considered the wealthiest man in the country. Construction was ongoing for decades after Conolly's death under a veritable parade of architects. The Guinness family pur-chased the house in the late 1970s and began the arduous restoration process. Now the estate is run by Dúchas, and the hour-long tour of Castletown is well worth the schlep out of Dublin. As a general rule, if you've toured one "big house" you've toured them all—grand sweep-ing staircases, intricate plasterwork, marble busts, and gilt furniture don't seem quite so splendid after a while—but if you visit only one Irish manse, let it be this one.

Castletown is 20 kilometers from Dublin; if driving, begin on the N4 west and take the Celbridge exit (putting you on the R403 for a few more kilometers). Otherwise, the **Dublin Bus** (tel. 01/873-4222, www. dublinbus.ie, #67 or #67A, 2-3 departures/hour Mon.-Sat., hourly on Sun.) will get you here from either the Pearse Street or Wood Quay stop in the city center.

Considering the presence of a national university, one might expect Maynooth (Maigh Nuad, "New Plain") to be full of hot-and-happenin' cafés and bars. Not quite. Perhaps the seminary—Ireland's largest—has something of a dampening effect on even ordinary students' social aspirations. That said, the pleasant tree-lined Main Street has a few shops and pubs worth checking out, and the National University of Ireland (NUI) Maynooth campus boasts some stunning neo-Gothic architecture. All in all, it's the most worthwhile stop in County Kildare.

Sights

Now a branch of the National University of Ireland, NUI Maynooth (tel. 01/708-6000, www.nuim.ie) was opened as a seminary at the close of the 18th century. From a humble inaugural class of 40 aspiring priests, Maynooth prospered into the world's largest seminary by the year 1895.

The seminary is still here, surrounded by all the trappings of a modern university in the age of technology. NUIM is divided into north and south campuses, though everything to interest the visitor is on the south campus.

The most important building on campus is the cavernous college chapel. With its elaborate frescoes, stained glass, and miserichordia, this grand and somber church is truly awe-inspiring. The chapel is clearly signposted from the university's front gate at Parson Street, a two-minute walk.

Guarding the entrance to the south NUI campus, the 13th-century Anglo-Norman Maynooth Castle (tel. 01/628-6744, 10am-6pm Mon.-Fri. and 1pm-6pm weekends June-Sept., 1pm-5pm Sun. in Oct., free), once the primary residence of the earls of Kildare, has been in a state of ruin since the 17th century. The castle is now administered by Dúchas. Seeing as it's free, you might as well take a few minutes to check out what's left of the keep and gatehouse.

There is an information point on the NUI campus (tel. 01/708-3576, 9am-5pm and 6pm-10pm daily).

Food

The cafeteria-style Coffee Mill (Mill St., tel. 01/601-6594, 8am-5pm weekdays, 8:30am-4pm Sat., under €8) is your average student hangout, offering basic sandwiches and salads. In fair weather you can sip your coffee on a pleasant stone patio out back. Easily the best restaurant in town, Stone Haven (1 Mill St., tel. 01/601-6594, www.stonehavenrestaurant.com, 5pm-9:30pm Tues.-Sun., €13-25, 3-course dinner €20) offers an eclectic menu in a romantic ambience.

Getting There and Around

Maynooth is 26 kilometers west of Dublin, just off the M4 motorway. Dublin Bus (tel. 01/873-4222, www.dublinbus.ie, #66, #66X, #67A, #67N, or #67X, frequent daily departures, 1-hour journey) can get you here from Wellington Quay in downtown Dublin. A quicker option is **Irish Rail** (Leinster St., tel. 01/836-6222, Dublin Connolly-Sligo line, at least 8/day Mon.-Sat., 4/day Sun., 25-minute journey).

Maynooth Express Cabs (tel. 01/628-9999) offers 24/7 service, with both cabs and minibuses.

Background

The Landscape

Ireland is 84,079 square kilometers (32,477 square miles); as a size comparison, you might fit the island within the state of New York. The island lies between the Atlantic Ocean to the west and the Irish Sea to the east, which separates Ireland from Great Britain. The Irish coastline is estimated to be 5,800 kilometers long.

CLIMATE

The North Atlantic Drift, a warm ocean current in the north Atlantic, contributes to Ireland's temperate climate; its temperatures are among the least extreme in Europe, and it rarely snows and even more rarely freezes. Yes, it rains two days out of three, and as Heinrich Böll once wrote, "The rain here is absolute, magnificent, and frightening." But the mild winters and wet summers allow for a green landscape all year long.

May and June are the sunniest months, with an average of six hours of sunlight per day; July and August are the warmest (average temp 14-16°C/57-60°F), though the temperature sometimes climbs into the 20s C/lower 80s F. December and January are the rainiest (70-75 millimeters monthly rainfall), January and February the coldest (4-7°C/39-44°F). August-November is also a very wet time of year (66-70 millimeters), and July and August bring the highest risk of thunderstorms, especially in the west (which is the rainiest region overall).

ENVIRONMENTAL ISSUES

Ireland has its share of pollution, much of it the product of industry and irresponsible agricultural practices. There is also an acute nationwide litter problem. Those rolling green hills are deceptively pristine, and it's precisely this traditional image of Ireland that is preventing or delaying much-needed reforms. Though a majority of Irish rivers and lakes offer good water quality, the Irish Sea is highly polluted (and there is some evidence that regular bathing in it is a cause of cancer). Plus, several tests have confirmed fecal contamination in the groundwater, but one example of the consequences of improper agricultural practice. Ireland is also well behind much of Europe when it comes to recycling, though the government finally initiated county-run recycling programs in 2005. There are glass receptacles in every strip mall parking lot and home collection for plastic and paper, but because the counties charge for this service, many citizens are not as diligent as they should be. For more information, visit the **Friends of the Irish Environment** (www.friendsoftheirishenvironment.org) or **An Taisce** (www.antaisce.org) on the web.

Previous: Dublin City Hall; the round tower in Glendalough.

Ireland has comparatively few plant and animal species because of its geological "youth": The island was created at the end of the last ice age.

Vegetation

Fewer than 1,000 plant species are unique to Ireland. Bogs—blanket and raised—feature prominently on the Irish landscape (12,000 square kilometers in all). They were formed when Neolithic farmers first cleared forests for farming: The treeless soil gradually became more acidic, forming heather and rushes; these plants decayed and formed a layer of organic matter on which new growth could begin. Logs of turf—essentially bricks of peat sliced from the bog and laid out to dry—have been a source of fuel since the 17th century. Ireland was heavily forested before the Stone Age, and after the Norman invasion the English exploited many remaining Irish forests for timber for shipbuilding.

Mammals

There are only 31 extant mammal species in Ireland, most of which have been introduced by humans over the last 8,000 years. Native species include the red fox, hedgehog, stoat, and badger. Several species, though not endangered, are found mostly in the country's national parks and nature reserves: the pine marten, red deer, and Irish hare. It's speculated that Neolithic settlers first brought cattle and sheep to Ireland sometime around 6500 BC. Rabbits were introduced by the Normans in the 12th century, and the two rat species and common mouse traveled here by boat as well.

Sealife

With all its lakes, rivers, tributaries, and coastlines, Ireland is an angler's paradise, and seafood is an integral part of the Irish diet. Salmon, pike, and brown trout are the primary freshwater species; marine species include bass, cod, haddock, hake, and turbot. Whales and dolphins frequent Irish waters, the common dolphin being the most frequently sighted species. Bottlenose dolphins are often very friendly, following boats for miles and lingering in harbors for long periods of time.

Birds

Most of the island's 400 recorded bird species are migratory, and there are more than 60 bird sanctuaries. For more information, contact the **Irish Wildbird Conservancy** (www.birdwatchireland.ie).

Reptiles and Amphibians

Ireland has very few reptiles. It's true that there are no snakes in Ireland, though St. Patrick probably had nothing to do with it! The island features only three amphibious species—the natterjack toad, smooth newt, and the common frog—and just one reptile, the common lizard.

PREHISTORY

We know relatively little about pre-Christian Ireland, and what we do is extrapolated from archaeology, mythology, oral tradition, and Roman records. The first human hunter-gatherers arrived between 10,000 to 8000 BC as the ice age ended and the oceans rose to separate Ireland from Britain and Europe. They arrived in small boats, though some may have crossed a narrowing isthmus. Agriculture was introduced from the continent around 4000 BC. Neolithic culture flourished, relics of which still punctuate the Irish landscape: large standing stones, dolmens, burial mounds, and stone circles, some cosmically aligned. The most impressive Neolithic passage tomb is **Newgrange** in County Meath, which predates the Great Pyramid in Egypt and features the famous tri-spiral motifs associated with Irish crafts to this day. Bronze Age artisans produced intricate gold work of a high quality renowned throughout Europe.

THE CELTS

Iron Age society in Ireland was dominated by druids, who functioned as spiritual leaders, doctors, poets, lawmakers, and teachers. The distinct rival kingdoms that began to emerge in Ireland at this time are survived today, more or less, in the traditional counties and provinces of Ireland. It is popularly believed that around this time Ireland underwent a large-scale invasion by the Celts, a creative if warlike race that originated in central Europe. It is more likely, however, that Celtic influences and culture were gradually adopted by the native Irish. Either way, from about 300 BC a strong Celtic society dominated Ireland over the following millennium, and their art and spiritualism are still considered an integral part of Irish culture. The Irish Celts followed an elaborate and surprisingly progressive civil legal system known as the **Brehon Laws,** though they were not above raiding the British coast and taking slaves.

While Ireland was never formally part of the Roman Empire, the island was influenced by, and engaged in trade with, the Romans. Frequent references to Hibernia, Ireland's Latin name, are found in Roman records, but it remains unclear what kind of relationship existed between Ireland and the vast empire.

EARLY CHRISTIAN IRELAND AND THE GOLDEN AGE

During the 5th century Irish pirates frequently raided the British coast, even forming colonies in Scotland, Wales, and England. Slaves were often taken, among them the adolescent who would become St. Patrick. Though he is popularly credited with single-handedly converting the Irish to Christianity, in fact there were other missionaries sent to Ireland long before and long after Patrick. And while he has had a lasting influence on Irish spirituality, Patrick cannot be solely credited with creating the particular variant of Christianity that embraced Irish traditions and laws (apart from those laws that directly contradicted Christian doctrine, of course). These influential clerics encouraged Ireland to unite its various rival kingdoms under a single authority, a high king.

Irish monasteries soon earned an excellent reputation as centers of Latin learning, and attracted scholars, scribes, and theologians from all over Europe. As scholarship and craftsmanship thrived in these monasteries, and as Christian values discouraged interkingdom warring, Ireland entered its Golden Age. The island's existing artisan traditions saw further advancement, and indeed the finest European artworks of the era were produced in Ireland's monasteries. Several impressive examples survive to this day, such as the delicately detailed **Ardagh Chalice,** on display in the National Museum of Archaeology and History, and the **Book of Kells,** an illuminated bible housed in Trinity College.

While the rest of Europe was ravaged by the Dark Ages, Latin learning (and Western civilization itself) was preserved in Irish monasteries like Glendalough in County Wicklow and Clonmacnoise in County Offaly. As Europe gradually stabilized, the "island of saints and scholars" sent missionaries back to mainland Europe, where they founded a great many monasteries.

THE VIKINGS

Such enormous wealth attracted barbarian attention, and in the 9th century Vikings from Norway arrived in their imposing longships, raiding the coasts and striking vulnerable towns and monasteries along the Shannon, Suir, and other strategic waterways.

The round tower, a style of refuge almost unique to Ireland, symbolizes this era. Eventually, some Vikings settled in Ireland, appreciating the milder winters. They founded towns along the coasts from which to attack the inland native strongholds, but successive generations embraced Irish culture and adopted Christianity, effectively becoming Hiberno-Norse. In the first decade of the 11th century, **Brian Boru** became high king. The title was mostly honorary for his predecessors, but Boru assumed actual authority over the island; he demanded tributes from the smaller kingdoms, which he used to rebuild churches and monasteries destroyed by the Vikings.

Brian Boru rallied the remaining Irish kingdoms in a bid to break Norse power over Ireland. His combined forces fought the climactic daylong **Battle of Clontarf** outside Viking Dublin in 1014, and Boru is traditionally credited with driving the Vikings "back into the sea." In reality, however, it was more a civil war between the Irish. (The "Viking" army was in the service of the king of Leinster and was composed mainly of Irish and Hiberno-Norse soldiers.) The elderly Boru did not survive the battle, and by this time the Viking and native cultures had already amalgamated. The Vikings had founded many of the seaports that would become Ireland's main towns and cities, including Dublin, Galway, and Cork. They also introduced the use of currency.

THE NORMANS

The second wave of invaders were to have an even more profound impact on Ireland's destiny. The Normans had previously settled in northern France, and in 1066 they conquered England. A century later Dermot MacMorrough, the exiled king of Leinster, petitioned England's Henry II to help him regain his kingdom. The Earl of Pembroke, Richard de Clare (popularly known as Strongbow) agreed to lead an invasion force in return for the hand of MacMorrough's daughter. By 1169 MacMorrough—often singled out as the greatest traitor in Irish history, which is no mean achievement—had retaken Leinster, and upon his death his Norman son-in-law ruled it.

Henry II felt threatened by this rival Norman kingdom growing across the channel and secured a papal bull in order to land a fleet in Ireland. Soon after Henry II arrived in Waterford in 1171, the Normans, with their superior weapons, armor and tactics, conquered the entire east coast and divided the taken land into earldoms as rewards for their knights. They built many distinctive towerlike castles all around the country.

By the 13th century, however, the Normans had retreated to the territory surrounding Dublin, known as **The Pale,** due to several factors. In 1315 Edward Bruce of Scotland invaded England; a long and bloody war ensued throughout the British Isles, in which the Gaelic lords sided against the English. Also, the Black Death hit the more densely populated Norman towns harder than their scattered Irish counterparts. Disconnected from a troubled England, the settled Normans began to consider themselves natives, and became "more Irish than the Irish themselves." Toward the end of the 16th century, England had lost virtually all its control over Ireland "beyond the Pale."

THE REFORMATION AND PROTESTANT ASCENDANCY

For Ireland, the Reformation spelled enduring catastrophe. Henry VIII of England cut all ties with the Catholic Church following his divorce from Catherine of Aragon; while the majority of England, Scotland, and Wales converted to Protestantism relatively painlessly, the more independent Ireland retained its deep-rooted Catholicism. Henry increasingly feared an Ireland-based invasion of either French or Spanish Catholic forces. So the king sought to undermine the most powerful dynasty in Ireland, the Fitzgeralds, who were the earls of Kildare. In 1543 Dublin was stormed by Silken Thomas, son of the reigning earl. This rebellion was quashed, Thomas and his men executed, and the Fitzgeralds' lands confiscated. Henry next turned his sights on the Catholic Church and pillaged several monasteries and churches, eventually "dissolving" them entirely (which is why virtually all of Ireland's pre-Reformation churches are Anglican). In 1541 Henry forced the Irish Parliament to declare him king of Ireland.

The Ulster province was the last outpost of Irish Catholic power, where Hugh O'Neill, Earl of Tyrone, initiated a rebellion. This erupted into the **Nine Years' War,** which raged through the reigns of Elizabeth I and her successor, James I. In 1601 the earls marched south and gathered a large army to meet the English in the **Battle of Kinsale.** The Irish were aided by a Spanish fleet, which besieged Kinsale seaside. Due mainly to misguided tactics, O'Neill and the earls were defeated, though some survived and fled to Europe, a turning point known as the **Flight of the Earls.**

For the first time in the centuries since the Norman invasion, England had resoundingly conquered Ireland. Elizabeth I implemented the **Plantation of Ireland,** where huge amounts of land confiscated from the earls were given to Protestant settlers in a bid to assimilate the Irish. Unlike previous settlers, these Protestants did not integrate with the angry and powerless Catholic majority. The native Irish were further oppressed by the **Penal Laws,** which outlawed all faiths except Protestantism. The majority of Catholics continued to practice their religion in secret.

OLIVER CROMWELL AND THE PENAL LAWS

The disenfranchised Irish supported Charles I, a Catholic, during the English Civil War against the Protestant Parliamentarians. Charles was defeated, and Oliver Cromwell, leader of the Parliamentarians, decided to restore English control of Ireland. There are few historical figures on whom history is more divided than Cromwell. The English thought him a hero of democracy, but his actions in Ireland have rightfully branded him a monster. Cromwell's forces landed in Drogheda in 1649 and cut a swath of destruction upward through the country. Cromwell's brutal campaign left more than a third of Ireland's population either dead or in exile. Approximately 20,000 square kilometers were seized from Irish Catholics and divided amongst Cromwell's supporters. Many of the dispossessed Irish relocated to the wilder, less fertile west. Cromwell's own infamous words were "to hell or to Connaught."

In 1689 Ireland hosted a second conflict between English monarchists and Parliamentarians. James II, also Catholic, arrived in Ireland and was recognized as king by the Irish Parliament. Preparations were made to restore property and status to Catholics. They laid siege to the city of Derry, which caused mass starvation within the city walls. The siege ended when James II was defeated at the Battle of the Boyne by the forces of William of Orange. William was actually James's Protestant son-in-law, invited to the throne by the English Parliament after James's departure.

The Penal Laws were reapplied, though harsher this time: They prevented Catholics from owning land and essentially outlawed all traces of Irish culture.

THE BIRTH OF NATIONALISM

Most of the 18th century was relatively peaceful in Ireland, though unrest escalated as the economic situation worsened. This combined with two very cold winters caused the first **famine** of 1740-1741, which caused the deaths of 400,000 people. Also fueling unrest were the American and French Revolutions, which inspired liberal thinking—even in the "planted" Protestant population, who were beginning to consider Ireland their home. The **United Irishmen** (under the leadership of **Theobald Wolfe Tone,** a high-minded Dublin Protestant) initially sought reform through nonviolent means, but as the French Revolution became increasingly gruesome, the society took on a more militaristic approach. In retaliation the Protestants formed the Orange Society, named in honor of William of Orange.

Tone accompanied the French in a failed attempt to land a fleet in Bantry Bay. The English government began a full-scale nationwide hunt for the United Irishmen, which caused widespread panic among Catholics. In 1798 a rebellion erupted in the traditionally peaceful county of Wexford, led by Father John Murphy. The rebellion was bloodily suppressed after a run of minor victories. Later in 1798 Tone and a second French fleet were defeated at sea. He was captured and committed suicide in prison.

THE ACT OF UNION AND CATHOLIC EMANCIPATION

The Irish Parliament was composed of an increasingly anxious Protestant gentry, and in 1800 the ruling body dissolved itself and joined the House of Commons. This consolidated government, the United Kingdom of Great Britain and Ireland, was an attempt to secure British authority.

Meanwhile, **Daniel O'Connell,** a young Catholic lawyer from County Kerry (though Catholics were denied education, wealthier families would send their sons to study in Europe), fought a successful campaign for the repeal of the Penal Laws. The British Parliament conceded **Catholic Emancipation** in 1826 after O'Connell won a parliamentary seat for County Clare. Though Catholics were not allowed to become members of Parliament, the government feared mass protests and permitted O'Connell to sit in Westminster.

O'Connell, hailed then and now as the "Great Liberator," went on to campaign for more reforms for Catholics, most notably an attempt to repeal the Act of Union. Though O'Connell had the popularity to rally "monster meetings" that drew as many as half a million Catholics, he eventually lost influence over the nationalist movement as it grew impatient with nonviolent methods.

FAMINE AND EMIGRATION

In 1845 a blight caused the failure of potato crops all over the island. This, coupled with exploitative and selfish economic structures, led to Ireland's worst tragedy, the **Great Famine** (1845-1849). The island's population

Tracing Your Roots

Looking for the names and old address of your great-great-grandparents from County Tipperary? Though each county has its own archive, it's more sensible to start at the **General Register Office** (Joyce House, Lombard St., Research Room, 2nd fl., tel. 01/635-4000, 9:30am-4:30pm Mon.-Fri.) in Dublin, where you can look up your ancestor's birth, marriage, or death certificate (all of which should list the addresses of the parties involved) no matter which county he or she came from; the records here start at 1864. The fees are nominal, though they can start to add up if you need to broaden your search: €2-4 per request (you can request up to five annual record books at a time), and €4 for a photocopy. Though the archive is always a hive of activity, the staff is willing to answer quick questions and offer search tips.

You can also check the census records and various databases at the **National Archives** (Bishop St., tel. 01/407-2300, www.nationalarchives. ie, 10am-5pm Mon.-Fri.). Another good starting point, particularly if you need help planning your search, is the **National Library Genealogy Advisory Service** (Kildare St., tel. 01/603-0200, www.nli.ie, 9:30am-5pm Mon.-Wed. and 9:30am-4:45pm Thurs.-Fri., plus 9:30am-12:45pm Sat. Mar.-Oct.). This office has a few databases on offer but is worth a visit mainly for the knowledgeable staff, who will provide you with thorough advice. No appointment is necessary.

The General Register Office in Dublin has birth, marriage, and death records for the Northern Ireland counties as well, but there is additional information available at the **Public Record Office of Northern Ireland** (66 Balmoral Ave., tel. 028/9025-5905, www.proni.gov.uk, 9am-4:45pm Mon.-Wed. and Fri., 10am-8:45pm Thurs.).

If you don't have the time to conduct extensive genealogical research, consider hiring a professional. Ask at the National Library office for a list of private researchers; most are based in Dublin.

dropped from eight to five million because of mass starvation and emigration. Though there was more than enough food in the country, most of it was exported to Britain and overseas. As historian Roy Foster explains it, "Traditionally, the Famine was seen as at worst a deliberate English policy of genocide, at best willful neglect on the part of the British government."

Under the Poor Laws landlords were responsible for the welfare of their tenants, yet many landlords exercised a less expensive option: paying for their tenants' passage to America. The conditions of the overcrowded and poorly managed ships were atrocious, and many emigrants did not survive the journey on these "coffin ships." The British government eventually granted some aid, but it was far from adequate, and emigration continued. At the turn of the 20th century the population was down to four million.

During this time the Irish language fell out of popular use; famine and emigration more heavily impacted Irish-speaking areas. Also, the recently introduced National School system taught only through English by order of the British government. Many Catholics—weary of poverty and observing the economic prosperity of English-speaking America and Britain—began to see Irish as a dying language. Irish was still spoken in the country's more rural and remote reaches, however. The regions in which Irish is still spoken as the primary language—Dingle, Connemara, Gweedore, Ring, and others—are known as the Gaeltachtaí.

PARNELL AND HOME RULE

In the wake of the Great Famine, Ireland's resentment of the British government grew, and several minor rebellions were staged by organizations such as the Fenians and the Irish Republican Brotherhood (IRB, a secret society that was to play a considerable role in the struggle for independence). Impoverished Catholic tenants were granted more rights—like the option to purchase the land they rented—by consecutive British governments under pressure from the Land League, headed by the IRB's Michael Davitt and Protestant landowner Charles Stewart Parnell, who organized boycotts of landlords who didn't comply with the league's conditions.

Parnell's firm belief in Irish sovereignty led him to found the Home Rule League, and in 1875 he was elected to the British Parliament—where he caused a lot of trouble. Though Parnell was an overwhelmingly popular and charismatic leader (he was referred to as the uncrowned king of Ireland, and he even convinced Prime Minister William Gladstone to back Home Rule twice), he fell from grace in 1890 when his affair with Kitty O'Shea, the wife of a fellow MP, became publicly known. The scandal greatly affected his health and he died the following year.

The wealthy Protestant population of eastern Ulster vehemently opposed the concept of Home Rule; as a heavily industrialized (rather than agrarian) society, they were spared the worst effects of the famine. Though Gladstone's second Home Rule Bill in 1892 had been defeated, they sensed the tides turning; in 1912 Sir Edward Carson founded the Ulster Volunteer Force (UVF, a vigilante offshoot of the Unionist Party). The UVF staged massive paramilitary rallies, threatening civil war in the face of Home Rule. In response to the UVF, Eoin O'Neill established the Irish Volunteers to defend Home Rule. But when World War I broke out in 1914, the threat of civil war was suspended.

THE EASTER RISING

In 1916 a small splinter group of Irish Volunteers, along with James Connolly's Irish Citizen Army (established in 1913 to protect peacefully demonstrating workers against the British police), staged an armed rebellion. The nationalists marched into Dublin on Easter Monday and took several landmark locations in the city, making the General Post Office their headquarters. From the steps of the GPO the poet Patrick Pearse read aloud the Proclamation of the Irish Republic, declaring his group of insurrectionists the provisional government of a new republic, the Volunteers its legitimate uniformed army. Initially most Dubliners condemned the rising, as a week of intense fighting between the rebels and the British Army (who responded with superior firepower and heavy artillery) had effectively wrecked the city. When the rebels finally surrendered to the

British, they had to be protected from the mobs of angry Dubliners they had intended to liberate.

The British exacerbated the situation when they executed 15 of the rebels (14 at Dublin's Kilmainham Jail, including Patrick Pearse and James Connolly, and one in London) and sentenced a further 76 to death. (Due to the mounting pressure of public sympathy for the rebels, the remaining death sentences were commuted to penal servitude.) This effectively made martyrs of the rebels, creating the very blood sacrifice the rising had intended and sparking a new wave of nationalism. Among the prisoners was Eamon de Valera, who was spared from execution by his American citizenship. He and his lieutenant, Michael Collins, a young civil servant from West Cork, were eventually released from prison on amnesty.

De Valera and other republicans formed a political party, **Sinn Féin** (meaning "We Ourselves"), and won the majority of the Irish seats in the 1918 general election. Rather than take their positions in Westminster, they declared Ireland independent and reformed the Volunteers into the Irish Republican Army (IRA), simultaneously declaring war on British troops on Irish soil.

THE WAR OF INDEPENDENCE

This entrenched war commenced with the murders of two Royal Irish Constabulary (RIC) men, on the same day the Dáil (the new independent Irish Parliament) convened: January 21, 1919. The British government tried to regain order by deploying a combined force to Ireland to assist the RIC: regular infantry, Army Auxiliaries, and an RIC reserve force, better known as the **Black and Tans.** This was a vicious and undisciplined paramilitary group comprising mainly ex-soldiers and prisoners, whose unchecked deeds further cemented the general population's embrace of republicanism. The Black and Tans retaliated with excessive force, burning and sacking several towns, including the Cork city center. Unable to engage the better-armed British forces directly with a front line, the IRA pioneered guerrilla and urban warfare, creating "flying columns" to ambush their enemy. This campaign was masterminded by Michael Collins, who in prison with other volunteers had effectively run a military training camp. Collins headed a delegation to London to negotiate, and in December 1921 both sides signed the **Anglo-Irish Treaty.** While granting Ireland considerable autonomy, the treaty allowed for the partition of the six counties that had a Protestant majority. This would create two new nations, each with Home Rule, though Northern Ireland would choose to remain part of the United Kingdom.

THE FREE STATE AND THE CIVIL WAR

The Dáil ratified the treaty in January 1922, forming the **Irish Free State,** and a general election that summer showed support for pro-treaty politicians. De Valera and his followers refused to accept the terms of the treaty, however, and stormed out of the Dáil. Soon afterward the Irish Free State

erupted into a treacherous civil war. Arthur Griffith, who had helped negotiate the treaty, became president of the Free State.

Now commander-in-chief of the Free State Army (formerly the IRA),
General Collins was forced to hunt down his former comrades and friends.
This is an often unspoken chapter in Ireland's history, as uncompromis-
ing idealism turned the country against itself—it divided communities
and even families down the middle—and atrocities were committed on
both sides. Griffith died of anxiety and General Collins was shot dead in
an ambush near his home parish in West Cork.

The anti-treaty forces laid down their arms in 1923, but the civil war
had cast a long shadow over the young nation. De Valera eventually recognized the government and formed a rival political party in 1927, Fianna
Fáil. They won several seats in the election of that year, and entered the Dáil
without taking the oath of allegiance to the British crown that had been a
controversial condition of the treaty. (The Free State was still a member of
the British Commonwealth.)

The Free State faced many difficulties in its early years. There was a
global economic depression in the wake of the Wall Street crash of 1929,
and several European states were turning to fascism to sustain themselves.
Fianna Fáil came into power in 1932—and since it was a peaceful change-
over, the Free State achieved a long-awaited sense of stability.

Though emigration, poverty, and unemployment levels were high,
Ireland remained a democracy during the uncertain decade. De Valera's
Ireland clung to several insular policies in an attempt at self-sufficiency.
He oversaw the large-scale cultivation of the bogs for peat as well as the
construction of the ambitious Ardnacrusha Hydroelectric Power Station
(or "Shannon Scheme"); at the time it was the largest project of its kind ever
attempted. De Valera also refused to pay land rates to Britain, contravening
yet another condition of the treaty.

The Catholic Church was as influential as de Valera; it directed the Free
State away from the liberal and inclusive ideals of the Proclamation of the
Irish Republic and toward an oppressively conservative Catholic climate.
The church ensured the banning of contraception, divorce, and other so-
called immoralities that affronted its dogma; at its bidding the Irish government censored and even banned a great many books and films. The church
also controlled the country's schools and hospitals. Many Protestants left
the Free State feeling intimidated in an overwhelmingly Catholic environment. Indeed, during the 1920s, a great many Protestant "big houses"—seen
as symbols of the Anglo-Irish Ascendancy—were burned to the ground.

In 1937 a new constitution was drawn up that affirmed Irish neutral-
ity and spared it from the ravages of World War II. Many Irish fought in
the war against fascism, however, and in truth the Free State was "neutral
in favor of Britain." Idiosyncratically, World War II was known as "The
Emergency" in Ireland, and heavy rationing was put in place.

THE IRISH REPUBLIC

After 16 years of political dominance, Fianna Fáil lost to Fine Gael, the successors to the original Free State government; Fine Gael quickly declared Ireland a republic and withdrew from the Commonwealth. Sean Lamass became Taoiseach (prime minister) in 1959, and he implemented sweeping new policies (such as free secondary education) to strengthen Ireland's economic prospects, competitiveness, and infrastructure—and to curb emigration. Successful and popular besides, Lamass was credited with laying the groundwork for Ireland's later economic vitality. Ireland also sought membership in the European Economic Community, but was not admitted until 1973 along with the United Kingdom. Membership initially proved beneficial, but toward the end of the 1970s a harsh downturn slowed the economy considerably. The 1980s were bleak indeed, characterized by high unemployment.

THE TROUBLES

Northern Ireland's first premier, James Craig, proclaimed it "a Protestant state for a Protestant people" in response to the overwhelmingly Catholic Free State south of the border. In the North, a policy of discrimination denied power, employment, and even decent housing to the Catholic minority. A corrupt electoral system and flagrant gerrymandering denied Catholics representation even in Derry, where they were in the majority by 10 percent.

A peaceful civil-rights movement emerged, following the example of Daniel O'Connell, Gandhi, and Martin Luther King Jr. But the Royal Ulster Constabulary and other militant unionists used violence to disperse a peaceful rights march in 1968, sparking counterviolence among the utterly disenfranchised Catholic population. Another march was attacked by a unionist mob in January of the following year, and the situation was only exacerbated by the police, who swept through the Catholic Bogside neighborhood of Derry City.

That August British troops were deployed to Northern Ireland to restore order. While the troops initially were welcomed by both sides, the Catholics soon realized the soldiers were an oppressive occupying force, an instrument of the Protestant majority. The situation came to a head with the events of January 30, 1972, **Bloody Sunday,** when 14 civilians were massacred by British troops during a civil-rights march. Many were shot in the back.

The IRA—not the original Irish Republican Army, but the ideological descendants of those who had rejected the Anglo-Irish Treaty—saw an exponential jump in recruitment and membership, as many Catholics believed these nationalist paramilitaries to be their lone, true defense force. In this poisonous atmosphere of sectarian hate and paranoia, the worst decade of the Troubles began.

The Troubles—a characteristically Irish euphemism—increased the size and power of various paramilitary groups on both sides, with various contrasting agendas. The IRA split into the Official IRA (OIRA) and the Provisional IRA (PIRA). In 1974 the more extreme Irish National Liberation Army was formed. On the unionist side, the UVF was joined by groups such as the Ulster Defense Association (UDA), the Ulster Freedom Fighters (UFF), and the Red Hand Commandos.

The Northern Irish Parliament was dissolved in 1972, and a new power-sharing system was almost put into place. A widespread strike by Protestant workers derailed the process, though, and for the next 27 years, Northern Ireland was under Direct Rule by the British Parliament. The paramilitary campaigns of both sides now featured bombings, which often resulted in civilian casualties.

The violence also spread beyond the borders of Northern Ireland, with the PIRA (also known as "the provos") setting off several bombs in London from 1973, and the UVF perpetrating bombings in Dublin and Monaghan on St. Patrick's Day 1974. Groups on both sides regularly committed sectarian murders. All such terrorist acts were condemned from both communities and from the British and Irish governments, but the cycle of violence and retribution was well underway. The Troubles reached a climax in 1981, when republican inmates in the infamous "H-blocks"—including 27-year-old elected MP Bobby Sands—went on a hunger strike in a plea to be recognized as political prisoners. Sands and nine others fasted to death, and to this day they are hailed as martyrs to the nationalist cause. The hunger strikers are often commemorated by Sinn Féin: originally de Valera's political party, now socialist in bent, and oft-accused of being the political wing of the Provisional IRA.

The presence of the British Army reserve and the (predominantly Protestant) Royal Ulster Constabulary (RUC), Northern Ireland's police force beginning in 1922, seemed to discourage ongoing violence—yet IRA splinter groups were preparing for a full-scale "long war," going as far as to procure large arms shipments from Libya. Even the majority of Catholics, who totally condemned the IRA and their methods, were unwilling to trust the British soldiers who'd treated them so horribly in the past. Catholics also suspected collusion between the armed forces and unionist paramilitaries, and in recent years much evidence has come to light to confirm this.

In 1986 the British and Irish governments signed the **Anglo-Irish Agreement,** by which they would work together to bring peace to the North. The 1990s brought economic prosperity to both sides of the border—which, combined with the waning authority of the Catholic Church, helped depolarize attitudes in the North. The Northern Ireland demographics were also moderating, with Catholics now making up 40 percent of the population.

Significant advances in the peace process of the early 1990s included the

Downing Street Declaration, which formally declared that Britain had no self-serving strategic or economic interest in Northern Ireland. In August 1994, Gerry Adams, leader of Sinn Féin, announced that the IRA was on a ceasefire. Two months later loyalist groups also announced a ceasefire. Actual peace talks never began, though, as demands from both sides were not met. The IRA refused to surrender its weapons unless British troops were withdrawn from Northern Ireland and its political prisoners were freed, all of which were demands the British government considered too high. The bombing of London's Canary Wharf in February 1996 brought an end to the first ceasefire.

A second IRA ceasefire was secured in 1997, and on April 10, 1998, negotiations resulted in the Good Friday Agreement. For the first time since the implementation of Direct Rule, a system of power-sharing was brought to the North, with both nationalists and unionists receiving legislative control in several areas of government.

The Good Friday Agreement was overshadowed by riots during unionist marches through nationalist neighborhoods, a rising internal unionist murder rate, and the worst bombing since the start of the Troubles: On August 15, the Real IRA (founded by former members of the PIRA who refused to accept the terms of the Good Friday Agreement) detonated a car bomb in Omagh, County Tyrone. Twenty-nine people were killed, both Catholic and Protestant. The Real IRA's actions were condemned by all governments and parties, including Sinn Féin.

Peace talks have progressed slowly in recent years; many contentious aspects of the Good Friday Agreement have yet to be resolved, such as paramilitary decommissioning and British military withdrawal. Also, since 2002 the power-sharing agreement has been suspended as a result of distrust between nationalist and unionist politicians. Another contributing factor is the recent rise in popularity of the more extreme nationalist (Sinn Féin) and unionist (Ian Paisley's Democratic Unionist Party) political parties over their more moderate counterparts.

The most recent and promising development came in July 2005, when the Provisional IRA announced that its armed campaign had come to an end. In September an international weapons inspector from Canada, John de Chastelain, oversaw the destruction of the PIRA's arsenal.

More than 3,000 soldiers and civilians have lost their lives over the course of the Troubles.

RECENT DEVELOPMENTS IN THE REPUBLIC OF IRELAND

The 1980s were a period of high unemployment and emigration, though policies and reforms were introduced that built on the infrastructures of the 1960s. Such policies finally paid off in the economic boom of the 1990s known as the "Celtic Tiger." The phrase, coined in 1994, refers to Ireland's remarkable period of economic growth between the early 1990s and 2001, which transformed the republic into one of Europe's wealthiest nations.

This success has been attributed to a variety of factors, including financial support from the European Union, conservative government spending, and low corporate tax rates (which encouraged many international businesses to open Irish branches). The wealth is not evenly distributed throughout the population, however; the east coast, particularly Dublin, has benefited the most. A global downturn in 2001 was followed by a rebounding Irish economy in 2004, but economists were spot on in their assertion that this second boom could not sustain itself as well as the original "Celtic Tiger." Sure enough, Ireland found itself in a financial crisis when the global recession hit at the end of 2008, and the recovery has been slow.

Birth control, illegalized in 1936, was made legally available again in 1992, and homosexuality was decriminalized the following year; divorce was legalized in 1996. Since these milestones of the mid-1990s Ireland has grown increasingly tolerant. The stigma associated with childbirth out of wedlock, for example, is pretty much a thing of the past in all but the most conservative circles. In keeping with these cultural shifts, Mass attendance has more than halved since 1995. Ireland's young (and young-in-spirit) liberals celebrated the positive outcome of the gay marriage referendum at the end of 2015.

Government and Economy

GOVERNMENT
The Irish Republic

Adopted in 1937 by referendum (thus replacing the Constitution of the Irish Free State in place since 1922), the Constitution of Ireland guarantees a democratic republic for its citizens. There is a bicameral legislature (or parliament) known as the Oireachtas ("o-ROCK-tas"), which comprises a lower house, the Dáil Éireann ("doll AY-rinn"), and a Senate-like house known as the Seanad Éireann ("SHAN-add AY-rinn," informally known as "the Senate"); both houses meet at Leinster House in Dublin. Unlike in the U.S. Congress, however, the Dáil exercises significantly more power than the Seanad. A member of the Oireachtas is known as a Teachta Dala ("TCHOCK-tuh DOLL-uh," abbreviated TD).

There are two primary political parties in the Irish system, the Fianna Fáil ("Soldiers of Destiny") and the Fine Gael ("Family of the Irish"). The former group was founded by Eamon de Valera in 1926 as a radical anti-treaty party, whereas the Fine Gael are the ideological descendants of the pro-treaty forces, founded in 1933 at the merging of three smaller parties. Fine Gael is traditionally considered moderate to conservative, while Fianna Fáil is moderate to liberal, though in reality the party lines are almost indistinguishable even to many native Irish. At time of writing the Fianna Fáil were the opposition party, holding 44 of the Dáil's 158 seats (Fine Gael holds 50).

Sinn Féin ("We Ourselves") is now the largest minority party in the republic, with 23 seats in the Dáil; traditionally considered the political arm of the Irish Republican Army and often associated with Marxism, this party is an even bigger player in Northern Ireland, where it is supported by most Catholic voters. Gerry Adams is the leader of the Sinn Féin party, whose ultimate goal is a united Ireland.

Other minority parties include Labour (founded by Easter rebel James Connolly in 1912), Anti-Austerity Alliance/People Before Profit, the new Independents 4 Change party, the Social Democrats, and the Green Party (founded in 1981 as the "Ecology Party of Ireland").

The Irish prime minister is known as the Taoiseach ("TEE-shock"), meaning "chieftain," and the Tánaiste ("taw-NESH-tah") is the deputy prime minister. The Taoiseach is the leader of his or her party, appointed by the president from among the members of the Dáil for a five-year term—or until the Taoiseach "loses the confidence" of the Dáil, at which time he or she may be compelled to resign (though this has never occurred). An Taoiseach—the formal title—nominates the Irish cabinet (as well as 11 members of the Seanad), and all cabinet members must also be members of the Oireachtas. At time of writing, Ireland's Taoiseach was Enda Kenny of the Fine Gael party; he took office in March 2011 and was reelected in 2016.

The Irish president (Uachtarán na hÉireann in Irish) is essentially a ceremonial figure, elected for a maximum of two seven-year terms. The poet Michael D. Higgins was elected ninth president of Ireland in 2011. Eamon de Valera was the first Taoiseach (and third president) of the Irish Republic, in office 1937-1948 (and president 1959-1973); Douglas Hyde was the first president, in office 1938-1945.

Northern Politics

Northern Ireland is governed by the British Parliament. The North's loyalist parties include the Ulster Unionist Party and the Democratic Unionist Party (DUP), the latter of which is now the largest in the province. Sinn Féin is Northern Ireland's primary republican and nationalist political party, the second being the Social Democratic and Labour Party (SDLP). The SDLP distinguished itself during the Troubles as antiterrorism, while Sinn Féin supported IRA violence as a means of achieving a unified Ireland. Other minority parties include the Green Party and People Before Profit Alliance on the left and the Traditional Unionist Voice (a DUP splinter group) on the right.

ECONOMY

Ireland's economic boom of the 1990s and early 2000s is a thing of memory now—the ghost of the Celtic Tiger is still licking its wounds after the global recession and €85 billion bailout from the European Union and International Monetary Fund. Agriculture has been Ireland's traditional lifeline, though in the last few decades tourism has become the number one industry—the island was welcoming well over seven million visitors a year in the early to mid-2000s. While tourism dropped off sharply in 2009, the figures are steadily climbing again.

Much of Ireland's white-collar workforce is engaged in the IT and investment sectors—international companies having been enticed here with tax incentives back in the boom times—and for a while many long-emigrated sisters and brothers were returning home to work. Ireland is no longer one of the richest nations in Europe, although it is slowly and steadily recovering.

People and Culture

DEMOGRAPHY

Since the recession, Ireland's population is no longer increasing by leaps and bounds. The current population of the republic is 4.7 million (by 2016 estimate), and approximately 1.8 million live in the six Northern counties (with 579,000 in the greater Belfast area). Though Dublin proper has roughly half a million inhabitants, almost 1.3 million Irish live in the greater metropolitan area, meaning that nearly 40 percent of the republic's population lives in the city and suburbs of the capital. The urban/rural population ratio is roughly 3:2, a reversal of the population distribution in the 1920s. Also, there are approximately 29,573 "Travellers," the politically correct term for the island's itinerant populations; each region has slightly different customs and dialect.

The **Central Statistics Office** (www.census.ie) has more interesting stats: Seeing as agriculture is such a historically integral part of the Irish economy, it's worth noting that approximately 6 percent of Irish farmers (who own their own farms) are under the age of 35. Divorce was legalized (by referendum) only in 1996, and today one in ten Irish marriages ends in divorce (the lowest divorce rate in the E.U.). The current life expectancy is 80.9 years: 79 for men and 83.5 for women.

IMMIGRATION

The influx of immigrants and refugees (from eastern Europe and Nigeria, mostly) since the advent of the "Celtic Tiger" economic boom is a remarkable irony: The Irish were so used to emigrating that they couldn't comprehend it when the foreigners started moving in! The percentage of Ireland's residents born elsewhere is roughly 20 percent, and a majority of those residents are eastern European; most successful visa applicants in recent years have been Indian, Russian, and Chinese. There is also a substantial population of African (mainly Nigerian) political refugees, whose children, when they speak, sound every bit as Irish as the Irish themselves.

RELIGION

The population of the republic is 84 percent Catholic and a little less than 3 percent Protestant. The Northern Ireland population is roughly 48 percent Protestant and 45 percent Catholic, and that split continues to even out as strict Catholics keep on having larger families (the Catholic Church still forbids the use of contraception). As you'd expect, the percentage of Irish citizens who identify themselves as non-Christian or atheist is extremely small; 0.03 percent are Jewish, 1.07 percent Muslim, and almost 6 percent report no religious beliefs (a further 1.6 percent are "unspecified").

In recent decades Ireland has veered away from its traditionally conservative climate and attitudes, partly due to growing disillusionment with the Catholic Church. Divorce, homosexuality, and most recently gay marriage were legalized through several referenda, birth control was made legally available again (though the Catholic Church still does not sanction its use), and allowances for abortion have been made in extreme circumstances. Church attendance has plummeted in recent decades, from more than 90 percent in the mid-1970s to 60 percent in the mid-1990s to roughly 40 percent in 2010 (and only 14 percent in Dublin). As in the United States and several other European nations, child abuse scandals are a huge reason why so many disillusioned Irish Catholics are no longer going to church on Sunday.

LANGUAGE

Irish (or Gaelic, as foreigners often call it) is the Republic of Ireland's first official language (though English is far more widely spoken, the Constitution recognizes it secondarily). Irish (Gaeilge in Irish) is an Indo-European language brought to the island by the Celts and related to the native tongues of Scotland, Wales, and the Isle of Man. The Gaelic language most similar to Irish is Scottish Gaelic; it is possible for a Donegal Irish speaker to hold an (albeit halting) conversation with a Scottish Gaelic speaker. Note that it is more precise to refer to the Irish language as "Irish" rather than "Gaelic," as "Gaelic" is more often used to refer to Scottish Gaelic.

Many people are working assiduously to avoid the death of the Irish language, and their hopes are looking up. The problem is that in the post-independence republic, students were "force-fed" Irish and punished if they did not speak it as well as they did English (a remarkable reversal from the age of the Penal Laws!), and as a result many middle-aged Irish retain a marked distaste for the language of their forebears. Outside the Gaeltachtaí, regions where Irish is the primary language, you'll hear it spoken fairly infrequently; another problem with sustaining the native tongue is that the Ulster (Donegal), Connaught (Mayo and Galway), and Munster (Cork and Kerry) dialects are different enough to incite confusion even among native speakers; there have been proponents of a standardized dialect, but unsurprisingly this movement has not progressed. Today there are approximately 70,000 native Irish speakers on the island, and though

Irish Expressions

You will probably notice that the Irish have a unique way of responding to a question; for example, if you ask "Did you go to the match today?" they'll say "I did" rather than "yes." This is because there are no real words in the Irish language for "yes" and "no." Instead, Irish-speakers reply with the same verb that was used to ask the question.

You may also notice that the Irish often drop their apostrophes—Murphy's Pub may read "Murphys Pub" above the doorway. Perhaps this also stems from the absence of apostrophes in the Irish language.

The first floor of a building is known as the "ground floor" in Ireland, and what Americans call a second floor is their first. Also, the Irish "ring" instead of "call" someone on their "mobile" rather than "cell phone." To "call on" people is to visit them in person.

Like the Brits, the Irish call french fries "chips" and potato chips "crisps." Soccer is "football" (which is not the same as Gaelic football), and fans are enthusiastic about "sport" rather than "sports."

"Your man" just means the particular person the speaker is referring to, not your boyfriend or husband.

The word *craic* (pronounced "crack") is fairly ubiquitous, and it has no direct translation—"fun" isn't quite adequate. "Fun with music and flowing pints" is more accurate. In any case, you'll brand yourself a tourist if you snicker when somebody uses it.

Here are a few more expressions you may need to know:

- "half-four"—4:30 (i.e., the time of day)

- "Monday week"—a week from Monday

- "fair play to you"—good job, nice going

---

40 percent of all those in the republic claim fluency in the language, most admit they use it pretty infrequently.

For more information on the Gaeltachtaí, check out the **Údarás na Gaeltachta** website (www.udaras.ie).

THE ARTS
Handicrafts

Ireland's traditional cottage industries include lace, linen, tweed, and knitting.

Kenmare in County Kerry was a center for the **lace-making** craft in the 19th century and today offers a historical lace exhibition in the heritage center. Virtually all the lace you find in stores now is machine-made, however.

The making of Irish **linen** goes back to the 11th century, when flax was first farmed here; from monastic annals we know that the fabric was worn by the upper classes. From the 17th through the 19th centuries, linen was an exclusively Northern industry, funded by the British government to encourage English and Scottish settlement; women and children toiled in the flax-spinning mills that lined Falls Road in Belfast, a staunchly Catholic neighborhood. Belfast's last linen factories closed in the early 1960s, though it's still possible to buy Irish-made linen products at upscale gift shops.

Donegal is the island's center for **tweed** production. Due to financial cutbacks, some of the county's tweed production is now completed abroad; look for the "made in" label when shopping for tweed.

Knitwear is another quintessentially Irish craft. Women on the Aran Islands in County Galway still knit their intricately cabled sweaters by hand, as they have for centuries. The vast majority of the "Aran sweaters" you'll find in Irish gift shops are machine-knit, but it's well worth spending a great deal more on a hand-knit jumper, if you can afford it.

Ireland—County Waterford in particular—is also renowned for its **crystal.** Many counties besides Waterford have their own crystal factories, including Kilkenny, Cavan, and Tipperary, and there are smaller workshops all over the country (many of them run by former Waterford master craftspeople). Waterford may be the most famous, but the crystal produced elsewhere can be every bit as beautiful (and is sometimes less expensive).

Though **pottery** is also a very popular souvenir, most Irish potters import their clay from England. A few do use a local variety of red daub earthenware clay, though, and some glazes used by Irish potters are produced using local materials as well.

Music and Dance

You may already be well acquainted with the music of U2, Van Morrison, the Cranberries, The Pogues, Enya, Damien Rice, and other popular Irish artists and groups, as well as the Riverdance phenomenon that began with the Eurovision performance in 1995 and all the other step-dance shows it's inspired since then. But you may not be as aware of the traditional music of Ireland.

The Irish traditional music session will always feature a fiddle, or two, or three, along with a bodhrán ("boh-RAWN"), a goatskin drum pounded with a two-ended wooden beater. Though they're not indigenous instruments—but to be accurate, very few quintessentially Irish instruments are—banjos, guitars, and bouzoukis are also common on the trad scene. The tin whistle is somewhat less popular despite its low startup (you can get a good whistle for €10) and portability. Accordions (and concertinas for the ladies) are becoming somewhat less common as well. It takes decades of practice to master the uilleann ("ILL-in") pipes, which is part of why uilleann pipers are few and far between these days. Harps are generally reserved for classical concerts and kitschy medieval banquets.

Regarding the music itself, most of the tunes you'll hear are jigs (6/8 time) and reels (4/4 time), with the occasional air—a song without time—thrown in for good measure (no pun intended). *Seán nós* is a traditional unaccompanied singing style, in Irish. Irish musicians have a strangely organic approach to their repertoires; often one in a group will begin to play and his or her fellow musicians will know which song it is, despite not having a name for it. Even if they don't know the song they will probably still be able to play along.

Traditional Irish dance consists of **step dancing,** in which dancers perform intricate tap dancing with stiff unmoving arms, and **set dancing,** a group dance resembling a quadrille. An evening of traditional music and dancing is called a **ceilidh,** though most of the ones you'll see as a tourist can have a somewhat over-the-top theatricality to them.

Literature

The Irish are consummate storytellers; just walk into a pub, sit beside a local, and wait for him or her to strike up a conversation. This longstanding reputation began with the bards of pre-Christian and medieval Ireland; they were some of the most revered members of society, patronized by petty chieftains and high kings. Until early Christian times Ireland's storytelling tradition was solely oral, but the first monks, learned in Latin as well as Irish, put nib to vellum and recorded many of the island's greatest epics, one of the more famous examples being the *Táin Bó Cúailnge* ("The Cattle Raid of Cooley").

Ireland's most famous writers have tended to be of the Anglo-Irish Ascendancy (not surprising, seeing as the vast majority of the dispossessed Irish were too busy trying to survive to produce much in the way of poetry and prose). Anglo-Irish writers of the 18th and 19th centuries still read today include Jonathan Swift (Dean of St. Patrick's Cathedral in Dublin, satirist, and author of the beloved *Gulliver's Travels*) and Maria Edgeworth, who produced fictions like *Castle Rackrent* to support her family estate in Longford. The 19th-century Anglo-Irish Gothic writers— Bram Stoker, Joseph Sheridan Le Fanu *(In a Glass Darkly)*, and Charles Maturin *(Melmoth the Wanderer)*—have been given short shrift in the realm of Irish literary criticism; it should be noted that Le Fanu's vampire novella *Carmilla* actually predates Stoker's enormously popular and influential *Dracula*. Maturin, an Anglican minister, was the great-uncle of Oscar Wilde, one of the country's greatest playwrights; Wilde would use the pseudonym "Sebastian Melmoth" when in exile in Paris.

Engineered by William Butler Yeats and his patron, Lady Augusta Gregory, the Irish Literary Revival of the early 20th century introduced more of the country's brightest luminaries, including John Millington Synge, George Bernard Shaw, and Sean O'Casey *(The Plough and the Stars)*. Today, James Joyce's doorstoppers, *Ulysses* and *Finnegan's Wake,* often eclipse the work of other fine writers of the early to mid-20th century on American college syllabi: Flann O'Brien, Sean O'Faolain, Patrick Kavanagh, Kate O'Brien, Elizabeth Bowen, and many others. Ironically, many of Ireland's greatest talents—Wilde, Yeats, Joyce, Samuel Beckett— spent most of their time abroad.

Playwright and author Brendan Behan *(The Borstal Boy)* was, like Wilde, a colorful figure renowned for his witty, self-revealing epigrams ("I only take a drink on two occasions: when I'm thirsty and when I'm not")—and

prolific despite an early death in 1964, at age 41. The country's most important contemporary playwrights include Tom Murphy *(The Gigli Concert)*
and Brian Friel *(Dancing at Lughnasa).*

Seamus Heaney is Ireland's most famous contemporary poet, having
translated *Beowulf* into English and produced an oeuvre worthy of the
1995 Nobel Prize in Literature. Other poets, like Nuala Ní Dhomnaill, write
exclusively in Irish (their volumes have English translations by other Irish
writers), and still other poets have gone back and forth between Irish and
English, like Michael Hartnett and Mícheál Ó Siadhail.

Television and Cinema

Until the founding of the Irish Film Board in 1981, British and American
companies produced most of the movies made in Ireland. Though John
Ford's *The Quiet Man,* filmed in Galway and Mayo in the summer of
1951, was seen as a Technicolor marvel at the time, the movie is thin on
plot and rife with stereotypes and absurd brogues. Fortunately, Irish film-
makers have more than made up for such early American-made blunders
with classics like *In the Name of the Father, The Field,* and *My Left Foot*
(all directed by Jim Sheridan), as well as *Michael Collins* and *The Crying
Game* (by Neil Jordan). Many American movies are filmed here each year
too (most recently the latest *Star Wars* installments), and though Irish actors get plenty of work in Hollywood, they tend to remember their roots.
Liam Neeson, a native of County Antrim, is the primary patron of the
Lyric Theatre in Belfast, the theater in which he learned his craft back
in the 1970s.

Architecture

Quaint thatched-roof whitewashed cottages aside, Ireland's most char-
acteristic architecture belongs to the distant past: the Iron Age ring forts
perched dramatically atop rocky promontories; the round towers and
simple one-room churches of the early Christian monasteries; the solid
medieval tower houses of the Gaelic chieftains and Norman conquerors.
Because domestic architecture was often of the wattle-and-daub variety,
the remnants of the island's prehistoric buildings are found mostly within
necropolises, the Brú na Bóinne site in County Meath being the most famous example. Archaeologists have also uncovered the stone foundations
of Neolithic farmhouses. Using such remains, some interpretive museums have been able to construct replicas of *crannógs*—artificial islands
built up with rocks and topped by a round thatched house—and other
ancient dwellings.

Though beehive huts, *clocháin,* are emblematic of the early Christian
monastic period—used as the monks' cells, for sleep or solitary prayer—
these corbelled structures were first erected in the Neolithic period. Round
towers—which functioned as a defense against Viking raiders (not for the
monks' lives so much as their treasures, jeweled reliquaries and illuminated manuscripts and suchlike) as well as a geographical touchstone for

An Architectural Glossary

From the Bronze Age to the opulent faux castles of the Victorian era, here's a rundown of the most common architectural terms. Architecture buffs should also check out **Archeire** (www.irish-architecture.com), an opinionated guide to Irish architecture from Norman castles to O'Donnell & Tuomey.

antae: a pilaster forming the end of a projecting lateral wall, as in some Greek temples, and constituting one boundary of the portico

bailey: a castle's outer wall

beehive hut: a small circular stone building shaped like a beehive

caher: a circular area enclosed by stone walls

cairn: a prehistoric grave covered by a mound of stones

cashel: a stone-walled circular fort

chancel: the eastern end of a church, where the altar is located

cheveaux de frise: a defensive field of sharp stone spikes around a fort, placed to impede the cavalry of an attacking army

clochán: a dry-stone beehive hut usually used for monks' solitary cells in the early Christian period

corbel: a triangular bracket, usually made of stone or brick, that projects from the face of a wall and is usually used to support a cornice or arch

cornice: a horizontal molded projection that crowns a building or wall

crannóg: an artificial island (piled up with rocks and debris) connected by a wooden bridge to the shore, usually containing a thatched house and barn surrounded by a palisade and created for ease of defense

cromlech: a tomb with two upright stones covered by a capstone, synonymous with dolmens; literally a "bent flagstone"

curtain wall: an exterior wall or a section of that wall between two gates or towers

dairtheach: in a monastery, a small room reserved for private prayer

demesne: the land surrounding a castle or manor house, often including gardens

dolmen: a prehistoric tomb made of two vertical stones topped by a capstone, giving the structure the vague appearance of a toadstool

fulacht fiadh: a Bronze Age hearth consisting of an earthen trough filled with water, into which fire-warmed stones would be placed, boiling whatever meats were submerged in the water; it is possible that such troughs were used for laundry, cloth-dyeing, and leather-making as well

gallery grave: a burial chamber shaped like a tunnel

Georgian: a relatively austere architectural style used from the 1710s to the 1830s, named for Britain's four King Georges and characterized by symmetry and proportion with a restrained use of classical Greek and Roman elements; examples abound in Irish domestic architecture, especially in Dublin and Limerick

pilgrims—are unique not only to the Christian monastic period, but to Ireland as well. You won't find any round towers except on this island.

Though the Vikings established their port cities at Dublin, Waterford, Wexford, and elsewhere in the 9th and 10th centuries, their extant architecture is limited to chunks of city walls. The Normans left Ireland with a tremendous architectural heritage, mostly in the form of the fortified

Gothic: an architectural style characterized by pointed arches, used in Irish castles and churches between the 12th and 16th centuries

keep: a castle's main tower, also called a donjon

machicolation: a projecting gallery at the top of a castle wall, supported by corbeled arches and having floor openings through which stones and boiling liquids were dropped on attackers

motte: an early Norman fortification with a raised, flattened mound topped with a keep; many motte-and-bailey structures were erected in the early 1200s

neoclassical: a movement beginning in the mid-18th century, inspired by ancient Greek and Roman architecture and a reaction against rococo and other ornate styles; examples include the Four Courts in Dublin

Palladian: the early 18th-century English revival of the style of 16th-century Italian architect Andrea Palladio, characterized by an adherence to mathematical proportions as well as architectural features like loggias and porticos; the foremost example of Irish Palladian architecture is Castletown in County Kildare

passage grave: a Celtic tomb reached by a passageway and buried beneath an earth and stone mound

ráth: a circular fort surrounded by a wooden wall and earthen banks

reredos: a decorative (usually wood-carved) partition in front of a church altar

ring fort: a circular stone structure with an embankment on all sides, built between the Bronze Age and medieval times

Romanesque: an architectural style characterized by rounded arches and vaulting, popular in Ireland in the 1100s; the style known as **Hiberno-Romanesque** incorporates Celtic motifs in its stone carvings as well as antae and high-pitched corbelled gables

round tower: a tall circular tower built in Irish monasteries between the 9th and 11th centuries, used for a lookout and refuge from Viking invaders (which is why the tower entrance was virtually always at least one story off the ground)

sheila-na-gig: a female effigy, similar to a prehistoric fertility figure in its exaggerated reproductive anatomy, carved in stone on the exterior of churches and castles (literally "Sheila of the teats")

souterrain: an underground chamber or passageway, usually used in ring and hill forts to provide storage for food or an escape route in an emergency

standing stone: a vertically placed stone set in the ground, dating across several time periods; their general purpose is unknown, though some were certainly used as grave markers

voussoir: one of the wedge-shaped stones forming the curve of an arch or vaulted ceiling

castles for which the country is perhaps best known. The Normans also brought the Gothic, which became the most pervasive style of ecclesiastical architecture in the centuries to follow.

The early 12th century heralded the popularity of the Romanesque style in Irish churches. Irish stonemasons created an amalgam of Romanesque and Celtic motifs to create a distinctive "Hiberno-Romanesque" style.

Through the 19th century (and well into the 20th) Roman Catholic churches went up in the neo-Gothic style, sometimes with Hiberno-Romanesque flourishes.

Opulent country houses built by English landlords run the gamut from neoclassical and Palladian styles to neo-Gothic manors to Victorian mansions. Ireland has a strong Georgian architectural heritage, and not just in cities like Dublin. Many smaller market towns were planned by the local landlord, so the extant architecture lining those tidy tree-lined squares echoes the prevailing aesthetics of the time.

Dublin's grandest architecture is also in the neoclassical style; take for example the president's home in Phoenix Park (Áras an Uachtaráin), designed by Francis Johnston, and the Customs House and the Four Courts by James Gandon. Some architects, like William Chambers (who designed the Casino Marino for the Earl of Charlemont), never even set foot on Irish soil. Though such structures as neoclassical Dublin City Hall and the Palladian Leinster House are examples of imperialist style and construction, they are nonetheless some of Ireland's finest architecture of the last 300 years.

SPORTS

Though you'll find plenty of fans of the British football teams, most Irish love to watch Gaelic football and hurling (camogie is the ladies' version of hurling). Formed in 1884 to promote these uniquely Irish pastimes, the **Gaelic Athletic Association** (www.gaa.ie) is headquartered at Croke Park in Dublin. For want of a better comparison, hurling looks like a cross between field hockey, baseball, and lacrosse, with a broad-ended stick used to balance the ball briefly before hitting it; players can also handle the ball. Gaelic football looks more like soccer than anything else. Horse and greyhound racing are popular with bettors.

Essentials

Transportation

GETTING THERE

Air

Transatlantic flights are available to **Dublin International Airport** (tel. 01/814-1111, www.dublinairport.com), which is 12 kilometers north of the city.

Airfares naturally vary greatly between seasons; when booking ahead for a summer holiday (round-trip, flying from the United States), expect to spend at least US$800; last-minute fares could cost you well over US$1,000. Fares in shoulder season are in the neighborhood of US$600-800. The sooner you purchase your ticket, the better the deal; the only exception is in mid-January through February, when Aer Lingus and other carriers offer very good last-minute fares (around US$500). Fares skyrocket again in the week leading up to St. Patrick's Day.

All ballpark figures noted above factor in taxes and fees.

FROM THE UNITED STATES AND CANADA

Aer Lingus (tel. 800/474-7424, www.aerlingus.com) and **United** (tel. 800/864-8331, www.united.com) offer the best service and options when flying from the United States. Both offer direct flights from New York (JFK or Newark), Boston, Denver, San Francisco, Los Angeles, and many other cities. **Delta** (tel. 800/241-4141, www.delta.com) also offers direct flights.

FROM THE UNITED KINGDOM AND CONTINENTAL EUROPE

Despite the inconvenience of flying out of secondary airports, low-cost air carriers are the way to go when flying from the United Kingdom and mainland Europe. **RyanAir** (www.ryanair.com) is far and away the most popular option, with **EasyJet** (www.easyjet.com) a close second. Aer Lingus offers frequent flights to Dublin from Heathrow, Gatwick, and London City, as well as Paris, Madrid, Milan, Rome, Naples, Frankfurt, Brussels, Amsterdam, Vienna, Budapest, Prague, Warsaw, Munich, and many more locations.

Sea

International ferry services are available, mostly from the United Kingdom, as well as Roscoff and Cherbourg in France. Booking online can save you as much as 10 percent, but note that not all ferries accept pedestrian passengers. **Irish Ferries** (tel. 01/638-3333, www.irishferries.com) sails from Dublin to Holyhead. **Steam Packet** (tel. 1800/805-055, www.steam-packet.

Previous: Temple Bar in Dublin; the Old Library at Trinity College Dublin.

com) sails to Dublin from the Isle of Man. Ferry service is available to Dún Laoghaire, 13 kilometers south of Dublin, via **Stena Line** (tel. 01/204-7777 or 01/204-7799, www.stenaline.ie) from Holyhead in Wales.

145

GETTING AROUND

Bus

The republic's national bus service, **Bus Éireann** (tel. 01/830-2222, www.buseireann.ie), has an extensive network of national routes, as well as local service in the larger towns and cities. An **Open Road** ticket allows unlimited bus travel within the republic during a certain period, three days out of six for €60 with each additional day costing €16.50.

Train

The Irish national train network is Iarnród Éireann, a.k.a. **Irish Rail** (tel. 01/836-3333, www.irishrail.ie), which serves most of the larger towns and cities. For the most part, the railway map looks like a starfish, with all lines leading from Dublin. Return fares are always a better value, day return fares especially, though prices rise at the weekend. If you're planning on a lot of train travel, purchase an **Irish Explorer Ticket,** a combination bus-and-train ticket that allows you five days of travel out of 15 (€160) within the republic. There's also a **Trekker pass** (€110) for unlimited train travel over a four-day period. Train passes are not available for purchase online; you can purchase them at any bus station ticket counter, though to be frank these tourist passes are not nearly as good a value as they used to be; tally up the ticket prices for your itinerary (using the website fare finder) and you may very well realize you won't be saving anything. For international train passes, visit **Eurail** online (www.eurail.com).

The **DART,** or Dublin Area Rapid Transit (www.dart.ie) is popular with commuters, and is very useful for visitors staying in Dublin who wish to see more of Counties Dublin and Wicklow. **Luas** (www.luas.ie) is a light-rail service within the city designed to cut down on gridlock.

Car

Driving on the left is a downright scary proposition, and the idiosyncrasies of the Irish roads can leave even the best drivers anxious and stressed out. If you plan to stick to larger towns and cities, you're best off using public transportation. But the Irish bus and rail networks do not serve many remote locations, and many wonderful attractions are difficult, even impossible, to reach without a car. Weigh the stress involved in driving on Irish roads against the benefit of going anywhere you like, anytime you like, and make a decision from there.

TRAFFIC REGULATIONS AND TIPS

First off, you'll be driving on the left (and don't make any wisecracks about "driving on the wrong side" at the Europcar desk!). In keeping with this, the right lane is the "fast" lane. The dread of every foreign driver is the roundabout, a common substitute for an intersection; traffic proceeds in a clockwise direction, and you enter the circle only when there are no vehicles oncoming from your right. The larger roundabouts also have traffic lights. When approaching the roundabout, stay in the left lane if you intend to take the first exit, the right lane for subsequent exits; you'll know which exit you want by reading the big green sign posted before the roundabout.

Parking is generally free in smaller places, though the larger towns and cities operate a "pay-and-display" policy. You buy a ticket from a blue kiosk to leave on your dashboard, €0.60-3/hour depending on the size of the town (not all accept credit cards, so be sure to carry several euros in change). Still other parking lots are "disc-operated," meaning you'll have to duck into the nearest newsagent to purchase a disc for about the same price. In some towns it's worth seeking out free parking spaces a bit farther from the center; in other situations you'll just have to fork it over. Spend a few minutes when you first arrive in a new place just getting your bearings and scoping out free parking opportunities. Some lots charge €3-3.50 for the whole day. After 6:30pm, though, you won't have to feed the car park kiosk.

In the republic, distances and speed limits are given in kilometers, with the exception of some very old signs still in need of replacement in more remote locales (you'll have no difficulty recognizing them). Always trust your map over the road signs; they're sometimes pointed in the wrong direction (through age and weather, not necessarily mischief). Though this book lists roads by official number ("N" indicating a national road, "R" a regional road, "L" a local road) for ease of navigation, the Irish don't always use them when giving directions—they tend to say "the Dublin road" instead of "the N3." Ireland has been hard at work building new motorways (noted by an "M") in recent years, so small-town bottlenecks aren't as ubiquitous or inevitable as they used to be. There are tolls (€2-7) along these motorways, so carry extra change (otherwise you have to park on the side of the highway and visit the office to use your credit card), although if you're driving the M50 you can pay your toll online using **eFlow** (www.eflow.ie).

It is polite to acknowledge the other drivers you pass on narrow back-country roads, especially if they pull to the side to let you pass first. Raise a finger or two off the steering wheel in a sort of benediction.

SAFETY

This may be a generalization, but there's a great deal of truth in it: Irish drivers are reckless. They are impatient, they drive too fast, and they take ridiculous risks. Also, the speed limits off the national roads and motorways are too high: 100 kph (62 mph) on a narrow, winding road where even a good driver would apply the brake liberally. Ireland's roads claim lives every weekend of the year, and until the government wises up, lowers the speed limits on regional roads, and then puts the guards on the streets to enforce them, these tragedies will continue to occur. Sadly, alcohol is often involved in such incidents. Avoid becoming a statistic by following all the usual commonsensible rules: Designate a sober driver who won't drink even a single beer, wear your seatbelts, and use the high beams on country roads (dim them if you see a car ahead, though). Drive only as fast as you feel comfortable; Irish drivers have no qualms about passing you, anyway!

CAR RENTALS

To rent an automobile, you must be over 23 years old and have been licensed for at least two years. There are numerous rental companies, most of which are international (and have desks at most airports): **Europcar** (www.europcar.ie), **Avis** (www.avis.ie), **Budget** (www.budget.ie), **Hertz** (www.hertz.ie), and **Enterprise** (www.enterprise.ie). GPS rental is universally available.

Theft insurance is an option, but because car theft is practically nonexistent in Ireland you'd do well to opt out and save yourself a few euros a day.

PACKAGE DEALS

You can find airfare-car rental combined rates on Expedia, Orbitz, and other websites. Otherwise, instead of booking directly through Avis, Europcar, or whichever, go through **AutoEurope** (tel. 01/659-0500, www.autoeurope.com). Clerks at the rental agencies admit that booking through AutoEurope will get you a better rate.

MAPS AND DIRECTIONS

Ordnance Survey (OS, www.osi.ie) publishes detailed scale maps of the national parks, cities, and the larger towns, which indicate one-way streets. Pick up a road atlas—the Collins or Ordnance Survey brands are recommended (about €9)—before leaving the airport, as the map the rental agency gives you isn't detailed enough.

Bike

Bicycle hire will usually run you €15-20 per day (or as much as €25 in Dublin). Weekly rental is a better value, roughly €50-60 per week. In addition, you're often required to leave a deposit and/or a form of ID. Some cycle shops provide one-way service for an additional fee; check out **Raleigh Rent-a-Bike** (www.raleigh.ie) for participating dealers. Serious cyclists will want to bring their own, of course; your bike will be factored into your baggage allowance. Irish buses usually allow bikes in the cargo hold, though you'll probably have to pay a surcharge. Especially with private companies, ring ahead to ensure you'll be able to bring your cycle along.

Tours

Keep in mind that most tours follow the well-trod tourist tracks. They are certainly convenient, but they generally provide only a very narrow tourist's view of Ireland. One of the most popular choices (popular with retirees) is **CIE** (www.cietours.com), offering coach tour packages in Ireland and elsewhere in Europe. In contrast, Con Moriarty at **Hidden Ireland Tours** (tel.

087/221-4002, www.hiddenirelandtours.com) offers active, often themed holidays. For the backpacking set, there's the **Paddywagon** (www.paddywagontours.com), a hop-on, hop-off bus tour, and **Shamrockers** (tel. 01/672-7651, www.shamrockeradventures.com).

Food and Accommodations

FOOD AND DRINK

Traditional Irish dishes like colcannon (mashed potatoes, butter, and cabbage or kale), boxty (potato pancakes), and lamb stew are fast disappearing off the pub menus, though black pudding, a sausage made from dried pigs' blood, is still served at B&Bs. When traditional meals do make an appearance, they're usually given the gourmet treatment in chic Continental restaurants, where your plate of bangers and mash (sausages and mashed potatoes) might come served with a sprig of some unidentifiable herb. This gourmet trend, encouraged by the Celtic Tiger, has resulted in hundreds of top-notch restaurants and "gastro-pubs" serving French- and Asian-inspired cuisine; the food is dubbed "Modern Irish" if it emphasizes local, often organic produce, meats (Kerry lamb, for instance), and seafood. Many native Irish chefs were trained on the Continent and have returned home to open their own eateries, and still other chef/owners are foreigners who recognize a growing market. Many pubs still serve defrosted fish-and-chips and gristly lamb stew, but they are becoming increasingly few and far between even in smaller villages. As ever, potatoes and brown bread are staples of the Irish diet.

Beverages

The Gaelic words for whiskey are *uisce beatha,* or "water of life"—which just goes to show you how much the Irish love to drink it. **Jameson** is the most popular brand, with **Bushmills** preferred by the Brits up North. Interestingly, it's said that you can tell the distillery's political affiliation by the shape of the bottle: square bottles are loyalist and round bottles (like Jameson's) are republican.

Of course, **Guinness** is far and away the most popular brand of Irish stout (also referred to as "porter" back in the day); **Beamish** and **Murphy's** are Cork brands, not readily available elsewhere in the country. Kilkenny-based **Smithwick's** is a popular ale (though it's now owned by Guinness). Imported beers are becoming increasingly commonplace in Irish pubs; favored brands include Stella Artois and Carlsberg. There are various cider brands available, though most of them are U.K. imports; Irish-brewed **Bulmer's** is the top brand (it's the same as Magner's in the United States).

Don't tip at the pub; unlike those back home, Irish bartenders make a regular wage. They'll actually be insulted if you try. Want to savor the music, but not the drink—or seriously short on cash? Try ordering a "blackcurrant," which is just a dollop of blackcurrant syrup in a pint glass of water. The bartender will charge you less than a euro for it, and it tastes like noncarbonated fruit soda.

The Irish do not use ice in their cold drinks, and if you ask for an "iced tea" they'll look at you like you're missing a few marbles (then inform you that "iced tea" is an oxymoron). Indeed, the Irish are fairly particular about their tea; few drink anything besides Barry's brand, and most people have at least one cup with pretty much every meal. Ireland's tea dependence originated in Britain; during the Industrial Revolution, English factory bosses recognized it as the ideal drink for their workers—inexpensive, caffeinated, and nonalcoholic. Low tea prices and comfort against the wet weather made it the natural choice in Irish homes as well. Despite declining tea sales, Barry's is still Ireland's most popular beverage. Indeed, this island has the world's highest per-capita tea consumption (four cups per day and seven pounds a year, to be exact).

And though coffee drinking is on the rise, java-lovers beware: many Irish B&Bs serve instant. In a nation of tea drinkers, very few people have ever seen (or heard of) a coffee grinder. Also, don't order a cocktail unless it's a posh sort of pub. Bartenders will often charge by the shot, meaning a Sex on the Beach could end up costing you €17.

Dining

Many bars offer a "pub grub" menu, featuring hearty traditional meat-and-potato meals at some places and more elegant, Continental-type fare at "gastro-pubs." Pub grub is less expensive than dinner at a regular restaurant, though most pub kitchens close by 9:30pm. The more upscale Irish restaurants generally offer a good-value two- or three-course early-bird menu.

Vegetarianism and Special Diets

Vegetarians, don't believe anyone who says you can't eat well in Ireland. Even halfway decent restaurants have at least one meat-free option, at worst an unimaginative pasta dish; gourmet eateries tend to offer only one choice, though it's generally as good as any other dish on the menu. And in the off chance you find yourself in a rural watering hole—miles from the nearest proper restaurant, with nothing on the pub grub menu but meat and fish—just ask the staff what they can whip up for you; they'll be happy to help you out. Vegans will likely have a tricky time of it outside the larger towns, however, since vegetarian dishes are usually quite heavy on the eggs and dairy. Worst-case scenario, you'll be served boring stirfries and "curries" consisting mostly of rice. (The concept of plant-based protein is not quite understood here yet, alas.) Consider planning your itinerary around the country's best vegan-friendly eateries (a trip to Cork City is a must), and/or using self-catering accommodations in rural areas so you can cook for yourself. For tips and resources, check out the **Vegetarian Society of Ireland** (www.vegetarian.ie), the **Vegan Society of Ireland** (www.vegan.

ie), and **Happy Cow** (www.happycow.net/europe/ireland) as you're planning your holiday.

Irish chefs (even in rural areas) are well informed when it comes to gluten allergies, and many menus mark their gluten-free options.

ACCOMMODATIONS
Hostels

Ireland has a rightful reputation for some of the best hostels in Europe. There are the inevitable stinkers, but the various hostelling organizations—**An Óige** (www.anoige.ie), the republic's youth hostel organization; **Independent Holiday Hostels in Ireland** (IHH, www.hostels-ireland.com); and **Independent Hostel Owners of Ireland** (IHI, www.independenthostelsireland.com)—generally ensure that hostels operating under their banners offer cleanliness and hospitality. Some hostels also have an adjacent campground, where you pay less for a site than you would for a bed but have access to the kitchens, showers, and sitting rooms. Many hostels arrange outdoor activities and other events; some include a light breakfast in the room price, and the very best hostels offer additional meals at dinner. Cramped bunk beds and communal showers can seem like negligible inconveniences when you consider how many new friends you can make while hostelling. Though most hostellers are under 30, generally travelers of all ages are welcomed. In recent years, some hostels have closed their doors to tourists to become immigrant or refugee housing (which is more profitable for the owner).

Also keep in mind that some hostels might start off with good management in the beginning, thus securing the IHH or IHI stamp of approval, only to decline after the business changes hands or for other reasons. A personal recommendation from a fellow traveler is ideal, but if that's not possible and you have your doubts about a particular establishment, ask for a brief tour of the hostel (including the dorm room you'd be staying in along with the shower room) before you check in. Also, most hostels don't issue dorm room keys, so be very careful with your valuables. Checkout is generally 10am.

Bed-and-Breakfasts

B&Bs, which are run out of a family home, are the most popular form of accommodation, and can be found in every nook and corner all over the country. Though B&B proprietors are among the friendliest, most knowledgeable, and helpful Irish people (after all, their livelihood depends upon it), there are several caveats: There's less privacy than in a hotel, and you may be forced to adjust to the owner's schedule, particularly regarding breakfast times. Also note that prices are per person, often with an unfortunate "supplement" for singles. Nevertheless, B&Bs are nearly always a better value than the hotels and much more comfortable than hostelling.

Also note that proprietors pay for those AA "diamond" ratings; if a B&B doesn't have one, it just means the owners didn't want to pay the AA inspector's fee. In the republic, the shamrock logo indicates the B&B has been approved by the tourist board, though many nonapproved B&Bs are excellent, too.

In theory, B&Bs serve a full Irish breakfast, but most owners skip the time-consuming items like mushrooms, blood sausage, and fresh fried potatoes. (Tinned baked beans may not sound very appetizing now, but you'll grow to like them.) Vegetarians need only ask; proprietors are happy to skip the bacon, and most offer cereal, yogurt, and/or fruit salad. Most places have a set breakfast time of one or two hours between 6:30am and 10am; your host will inform you of these hours. A few B&Bs serve evening meals, mostly in rural areas where there are few restaurants.

Many B&Bs do not accept credit cards, since the fees eat up a percentage of their profits, and those that do sometimes impose a small service charge (2-3 percent). It is customary to pay on the morning of your departure, though, so there's no need to search for the nearest ATM before you check in. Checkout time is generally 11am.

Over the past few years **AirBnB** (www.airbnb.com) has become a very popular alternative—sometimes even traditional B&Bs have listings there. Even if you're going mostly with AirBnB accommodations, you might want to spend at least one or two nights in an old-fashioned B&B to soak up the atmosphere.

Hotels

The more established Irish hotels can be quite grand, old-fashioned, and lovely, but compared to B&Bs they're generally not a great value for the money. Prices range from €40 in remote locales to well over €200 or €300 in converted castles or manor houses, though the higher price bracket is often per room rather than per person. Some hotels have moved away from an inclusive full breakfast, so ask before making a reservation. Checkout time is generally at noon.

Self-Catering Accommodations

If you plan to "stay put" in one place for a week or more, taking day trips rather than moving from town to town, a self-catering cottage or apartment may be a good choice. Some self-catering digs are brand-new apartments or holiday homes; others are quaint thatched-roof cottages. Purpose-built "holiday homes" in highly touristed areas are often excessively priced, though, so look for individuals who rent out a few small properties as a way of making extra cash. Helpful websites with properties nationwide include **Trident Holiday Homes** (www.selfcatering-ireland.com) and **Dream Ireland** (www.dreamireland.com). Another site, **Rent an Irish Cottage** (www.rentacottage.ie), offers rentals in the western counties from Mayo to Cork (excluding Galway). Some proprietors will charge you for the heat and electricity used over the week, so ask about this beforehand.

VISAS AND OFFICIALDOM

Passports and Visas

Unless you are a citizen of the European Union, you'll need a passport to enter the country (and even if you are, it's smart to carry it anyway). North American visitors' passports are stamped with a tourist visa, which allows them a stay of three months. If you plan to remain in the Republic of Ireland for longer than three months, contact the Irish police, the **Garda Síochána** (tel. 01/666-9100, www.garda.ie), to register for a student or work visa. If you ask at the customs desk, they'll provide you with the address of the *garda* station at your destination. Both the Garda National Immigration Bureau (GNIB) and the Irish Naturalisation and Immigration Service are at 13/14 Burgh Quay in the Dublin city center.

Customs

When leaving Ireland, E.U. citizens have no limit to the monetary value of goods purchased while in Ireland, so long as the items purchased are not for commercial use. Citizens of the United States, however, are subject to U.S. Customs restrictions: You're allowed only $400 worth of goods tax free (that's $400 per person), and there's a 10 percent tax imposed thereafter. It's possible to mail up to an additional $200 worth of goods home without paying the duty, but your purchases in the duty-free shops in Irish airports count toward that $400 monthly total (that is, you're not paying tax in Ireland, but you may still be required to do so on those same goods upon return to the United States). There are also limits imposed upon cigarettes (200 maximum) and alcohol (one liter maximum). In addition, U.S. citizens should note that bringing fresh food or plants home is not permitted. For more information, visit the U.S. Customs website (www.customs.gov).

CONDUCT AND CUSTOMS

While the atmosphere in most pubs may seem informal enough, and plenty of people lapse into the use of excessive expletives when they've had too much to drink, you should always try to keep your language as clean as possible. The Irish make allowances for those silly drunkards, but they won't consider you very mannerly if you use the same language their inebriated friend does. It's also smart to avoid talking politics, unless you're sure your views won't clash with those of your companions.

During music sessions in the pub, it is polite to pause in conversation to clap for the musicians when a song ends. And if a new friend is kind enough to buy you a pint, it goes without saying that the next round is on you!

Visitors should never make assumptions about the sexual mores of their new friends—suggestive advertising, frank talk on TV and in social situations, and other purported signs of a sexually liberated culture can belie deep-rooted conservative values.

SIGHTSEEING PASSES AND DISCOUNTS

If you plan to do much sightseeing, the **Dúchas Heritage Card** (www.heritageireland.com) is a must-have. For €25 (€10 for students!), you can get into any of the Office of Public Works' 70-plus sites for a full year. Seeing as Newgrange-Knowth combo admission costs €11 now (and many other sites are €4-7 apiece), you'll recoup that money in just a few visits. Obviously, students should pick up the card even if they're planning to use it only a few times. Purchase the card at the reception desk of any site.

Another option is the **Heritage Island Explorer Touring Guide** (www.heritageisland.com); buy the €8 info brochure and show it at more than 90 sites for a 2-for-1 or percentage discount. Most discounts are the former, though, so it makes more sense to buy this one if you're traveling in pairs.

ACCESS FOR TRAVELERS WITH DISABILITIES

Guesthouses, museums, and so forth are gradually becoming more accessible for visitors with disabilities. Bord Fáilte publishes an annual accommodations guide, available at any tourist office, that specifies which hotels and B&Bs offer special access. The Dúchas website (www.heritageireland.ie) details which heritage sites are wheelchair-accessible.

Renting a car is probably the way to go, as navigating the public transportation systems can be difficult at best. Irish buses are not wheelchair-accessible, though the trains are possible to ride with some assistance. Iarnród Éireann's official policy provides for this, but you must call ahead (tel. 01/836-3333).

For information or assistance, contact **Enable Ireland** (tel. 01/872-7155, www.enableireland.ie), a nonprofit organization in the republic. If you are in need of a wheelchair, contact **The Irish Wheelchair Association** (24 Blackheath Dr., Dublin, tel. 01/833-8241, www.iwa.ie).

TRAVELING WITH CHILDREN

Virtually all sightseeing attractions offer a family admission rate, as do some modes of public transportation (with one or two adults and up to three children under the age of 16). Otherwise, B&Bs and hotels generally offer cots at no extra charge, as well as a children's discount of 20-50 percent.

By law, those under the age of 18 are not allowed in the pubs after 10pm in summer and 9pm in winter. This cutoff time might be earlier depending on the establishment (look for a sign above the bar).

WOMEN TRAVELING ALONE

Ireland is one of the safest places on earth for the single female traveler. The psychological intricacies of the stereotypical Irishman aside, the men of this island are almost always genuinely friendly and eager to help you in any way they can.

Since you will need your sweaters even in July and August, the question of how revealing one can dress when out pubbing and clubbing is pretty much moot. While the occasional eccentric Englishwoman can be found sunbathing in the nude at some of the less touristy beaches, this kind of activity is not recommended. Nor is hitchhiking—though if you must, hitching in Ireland is safer than anywhere else. That said, caution and common sense are your greatest assets. Some parts of Dublin simply aren't safe for lone women pedestrians after dark, and incidents can occur even in quiet suburban neighborhoods.

If you will be hostelling during your trip, note that many Irish hostels now offer predominantly mixed-gender dormitories. If you would prefer a girls-only dorm room, be sure to mention that when you check in.

GAY AND LESBIAN TRAVELERS

Ireland has grown increasingly tolerant and open minded regarding homosexuality, as evidenced by the happy outcome of the same-sex marriage referendum in 2015. The local church is mum on the matter, and, thankfully, bigotry is limited to isolated incidents.

Excellent resources include **Outhouse** (tel. 01/873-4932, www.outhouse.ie), **Gaire** (www.gaire.com), and **The Outmost** (www.theoutmost.com). **QueerID** (www.queerid.com) is Dublin-centric. For information on the summer Gay Pride Parade in Dublin (and plenty more), check out **Dublin Pride** (www.dublinpride.org).

There are a couple of switchboards in Dublin: **Gay Switchboard Dublin** (tel. 01/872-1055, www.gayswitchboard.ie, 8pm-10pm daily, except for 3:30pm-6pm Sat.) and **Lesbian Line Dublin** (tel. 01/872-9911, www.dublinlesbianline.ie, 7pm-9pm Thurs.).

STD cases are on the rise, especially in Dublin—take all necessary precautions. **The Gay Men's Health Project** (tel. 01/660-2189, www.gmhs.ie), which operates a clinic in the Baggot Street Hospital in Dublin, can offer more information, as can the sites listed above.

SENIOR TRAVELERS

Visitors over the age of 60 are entitled to discounts at museums and other sights as well as on most forms of public transit (including Bus Éireann and Irish Rail). The bus or train may be the best way to go, as car-rental companies will not rent automobiles to drivers over the age of 75 (and usually impose a surcharge for drivers ages 70 to 74).

BUSINESS HOURS

Irish banks are generally open 9am or 10am to 4pm or 5pm Monday to Friday; post offices keep the same hours, closing 1pm-2pm for lunch. Many smaller businesses close during this hour, too, so keep this in mind when running errands. Bookstores, boutiques, and many other shops close at 6pm, and most stores still close on Sunday, especially in the smaller towns and villages.

LAUNDRY

Irish launderettes are mostly full service, and will run you €8-12 per load. Some offer a same-day tourist service. Many accommodations offer laundry service for an additional fee (often less than that of a launderette), so ask at your B&B before looking for a cleaners in town.

TOILETS

Most sizable Irish towns offer public toilets. Those not coin-operated are very basic (not to mention grotty), so always carry a bottle of hand sanitizer. Most establishments reserve their restrooms for customers only, though this rule is often bypassed in pubs by the truly desperate traveler.

The Irish words for "men" and "women" often appear on restroom doors: the men's room is labeled *fir* and the women's is *mna*. The Irish for "toilets" is *leithreas*.

Information and Services

HEALTH AND SAFETY

In the event of an emergency, dial 999 on your cell phone or nearest pay phone, which will connect you with the local police (or *gardaí*) and ambulance.

There is a choice of pharmacies even in the smaller Irish towns, though not all are open on Sunday; general hours of operation are 9am-6pm, and many places are open until 8pm or 9pm at least a few days a week. Your accommodation can direct you to the nearest seven-day pharmacy, if you end up needing medication over the weekend. Condoms are now available at any pharmacy.

Ireland is a very safe country—the vast majority of violent crimes are drug-related, and fortunately this is a world tourists seldom come into contact with. Your biggest safety concern regards your rental car, as there are a staggering number of motor accidents on a daily basis: 1,000 people are injured per month, with an average monthly death toll of 30. Drive conservatively no matter how many speed demons pass you on those narrow roads.

It goes without saying that you should never drink to excess—no matter if your B&B is a five-minute walk up the road, and regardless of how many free pints you're handed. If at all possible, avoid driving late at night even if you're the designated driver; many other motorists won't be so conscientious. And while it seldom happens that blackout drugs are slipped into nightclub drinks when a girl's back is turned, you should still keep your drink with you at all times.

MONEY

Currency

The Irish punt is long gone—the euro has been the official currency since

February 2002. Check on the exchange rate before you leave using Google or the **Universal Currency Converter** (www.xe.com/ucc); at time of writing the U.S. dollar was a bit stronger against the euro (compared to before the economic downturn), €1 equaling $1.13.

Using your credit or ATM card gets you the best exchange rate, but if you need to change money, visit a bureau de change at a bank. (Bureaux de change at tourist offices, hotels, and commercial agencies offer a poorer rate of exchange, plus commission.)

Taxes

You are entitled to a VAT (value added tax) refund on all goods purchased in the republic upon departure, so long as you aren't an E.U. citizen—saving you 17.36 percent off the original price. Whenever you make a purchase at a gift shop, just ask for a voucher. (Note that it's the VAT on goods, not services, that is refundable.) Fill all your forms in before you get to the airport, then visit the Global Refund Desk, which is located between the security and immigration checkpoints. You'll receive a refund in cash or by credit card, though a credit refund can take as long as two months to process.

Tipping

As bartenders are paid a regular wage in Ireland, there is no need to tip them.

At restaurants, your credit card slip will include a gratuity line. Tip only if your service has been better than average (and if you aren't being served by the owner of the establishment), and do not feel compelled to leave 15 or 20 percent even for excellent service. (Remember that unlike American servers, your waiter is making at least minimum wage.) Also, if a restaurant has imposed a service charge (10-15 percent) and you weren't satisfied with the service, don't hesitate to request the charge be removed from your bill.

Though it isn't necessary to tip Irish taxi drivers, you might want to add a euro or two if he or she has been especially helpful. If you have luggage, there's an automatic surcharge of approximately three euros, which is fair considering the driver will almost always load and unload your bags, and may even carry them to the door for you unasked.

COMMUNICATIONS AND MEDIA

Telephone

Phone numbers in the republic can be five, six, or seven digits. The area codes 083, 085, 086, 087, or 089 indicate the number belongs to a cell phone (Three, Meteor, Vodafone, or Tesco Mobile).

When calling Ireland from the United States, note that the Republic of Ireland's country code is 353, and you must omit the zero from the area code when dialing. For example, to reach Dublin (area code 01) from the United States, you would dial 011-353-1-555-555.

If you are planning to stay for longer than a few weeks and need to use a phone regularly for reservations, taxis, and so forth, it might pay you to get your home cell phone "unlocked" (for a fee of €10) and then spend €10-20 for a new simcard and pay-as-you-go plan. Having said all this, since wireless Internet access is now widely available, you can get by using Skype whenever you're online.

Internet Access

Wireless Internet access is now widely available (and virtually always free of charge) in pubs, restaurants, and accommodations on both sides of the border, rendering the Internet "cafés" of the 1990s and early 2000s more or less obsolete. There's usually a password to log in, so ask a staff member if it isn't posted.

Media

The Irish get their television and radio news from **RTÉ**, Radio Telefís Éireann. **TG4**, pronounced "tee gee CAH-her," is the Irish-language television network, though it does run some English-language programs (and includes subtitles for most of the rest).

The Irish Times (www.ireland.com) is the republic's primary newspaper, available at newsagents nationwide.

MAPS AND TOURIST INFORMATION

The tourist board in the Republic of Ireland is **Fáilte Ireland** (www.failteireland.ie). Though tourist offices provide information to visitors, they pretty much exist to arrange accommodations (for a small fee, of course), sell books and maps, and provide other profit-based services. Indeed, a tourist office always doubles as a gift shop. Tourist office opening hours vary from season to season; some are closed in winter, and many close for lunch (1pm-2pm).

Ordnance Survey maps (www.osi.ie) are available at tourist offices and bookstores. The OS Discovery Series consists of 89 maps covering the country; at 1:50,000, they detail practically every stone in the road. If you are doing any walking, cycling, or in-depth sightseeing, be sure to pick up the appropriate map (they run about €9). Unfortunately, bookstores and tourist offices generally stock only maps covering the immediate area, though it is possible to order online.

WEIGHTS, MEASURES, AND TIME

Ireland is officially on the metric system, but in reality, measurements of weight and distance are inconsistent. Meat and produce are weighed and priced in kilograms, but Guinness will be poured in pints until the last day of the world. If you hear something like "I lost three stone on this new diet," know that one stone is roughly 14 pounds.

In the republic, all speed limit signs are given in kilometers.

Before you leave home, pick up a three flat-pin adapter from an electronics store so you can use your laptop and other electrical gadgets. Ireland's standard voltage is 220 volts at 50 hertz, and you will need to purchase a voltage converter if any of your appliances are not compliant (though most likely you'll be fine with just an adapter). If you have any doubts, contact the manufacturer of the device in question before departure.

Ireland is on Greenwich mean time (GMT) and uses daylight saving time (GMT plus one hour in summer), though the country goes to daylight saving time two weeks ahead of the United States. Ireland is five hours ahead of America's east coast and eight hours ahead of the west coast, apart from those two weeks (when it is six and nine hours ahead).

Ireland is one hour behind Spain, France, and Italy, and nine and ten hours behind Australia (nine in Brisbane, ten in Sydney and Melbourne). To check the time difference between Ireland and other locations, you might try the helpful website **The World Clock** (www.timeanddate.com/worldclock).

Resources

Glossary

This compilation includes slang and common cultural and historical references in both Irish and English.

afters: dessert

Anglo-Irish: a land-owning Protestant family of English descent, or any descendants thereof

Anglo-Irish Treaty: the 1921 agreement that divided Ireland into British-controlled Northern Ireland and the independent republic in the south; the cause of the Irish Civil War (1922-1923)

ard rí **(ard REE):** high king

bank holiday: an official three-day weekend when banks close and everyone's off work on the Monday; expect crowds at pubs, restaurants, and hostels

banoffee pie: a dessert made from toffee and bananas that originated in England and is now quite popular on Irish menus

banshee: a female spirit whose shrieking and wailing augurs an impending death

bap: a lunch roll, like a seedless hamburger bun

bawn: a yard enclosed by a fortified house

big house: a term used (usually disparagingly) to refer to the home of the local landlord, who would be a member of the Protestant ascendancy

Black and Tans: a brutal and undisciplined British paramilitary force in 1920 and 1921, sent to Ireland to suppress all rebels (especially the IRA)

black pudding: sausage made from dried pigs' blood

Blue Flag: an "eco-label" awarded by an independent group, the Foundation for Environmental Education, that indicates the beach in question is very clean and safe

bodhrán (boh-RAWN): a hand-held goatskin drum used in traditional Irish music

bog: wet terrain with thick spongy layers of moss and other vegetable matter; also slang for toilet

bridle way: path for walkers, cyclists, and horseback riders

camogie: the women's version of hurling

caravan: a trailer or mobile home

céad míle fáilte **(kayd MEE-leh FAWL-cheh):** traditional greeting, meaning "a hundred thousand welcomes"

ceilidh (KAY-lee): a session of traditional dance and music

champ: mashed potatoes and onions

chemist: pharmacist

chipper: a fish-and-chips shop

cider: alcoholic apple cider

clearway: a road without a shoulder

coach: long-distance charter bus, usually for large tourist groups

concession: discounted admission

Connaught: one of the four ancient Irish provinces, encompassing Counties Galway, Mayo, Sligo, Roscommon, and Leitrim

control zone: the area of a town center where cars must not be left unattended

craic **(crack):** a fun time, good music and conversation; sometimes used in greeting, as in "What's the *craic*?"

culchie **(CULL-chee):** an urbanite's derogatory term for a person from the country; a "country bumpkin"

curragh: a rowboat covered with tarred canvas, traditionally used for fishing

Dáil (doll): the lower house of the Irish Parliament

DART: Dublin Area Rapid Transit, the commuter train line running from Howth through Dublin south to Bray in County Wicklow

diamond: town square

drink: alcohol (often called "the drink")

drisheen: pudding made from pigs' blood, a traditional Irish breakfast food

dual carriageway: a divided four-lane highway

Dubs: short for Dubliners

DUP: the Democratic Unionist Party, a hardline unionist (and exclusively Protestant) political group formed by Ian Paisley in the early 1970s

drumlin: a gentle hill formed long ago by retreating glaciers

Éire (air): the Irish name for the Republic of Ireland

eolas **(OH-lahs):** information

feis **(fesh):** a gathering

feis ceoil **(fesh kyohl):** a festival of music

Fenians: a nickname for members of the Irish Republican Brotherhood (IRB), a militant nationalist group founded in 1858; predecessors of the IRA

Fianna (FEE-uh-nuh): a group of mythical warriors whose exploits feature in many Irish legends

Fianna Fáil (FEE-uh-nuh FALL): a centrist political party formed by those nationalists who did not want to accept the compromise of continued British rule in the North

Fine Gael (FEE-nuh GALE): a centrist political party formed by those nationalists who were willing to accept continued British rule in the North to be able to form an independent republic

fir **(fihr):** men; used on toilet doors (singular *fear*)

freephone number: toll-free telephone number

GAA: abbreviation for the Gaelic Athletic Association, the organization founded in 1884 to promote the native pastimes of hurling, Gaelic football, and other sports

Gaeltacht (GALE-tahckt or GWALE-tahckt): a region where Irish is the primary language spoken (plural Gaeltachtaí)

gangway: aisle

gansey: sweater

garda, gardaí (GAR-da, gar-DEE): the Irish police, the full name being An Garda Síochána, "Guardian of the Peace"

H-blocks: literally refers to the H-shaped layout of British prisons, though the term is generally used in regard to the IRA members who as H-block inmates conducted a widespread hunger strike in 1981 in hopes of being reclassified as political prisoners

Hibernia: the Roman name for Ireland; literally "Land of Winter," so misnamed because the Romans thought they had discovered Iceland

homely: cozy, homey, homelike (never means "ugly"!)

hooker: a traditional Galway sailing ship, from the Irish *húicéir*

hurling: a traditional Irish sport, one of the fastest games in the world; a cross between hockey, lacrosse, and soccer

IHH: Independent Holiday Hostels of Ireland; a hostel's membership in this organization is indicative of high standards in safety, cleanliness, and hospitality

interval: intermission

IRA: the Irish Republican Army, the largest republican paramilitary group, founded in 1919 with the aim of a reunited Ireland, achieved by force if necessary

jacks: toilet

jars: alcoholic drinks

jumper: sweater

kerb: just another spelling of "curb"

kipper: smoked herring

knickers: ladies' underwear

leabharlann **(LORE-lahn):** library

Leinster: one of the four ancient Irish provinces, encompassing the southeastern section of the country from Louth down to Kilkenny and Wexford

loo: toilet

lough (lock): a lake or narrow sea inlet

loyalist: one (usually a Protestant) who supports Northern Ireland's continued existence as part of Great Britain; another word for unionist

Luas: the light-rail system through suburban and downtown Dublin

marching season: the time of year between Easter and mid-June when the Northern Irish calendar is filled with loyalist marches in celebration of the victory of William of Orange at the Battle of the Boyne in 1690

minced meat: hamburger

mná **(m'NAH):** women; used on toilet door (singular *bean*)

mobile (MOH-bile): cell phone

MP: member of Parliament (British)

Munster: one of the four ancient Irish provinces, encompassing Counties Clare, Limerick, Kerry, Cork, Tipperary, and Waterford

musha **(MUSH-ah):** indeed (archaic)

naomh **(nave):** saint

nationalism: the belief that Ireland should be reunited; its proponents are called nationalists

off-license: liquor store

ogham (OH-um): Ireland's earliest form of writing (dating from the 5th to the early 7th century), consisting of an alphabetic system of lines for consonants and notches for vowels, usually carved in stone

Oireachtas: the bicameral Parliament of the Irish Republic, consisting of the Dáil (lower house) and the Seanad Éireann (upper house, or Senate)

OPW: Office of Public Works, the republic's governmental agency for town planning as well as conservation and restoration efforts

Orange Order: the largest Protestant group in Northern Ireland, established in 1795

OS: Ordnance Survey, Britain's national mapping agency; Ordnance Survey Ireland (OSi) issues detailed region maps for all Ireland

Partition of Ireland: the division of Ireland into Northern Ireland and the Irish Republic in 1921

pasty (rhymes with "nasty"): a meat pie with a crust

pay-and-display parking: the paid hourly parking system in most Irish towns, whereby motorists are required to purchase a ticket from a blue kiosk to display on their "windscreens"

peat: partially carbonized vegetable matter, found in bogs, that has traditionally been dried and used for fuel; now also comes in briquette form for household use

Penal Laws: laws passed in the 18th century that forbid all Catholics from gathering for Mass, owning land, holding public office, and so forth; officially known as "Laws in Ireland for the Suppression of Popery"

petrol: gas (as in fuel)

Plantation: the settlement of English immigrants on lands confiscated from Irish Catholic farmers in the 17th century

plaster: a Band-Aid

poteen (po-CHEEN): illegal whiskey, potent enough to kill in large quantities, that was usually brewed by dispossessed Irish farmers to make extra money; from the Irish *poitín*

Prod: a Northern Irish Protestant

quay (key): a street along a river or harbor

queue (cue): a line (at the bank, the supermarket, etc.)

quid: slang for pounds (now euros), though it isn't used as often since the conversion

rashers: bacon

republicanism: the militant belief in a reunited Ireland

return ticket: a round-trip fare

roundabout: traffic circle

Rover pass: a euro-saving Bus Éireann bus pass good for 3 days' travel out of 8 consecutive days, 8 days out of 15, and so on

RTE: Ireland's broadcast network, the acronym for Radio Telefís Éireann

rubber: eraser

scrummy: short for scrumptious

SDLP: Social Democratic and Labour Party, the largest nationalist political party in the Northern Ireland assembly

sean nós **(shawn NOHSS):** a style of traditional song with three primary characteristics: the songs are unaccompanied, performed solo, and always sung in the Irish language; literally, "in the old way"

seisún: a traditional music session

single ticket: a one-way fare

síbín **(shuh-BEAN):** an illicit tavern or speakeasy; "shebeen" in English

Sinn Féin: a republican political party whose longstanding goal is a reunited Ireland; it is usually considered the political arm of the IRA despite its assertion that the two organizations are unaffiliated

slagging (off): making fun of someone

slí **(shlee):** literally "way," a hiking trail

slieve: a mountain, from the Irish *sliabh*

smalls: underwear

snug: a booth tucked away in a pub, meant for a bit of privacy

strand: beach

subway: an underground passageway for pedestrians

Taoiseach (TEE-shock): prime minister of the Republic of Ireland; literally, a chieftain

takeaway: takeout food

taking the piss: making fun of someone

Tánaiste (TAHN-ish-tcheh or TAHN-iss-teh): deputy prime minister of the Irish Republic

Teachta Dala (TCHOCK-tuh DOLL-uh): a member of the Irish Parliament, abbreviated TD

teach, tí, tigh **(tchock, tchee):** house (often used as in a public house, i.e., pub)

teampall **(TCHYEM-pull):** church

tinker: a now politically incorrect (and even offensive) term for an Irish person who lives a nomadic lifestyle, traveling in caravans and traditionally making a living as a smith; also (inaccurately) called gypsies

top up: to fill up a drink, or to add credit to your mobile phone account

torc: a neck or wrist ornament made of a band of twisted bronze or other metal, a type of jewelry introduced by the ancient Celts; most Irish examples date from the late Bronze Age and early Iron Age

Tory: the term for a conservative politician in Britain comes from the Irish *toiride*, meaning "pursuer," a word that originally referred to a highwayman

trad: short for traditional music

Traveller: the politically correct word for one of a group of nomadic Irish-people who travel in caravans and speak a separate language (called Shelta) in addition to English; there are approximately 25,000 Travellers in Ireland today

Tricolour: the green, white, and orange Irish flag symbolizing peace between the (green) Catholic Irish and the (orange) Protestant Irish

turf: another word for peat

turlough (TUR-lock): a small lake that disappears in dry weather

uilleann pipes (ILL-inn): the Irish bagpipes, which are inflated by a bellows and have a range of two octaves

uisce **(ISH-keh):** water

uisce beatha **(ISH-keh BAH-hah):** whiskey; literally, "water of life"

Ulster: one of the four ancient Irish provinces, encompassing the six counties of Northern Ireland (Antrim, Armagh, Derry, Down, Fermanagh, and Tyrone) along with three counties in the republic (Cavan, Monaghan, and Donegal); sometimes used to refer to Northern Ireland (especially by the British government)

UVF: Ulster Volunteer Force, a unionist paramilitary group established in 1966

unionist: one (usually a Protestant) who supports Northern Ireland's continued existence as part of Great Britain; synonym for loyalist

victualler: butcher

Wellingtons: knee-high rubber boots, also known as wellies

PLACE-NAMES

Here are Irish words that form place-names in English.

ard: high

baile **(BAL-ee or BALL-yuh):** village, town

beag **(beg):** small

bothár **(BOH-hir):** road

caislean **(CASH-lin):** castle

carraig **(KAR-rig):** rock

cath **(kah):** battle

cill **(kill):** church

dún **(doon):** fort

gort: field

lough **(lock):** lake

mór **(more):** big

slí **(shlee):** path, way

teach **(tchock):** house

HISTORY

Duffy, Sean. *The Concise History of Ireland.* Dublin: Gill & MacMillan, 2005. Just what it says on the tin, from a specialist in medieval history.

Harbison, Peter. *Guide to National and Historic Monuments of Ireland,* 3rd ed. Dublin: Gill & Macmillan, 1998. This guide will prove invaluable if you plan to visit archaeological sites.

LITERATURE

Here is an assortment of the contemporary and the classic. Ask at a local bookshop for more recommendations.

Banville, John. *The Sea.* New York: Knopf, 2005. The prolific Banville is one of today's best Irish literary novelists. *The Sea* won the 2005 Booker Prize.

Behan, Brendan. *The Complete Plays: The Hostage, the Quare Fellow, Richard's Cork Leg, Moving Out, A Garden Party, The Big House.* New York: Grove/Atlantic, 1978. Considering all the time he spent in jail (and in the pubs), hard-drinking IRA member Behan was able to write a load of plays and fiction in his 41 years; this volume is a must-have for theatergoers.

Delaney, Frank. *Ireland.* New York: Harper, 2008. Delaney's a master at telling stories within the story.

Enright, Anne. *The Green Road.* New York: Norton, 2016. Enright is one of Ireland's foremost fiction writers, having won the Booker Prize for her novel *The Gathering* in 2007.

Frawley, Oona. *Flight.* Dublin: Tramp Press, 2014. This beautifully written novel portrays the various hardships of Ireland's immigrant population in a very compassionate way.

Joyce, James. *Dubliners.* Many consider Joyce the greatest Irish writer of all time and others find his work pretentious. If *Ulysses* isn't your cup of tea, try this collection of short stories. The final tale, *The Dead,* was inspired by the childhood love of his wife, Nora Barnacle, and the 1987 film version was director John Huston's last.

Keane, Molly. *Good Behaviour.* London: Virago Press, 2001. This ironically titled novel, set in the 1920s, offers up black comedy at the expense of the Irish Ascendancy.

Kinsella, Thomas. *The Tain: From the Irish Epic Táin Bó Cuailnge.* Oxford: Oxford University Press, 1969. The definitive translation of the

8th-century Irish epic featuring the hero Cúchulainn and his nemesis, Medb, the scheming queen of Connaught.

Le Fanu, Sheridan. *In a Glass Darkly* (Oxford World's Classics). Oxford: Oxford University Press, 1999. Dubbed "The Invisible Prince" by his Dublin neighbors, Le Fanu funneled his obsession with the occult into an awesome collection of horror stories, including the vampire tale "Carmilla," for which he is best known.

McCormack, Mike. *Notes from a Coma.* London: Jonathan Cape, 2005. A fine novel, described (albeit simplistically) as a cross between *1984* and *The X-Files,* from one of a younger generation of Irish prose writers.

McGahern, John. *By the Lake.* New York: Knopf, 2003. It may not have much of a plot, but in this gorgeously atmospheric novel (titled *That They May Face the Rising Sun* in Ireland and Britain) it's hardly a flaw. The much-revered McGahern, who passed away in 2006, is known for darker works than this (such as *The Dark,* which was banned in 1965).

Ní Dhomhnaill, Nuala. *Selected Poems: Rogha Dánta.* Dublin: New Island, 2000. Many of Ireland's finest poets are writing exclusively in Irish, and Ní Dhomhnaill is perhaps the most beloved among them. (Original Irish on the left page and the English translation on the right.)

O'Brien, Kate. *The Land of Spices.* London: Virago Modern Classics, 1988. Banned in Ireland in 1941 for its fleeting and euphemistic mention of a homosexual tryst, this is one of the best Irish novels of the 20th century.

Ó Cadhain, Máirtín. *Cré na Cille* (*Graveyard Clay*), trans. Liam Mac Con Iomaire and Tim Robinson. New Haven: Yale University Press, 2016. Set in a Connemara graveyard, this 1949 novel follows the grudges and rivalries of the ghosts who linger there.

O'Casey, Sean. *Three Dublin Plays: The Shadow of a Gunman, Juno and the Paycock, and the Plough and the Stars.* New York: Faber and Faber, 2000. These three early plays, generally considered O'Casey's best work, provide a window into inner-city life that only a man born there could have achieved.

Synge, John Millington. *The Aran Islands.* New York: Penguin, 1992. Synge's travel writing isn't as well known as his dramatic works, but this volume is a must-read for Aran enthusiasts and armchair travelers alike.

Synge, John Millington. *Playboy of the Western World and Other Plays.* Oxford: Oxford University Press, 1998. This edition features all of Synge's published plays.

Wilde, Oscar. *The Best of Oscar Wilde: Selected Plays and Writings.* New York: Penguin, 2004. This collection includes *An Ideal Husband* along with four more well-known plays and several pieces of Wilde's literary criticism.

Wilde, Oscar. *The Picture of Dorian Gray.* New York: Random House, 1998. This edition features an introduction by Pulitzer Prize winner Jeffrey Eugenides.

Yeats, William Butler. *Selected Poems and Four Plays,* 4th ed. New York: Scribner, 1996. If you buy only one compilation of Yeats's work, this is a solid choice.

ART HISTORY

Bowe, Nicola Gordon. *The Life and Work of Harry Clarke.* Dublin: Irish Academic Press, 1989. An illuminating study of Clarke, Ireland's greatest stained-glass artist, by a professor at the National College of Art and Design in Dublin.

THE IRISH LANGUAGE

Ó Siadhail, Mícheál. *Learning Irish: An Introductory Self-Tutor,* 3rd ed. New Haven: Yale University Press, 1995. This is one of the best introductory Irish textbooks; it uses Connaught Irish rather than the standard dialect.

FOOD AND DRINK

Arnold, Hugo, and Georgia Glynn. *A Year at Avoca: Cooking for Ireland.* Dublin: Gloss Publications, 2010. Modern Irish cuisine from the country's favorite gourmet chain restaurant.

Cotter, Denis. *For the Love of Food.* New York: Collins, 2011. A fabulous cookbook from the owner/chef of Cork City's famous vegetarian restaurant, Café Paradiso.

NATURE AND WALKING GUIDES

Booth, Frank. *The Independent Walker's Guide to Ireland.* New York: Interlink, 1999. This guide features 35 day hikes nationwide, all 3-15 kilometers long.

Lynham, Joss, ed. *Best Irish Walks,* 3rd ed. Dublin: Gill & Macmillan, 2001. This volume offers 75 hiking routes that are generally longer and more challenging than those in the Booth guide.

LIVING IN IRELAND

McDonald, Christina. *Living Abroad in Ireland*. Berkeley, CA: Avalon Travel, 2012. Whether you intend to stay six months or a lifetime, this book provides all the resources you need to put down roots.

Internet Resources

ENTERTAINMENT

www.entertainment.ie
Entertainment Ireland has the lowdown on clubs, theaters, festivals, concerts, films, etc.

www.todayfm.com
One of the republic's most listened-to radio stations plays mostly "top 40" interspersed with lots of entertaining chitchat.

SIGHTSEEING AND TOURIST INFORMATION

www.ecotourismireland.ie
A new organization dedicated to promoting environmentally friendly tourism, primarily through walking and cycling holidays.

www.heritageireland.ie
Dúchas, Ireland's Office of Public Works, offers photos, background, and information on national parks and monuments on its official site.

www.lovindublin.com
A popular Dublin-centric blog offering reviews of new and trendy restaurants along with entertainment listings.

www.megalithomania.com
An informative and opinionated gazetteer on the country's megalithic and early Christian remains, including fine color photos.

www.failteireland.ie
The official site of Bord Fáilte in the Republic of Ireland.

ACTIVITIES AND RECREATION

www.irelandwalkhikebike.com
This is your site if you're looking for a guided walking or cycling tour. All tour operators are Tourist Board-approved.

www.irishtrails.ie
The Irish Sports Council provides maps, trail descriptions, and other resources for long-distance walkers.

www.mountaineering.ie
Virtual home of the Mountaineering Council of Ireland.

www.mountainviews.ie
Before you go, view pictures and tips of individual mountains posted by seasoned hill-walkers.

www.npws.ie
For all you bird-watchers and walkers, the National Parks & Wildlife Service website lists nature reserves and conservation sites in the republic.

TRANSPORTATION

www.aaroadwatch.ie
The Automotive Association website includes a route planner, invaluable for mapping out your road trip.

www.transportforireland.ie/taxi/taxi-fare-estimator
Check out this site if you're not renting a car. It very helpfully provides a list of the maximum fares (by location) that a taxi driver can legally charge you.

NEWS AND PUBLICATIONS

www.breakingnews.ie
Just as it says, this slightly sensationalist news source lists Irish news first.

www.ireland.com
The *Irish Times,* the best source for nationwide news online and in print.

www.rte.ie
The official site of Radio Telefís Éireann, the republic's radio and television service.

List of Maps

Dublin

Around Dublin

Photo Credits

Also Available

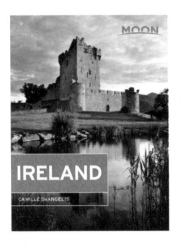

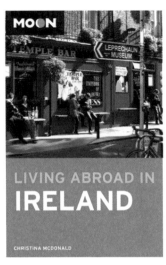

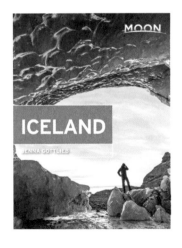

MAP SYMBOLS

Expressway	★	Highlight	✗	Airfield	⚓	Golf Course
Primary Road	○	City/Town	✈	Airport	🅿	Parking Area
Secondary Road	⊙	State Capital	▲	Mountain	⛰	Archaeological Site
Unpaved Road	◉	National Capital	✛	Unique Natural Feature	🍶	Church
Trail	★	Point of Interest			🏠	Gas Station
Ferry	•	Accommodation	🐚	Waterfall		Glacier
Railroad	▼	Restaurant/Bar	⚑	Park		Mangrove
Pedestrian Walkway	■	Other Location	🚩	Trailhead		Reef
Stairs	△	Campground	⛷	Skiing Area		Swamp

CONVERSION TABLES

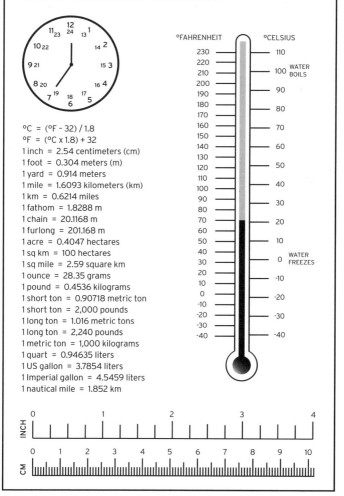

°C = (°F - 32) / 1.8
°F = (°C x 1.8) + 32
1 inch = 2.54 centimeters (cm)
1 foot = 0.304 meters (m)
1 yard = 0.914 meters
1 mile = 1.6093 kilometers (km)
1 km = 0.6214 miles
1 fathom = 1.8288 m
1 chain = 20.1168 m
1 furlong = 201.168 m
1 acre = 0.4047 hectares
1 sq km = 100 hectares
1 sq mile = 2.59 square km
1 ounce = 28.35 grams
1 pound = 0.4536 kilograms
1 short ton = 0.90718 metric ton
1 short ton = 2,000 pounds
1 long ton = 1.016 metric tons
1 long ton = 2,240 pounds
1 metric ton = 1,000 kilograms
1 quart = 0.94635 liters
1 US gallon = 3.7854 liters
1 Imperial gallon = 4.5459 liters
1 nautical mile = 1.852 km

MOON DUBLIN
Avalon Travel
An imprint of Perseus Books
A Hachette Book Group company
1700 Fourth Street
Berkeley, CA 94710, USA
www.moon.com

Editor and Series Manager: Kathryn Ettinger
Copy Editor: Deana Shields
Graphics Coordinator: Darren Alessi
Production Coordinator: Darren Alessi
Cover Design: Faceout Studios, Charles Brock
Interior Design: Domini Dragoone
Moon Logo: Tim McGrath
Map Editor: Kat Bennett
Cartographers: Brian Shotwell, Karin Dahl, Kat Smith
Indexer: Deana Shields

ISBN-13: 978-1-63121-657-2

Printing History
1st Edition — June 2017
5 4 3 2 1